1/16

LEARN TO PROGRAM
WITH MINECRAFT®

LEARN TO PROGRAM WITH MINECRAFT®

TRANSFORM YOUR WORLD WITH THE POWER OF PYTHON

BY CRAIG RICHARDSON

**no starch
press**

San Francisco

Printed on demand in USA.

ISBN-10: 1-59327-670-2
ISBN-13: 978-1-59327-670-6

Publisher: William Pollock
Production Editor: Riley Hoffman
Cover Illustration: Josh Ellingson
Developmental Editors: Hayley Baker and Tyler Ortman
Technical Reviewer: John Lutz
Copyeditor: Anne Marie Walker
Compositor: Riley Hoffman
Proofreader: Paula L. Fleming

For information on distribution, translations, or bulk sales, please contact No Starch Press, Inc. directly:

No Starch Press, Inc.
245 8th Street, San Francisco, CA 94103
phone: 415.863.9900; info@nostarch.com
www.nostarch.com

Library of Congress Cataloging-in-Publication Data

```
Names: Richardson, Craig (Software developer), author.
Title: Learn to program with Minecraft : transform your world with the power
   of python / by Craig Richardson.
Description: San Francisco : No Starch Press, [2016] | Includes index.
Identifiers: LCCN 2015035298| ISBN 9781593276706 | ISBN 1593276702
Subjects: LCSH: Python (Computer program language) | Computer
   games--Programming. | Minecraft (Game) | Raspberry Pi (Computer)
Classification: LCC QA76.73.P98 R53  2016 | DDC 005.13/3--dc23
LC record available at http://lccn.loc.gov/2015035298
```

To the countless adults and children that read the early drafts
of this book, used my recipe cards, and attended my talks and
workshops: thank you so much for your enthusiasm and support.
This book is for you.

ABOUT THE AUTHOR

Craig Richardson is a software developer and Python educator. He has worked for the Raspberry Pi Foundation, taught high school computing classes, and led many workshops on Python programming with Minecraft.

ABOUT THE TECHNICAL REVIEWER

John Lutz is a math teacher in the New Orleans public school system, where he also teaches extracurricular courses on Scratch, Arduino robotics, and 3D printing. He piloted his school's computer science program, which continues to grow and attract bright new minds to coding. Since helping with this book, John is working on a Python program that will destroy all baby zombies in his Minecraft world, forever.

BRIEF CONTENTS

Acknowledgments xvii

Introduction xix

Chapter 1: Setting Up for Your Adventure 1

Chapter 2: Teleporting with Variables 27

Chapter 3: Building Quickly and Traveling Far with Math 47

Chapter 4: Chatting with Strings 65

Chapter 5: Figuring Out What's True and False with Booleans 81

Chapter 6: Making Mini-Games with if Statements 103

Chapter 7: Dance Parties and Flower Parades with while Loops. 123

Chapter 8: Functions Give You Superpowers. 145

Chapter 9: Hitting Things with Lists and Dictionaries. 167

Chapter 10: Minecraft Magic with for Loops 195

Chapter 11: Saving and Loading Buildings with Files and Modules 231

Chapter 12: Getting Classy with Object-Oriented Programming 257

Afterword 283

Block ID Cheat Sheet 285

Index 291

CONTENTS IN DETAIL

ACKNOWLEDGMENTS   XVII

INTRODUCTION   XIX

Why Learn to Program? xx
Why Python? xx
Why Minecraft? xx
What's in This Book? xx
Online Resources xxii
Let the Adventure Begin! xxii

1
SETTING UP FOR YOUR ADVENTURE   1

Setting Up Your Windows PC 2
    Installing Minecraft 2
    Installing Python 3
    Installing Java 4
    Installing the Minecraft Python API and Spigot 6
    Running Spigot and Creating a Game 7
    Starting Over with a New World 8
    Playing Offline 9
    Switching to Survival Mode 10
Setting Up Your Mac 11
    Installing Minecraft 12
    Installing Python 13
    Installing Java 14
    Installing the Minecraft Python API and Spigot 15
    Running Spigot and Creating a Game 16
    Starting Over with a New World 17
    Playing Offline 18
    Switching to Survival Mode 18
Setting Up Your Raspberry Pi 18
Getting to Know IDLE 20
    Getting to Know the Python Shell 20
    Say Hello to IDLE's Text Editor 21
    When to Use the Python Shell and When to Use the Text Editor 23
    The Prompts Used in This Book 23
Testing Your Minecraft Python Setup 24

2
TELEPORTING WITH VARIABLES   27

What Is a Program?. 27
Storing Data with Variables. 28
     The Structure of Programming Languages. 29
     Syntax Rules for Variables 30
     Changing the Values of Variables 30
     Integers 31
     Mission #1: Teleport the Player **31**
     Floats 37
     Mission #2: Go Exactly Where You Want. **38**
Slowing Down Teleportation Using the time Module. 39
     Mission #3: Teleportation Tour **40**
Debugging 42
     Mission #4: Fix the Buggy Teleportation. **43**
What You Learned 45

3
BUILDING QUICKLY AND TRAVELING FAR WITH MATH   47

Expressions and Statements. 47
Operators. 48
     Addition 48
     Mission #5: Stack Blocks. **49**
     Mission #6: Super Jump **51**
     Subtraction. 52
     Mission #7: Change the Blocks Under You **52**
     Using Math Operators in Arguments 54
     Mission #8: Speed Building. **55**
     Multiplication 58
     Division 58
     Mission #9: Spectacular Spires **58**
Exponents 60
Parentheses and Order of Operations 61
Handy Math Tricks. 62
     Shorthand Operators. 62
     Playing with Random Numbers 62
     Mission #10: Super Jump Somewhere New! **63**
What You Learned 64

4
CHATTING WITH STRINGS   65

What Are Strings? 66
The print() Function. 66
     Mission #11: Hello, Minecraft World **67**
The input() Function 68
     Mission #12: Write Your Own Chat Message. **69**
Joining Strings. 71
     Converting Numbers to Strings 71
     Concatenating Integers and Floats. 72
     Mission #13: Add Usernames to Chat **72**

Converting Strings to Integers with int() 74
    Mission #14: Create a Block with input **74**
Bounce Back from Errors 76
    Mission #15: Only Numbers Allowed **77**
    Mission #16: Sprint Record **78**
What You Learned 80

5
FIGURING OUT WHAT'S TRUE AND FALSE
WITH BOOLEANS   81

Boolean Basics 82
    Mission #17: Stop Smashing Blocks! **82**
Concatenating Booleans 83
Comparators 83
    Equal To 84
    Mission #18: Am I Swimming? **85**
    Not Equal To 86
    Mission #19: Am I Standing in Something Other Than Air? **87**
    Greater Than and Less Than 88
    Greater Than or Equal To and Less Than or Equal To. 89
    Mission #20: Am I Above the Ground? **90**
    Mission #21: Am I Close to Home? **91**
Logical Operators 92
    and 93
    Mission #22: Am I Entirely Underwater? **93**
    or 95
    Mission #23: Am I in a Tree? **95**
    not 96
    Mission #24: Is This Block Not a Melon? **97**
    Logical Operator Order 98
    Is My Number Between Two Others? 99
    Mission #25: Am I in the House? **100**
What You Learned 101

6
MAKING MINI-GAMES WITH IF STATEMENTS   103

Using if Statements. 104
    Mission #26: Blast a Crater **105**
    else Statements 107
    Mission #27: Prevent Smashing, or Not **108**
    elif Statements 109
    Mission #28: Offer a Gift **110**
    Chaining Together elif Statements 112
    Mission #29: Teleport to the Right Place **113**
    Nested if Statements 115
    Mission #30: Open a Secret Passage **115**
Using if Statements to Test a Range of Values 117
    Mission #31: Restrict Teleport Locations **118**
Boolean Operators and if Statements 119
    Mission #32: Take a Shower **120**
What You Learned 122

7
DANCE PARTIES AND FLOWER PARADES WITH WHILE LOOPS   123

A Simple while Loop. 123
    Mission #33: A Random Teleportation Tour 125
Controlling Loops with a Count Variable. 127
    Mission #34: The Watery Curse. 128
    Infinite while Loops 130
    Mission #35: Flower Trail 130
Fancy Conditions 131
    Mission #36: Diving Contest 132
    Boolean Operators and while Loops 134
    Checking a Range of Values in while Loops 135
    Mission #37: Make a Dance Floor 135
    Nested if Statements and while Loops 137
    Mission #38: The Midas Touch. 138
Ending a while Loop with break. 139
    Mission #39: Create a Persistent Chat with a Loop 139
    while-else Statements 141
    Mission #40: Hot and Cold 141
What You Learned. 144

8
FUNCTIONS GIVE YOU SUPERPOWERS   145

Defining Your Own Functions 146
    Calling a Function. 146
    Functions Take Arguments 147
    Mission #41: Build a Forest. 148
    Refactoring a Program. 150
    Mission #42: Refactor Away 151
    Commenting with Docstrings 152
    Line Breaks in Arguments 153
    Function Return Values. 153
    Mission #43: Block ID Reminder 155
Using if Statements and while Loops in Functions 157
    if Statements. 157
    Mission #44: Wool Color Helper 158
    while Loops 159
    Mission #45: Blocks, Everywhere. 160
Global and Local Variables. 162
    Mission #46: A Moving Block 163
What You Learned. 165

9
HITTING THINGS WITH LISTS AND DICTIONARIES   167

Using Lists. 168
    Accessing a List Item 168
    Changing a List Item 169
    Mission #47: High and Low.. 169

Manipulating Lists 171
    Adding an Item 171
    Inserting an Item 172
    Deleting an Item 172
    Mission #48: Progress Bar **173**
Treating Strings like Lists 175
Tuples 175
    Setting Variables with Tuples 176
    Mission #49: Sliding **177**
    Returning a Tuple 179
Other Useful Features of Lists 179
    List Length 179
    Mission #50: Block Hits **180**
    Randomly Choosing an Item 182
    Mission #51: Random Block **183**
    Copying a List 183
    Items and if Statements 185
    Mission #52: Night Vision Sword **186**
Dictionaries 188
    Defining a Dictionary 188
    Accessing Items in Dictionaries 189
    Mission #53: Sightseeing Guide **190**
    Changing or Adding an Item in a Dictionary 191
    Deleting Items in Dictionaries 192
    Mission #54: Block Hits Score **192**
What You Learned 194

10
MINECRAFT MAGIC WITH FOR LOOPS 195

A Simple for Loop 195
    Mission #55: Magic Wand **196**
    The range() Function 198
    Mission #56: Magic Stairs **199**
    Playing Around with range() 200
Other List Functions 201
    Mission #57: Pillars **202**
    Mission #58: Pyramid **203**
Looping Over a Dictionary 205
    Mission #59: Scoreboard **205**
for-else Loops 206
    Breaking a for-else Loop 207
    Mission #60: The Diamond Prospector **207**
Nested for Loops and Multidimensional Lists 208
    Thinking in Two Dimensions 209
    Accessing Values in 2D Lists 213
    Mission #61: Pixel Art **214**
    Generating 2D Lists with Loops 216
    Mission #62: A Weather-Worn Wall **217**
    Thinking in Three Dimensions 218
    Outputting 3D Lists 219

Accessing Values in 3D Lists 223
Mission #63: Duplicate a Building **225**
What You Learned 230

11
SAVING AND LOADING BUILDINGS WITH
FILES AND MODULES
231

Using Files 232
Opening a File 232
Writing to and Saving a File 233
Reading a File 234
Reading a Line of a File 234
Mission #64: To-Do List **235**
Part 1: Writing the To-Do List 235
Part 2: Displaying the To-Do List 237
Using Modules 238
The pickle Module 238
Importing pickle 238
Importing One Function with the from Clause 240
Importing All Functions with * 241
Giving a Module a Nickname 241
Mission #65: Save a Building **242**
Part 1: Saving the Building 242
Part 2: Loading the Building 245
Storing Lots of Data with the shelve Module 247
Opening a File with shelve 247
Adding, Modifying, and Accessing Items with shelve 247
Mission #66: Save a Collection of Structures **248**
Part 1: Saving a Structure to a Collection 248
Part 2: Loading a Structure from a Collection 249
Installing New Modules with pip 252
Using pip on Windows 252
Using pip on a Mac or Raspberry Pi 253
Using a Module from pip: Flask 253
Mission #67: Position Website **255**
What You Learned 256

12
GETTING CLASSY WITH OBJECT-ORIENTED
PROGRAMMING
257

Object-Oriented Basics 258
Creating a Class 258
Creating an Object 259
Accessing Attributes 259
Mission #68: Location Objects **260**
Understanding Methods 261
Mission #69: Ghost House **263**
Returning Values with Methods 266
Mission #70: Ghost Castle **266**

Creating Multiple Objects 269
    Mission #71: Ghost Town **269**
Class Attributes 271
Understanding Inheritance. 273
    Inheriting a Class 274
    Adding New Methods to Subclasses 275
    Mission #72: Ghost Hotel **275**
Overriding Methods and Attributes. 278
    Mission #73: Ghost Tree **280**
What You Learned 282

AFTERWORD   283

BLOCK ID CHEAT SHEET   285

INDEX   291

ACKNOWLEDGMENTS

Massive thanks to the fine people at No Starch Press—Riley Hoffman, Hayley Baker, Tyler Ortman, and Jennifer Griffith-Delgado—and the very dedicated technical reviewer John Lutz.

Thanks to David Whale and Martin O'Hanlon who were immensely helpful whenever I had a technical issue. I'd also like to thank Mojang for releasing the Minecraft: Pi Edition (which had the original implementation of the Minecraft Python API) for free. Without the people who dedicate their free time to Spigot and CanaryMod, this book would not have been possible. The same goes for the fine people who updated the Minecraft API to Python 3 and also Alex Bradbury for his work on Raspbian.

If you ever meet David Whale, Matthew Timmons Brown, David Honess, Rachel Rayns, Andrew Robinson, or Jenny Brennan, give them a round of applause for helping out at Minecraft and Python workshops. Likewise, a round of applause for Tim Richardson, Michael Horne, Alan O'Donohoe, and Laura Dixon for arranging events that helped these workshops reach young people across the country.

Without Brian Corteil, the Minecraft mission that uses Flask would have been a lot more boring. Charlotte Godley helped immensely by loaning me her Mac so I could write the Mac installation instructions for this book.

Finally, to all my friends, family, and colleagues, I am forever grateful for your support during my various phases of bearded reclusiveness.

INTRODUCTION

Welcome to *Learn to Program with Minecraft*! In this book, you'll learn how to write programs with a programming language called Python to control what happens in your Minecraft world. You'll learn how programming works, and then use what you learn to create buildings with code, write mini-games, and transform boring Minecraft items into exciting new toys. By the end of the book, you should have the skills you need to bring all of your wildest ideas to life.

Programming is creative and imaginative, just like Minecraft. With the skills you learn in this book, you'll be able to make all kinds of things (like games, apps, and useful tools) beyond programs that use Minecraft. This is the first step in your journey to becoming an amazing programmer and a Minecraft master!

WHY LEARN TO PROGRAM?

One of the main reasons to learn to program is that it teaches you how to solve problems. You'll discover how to break down big problems into smaller parts to make them easier to tackle. Many of the problems you try to solve will require you to think in creative ways and test different ideas.

Another benefit of programming is that it teaches you to think logically to better understand and plan the structure and flow of your programs. Even when you're not working with computer code, problem solving, creativity, and thinking logically are valuable skills to have.

Careers in programming are very rewarding, too. Every day you get to come up with creative solutions to problems. Even if you don't choose to become a programmer, programming as a hobby is engaging and entertaining. In fact, I started programming as a hobby and it led to a full-time job.

Most importantly, programming can be loads of fun! Nothing is more satisfying than seeing a program you've created do something cool!

WHY PYTHON?

So, why should you learn to program with Python? Python is a great first language for any beginning programmer. It's easy to read and write, and it's powerful enough to create real computer programs. Python is one of the most popular programming languages in the world!

WHY MINECRAFT?

Minecraft is very popular because it's fun and creative. In your Minecraft world, you have total freedom over what you create. You can let your imagination run free. By integrating Minecraft with your own Python programs, you can take even more control of Minecraft and unlock even more of your creativity. You'll be able to do things (like constructing a huge building in just seconds) that are not possible with Minecraft alone.

Sometimes it's difficult to begin programming because you have to learn a bunch of code that doesn't do anything exciting. But by combining Python and Minecraft, you'll be able to see the results of your awesome programs instantly in your Minecraft world.

WHAT'S IN THIS BOOK?

Each chapter focuses on a single Python concept. As you progress through the book, you'll build on your knowledge of Python programming. Included in each chapter are explanations of how Python works, examples that show Python in action, and Minecraft missions. In the missions, you'll write programs that interact with Minecraft. I'll provide you with some skeleton code, and it will be up to you to fill in the gaps and complete the programs. As a result, you'll develop the problem-solving skills that are essential for any programmer.

Let's review what you'll explore in each chapter.

- **Chapter 1: Setting Up for Your Adventure** helps you set up Python and Minecraft so you're ready to forge ahead and get started programming!

- **Chapter 2: Teleporting with Variables** teaches you how to instantly teleport your player by manipulating variables. You'll learn about variables and how they remember data in your programs. You'll even build on your fancy teleportation skills to go on a magical teleportation tour of your world.

- **Chapter 3: Building Quickly and Traveling Far with Math** shows you how to use math to grant yourself superpowers and build your creations at superfast speeds. Do you want to build a Minecraft house in less than a second? Math operators can help you do that. Do you want to jump super high in the air? Math operators have your back!

- In **Chapter 4: Chatting with Strings**, you'll learn all about strings to make an interactive chat. In programming, a *string* means text. You'll learn how to write Minecraft Python programs that deliver messages to you and your players.

- **Chapter 5: Figuring Out What's True and False with Booleans** teaches you how to use Booleans and logic so your programs can answer questions. In other words, you'll be able to make your programs tell you whether something is true or false. Your Minecraft Python programs can answer all kinds of questions: Am I underwater? Am I in a tree? Am I near my house?

- **Chapter 6: Making Mini-Games with if Statements** takes Boolean logic to the next level. Using if statements, you'll learn how to create programs that make decisions based on the data they're given. Have you ever wanted a secret passage to open in Minecraft when you put a certain block in a certain place? You can do that using if statements!

- **Chapter 7: Dance Parties and Flower Parades with while Loops** shows you a very cool way to make your programs repeat using loops. You'll be able to automate code to make amazing things happen. For example, imagine a trail of flowers following the player or a magical dance floor that flashes different colors. These are some of my favorite programs to show off to people.

- In **Chapter 8: Functions Give You Superpowers**, you'll learn to build entire forests and cities instantly by using functions. You'll also learn how to make your programming life easier by reusing parts of your programs.

- In **Chapter 9: Hitting Things with Lists and Dictionaries**, you'll learn to make mini-games with lists. Lists are a powerful programming concept because they let you store important information in one place. You'll use lists to make your program remember all the blocks you hit with your sword, and with a few extra lines of code, you'll turn that into a mini-game. Pretty neat!

- **Chapter 10: Minecraft Magic with for Loops** shows you how to build structures, such as pyramids, using for loops. You can even use for loops to draw pixel art or duplicate your Minecraft buildings. You can build a glorious statue, and then duplicate it to create an entire army of statues!

- In **Chapter 11: Saving and Loading Buildings with Files and Modules**, you'll use your programs to create and edit files to save objects that you build, and then load them into different game worlds. In other words, you'll convert your buildings into files that you can transfer anywhere. Do you want to save that incredible mansion you built? No problem! With files, you'll be able to save it and load it wherever you go.

- **Chapter 12: Getting Classy with Object-Oriented Programming** introduces some advanced topics: classes, objects, and inheritance. When you've finished this chapter, you'll be a Python master. In the missions, you'll start with some code that builds a building. Then you'll use classes, objects, and inheritance to easily build duplicates and variations, like villages and hotels, with only a couple extra lines of code.

- The **Block ID Cheat Sheet** is a handy reference of Minecraft block IDs that you can use in your programs.

ONLINE RESOURCES

All the code and resources for this book are available on its companion website, *https://www.nostarch.com/pythonwithminecraft/*. Download the code for the Minecraft missions if you get stuck and want to check out the solutions—or if you want to modify the code to create your own awesome programs! You can also download the setup files—I'll walk you through the setup in Chapter 1.

LET THE ADVENTURE BEGIN!

I hope you're as excited as I am to get going. I've really enjoyed writing this book and making all the Minecraft missions that will help you learn to program. Let's get started!

1

SETTING UP FOR YOUR ADVENTURE

Before you can start making cool Python programs for your Minecraft world, you need to set up Minecraft, Python, and a few other things on your computer. In this chapter, I'll show you how to install and run all the required software.

You can use Minecraft on your Windows PC or Mac, or you can use Minecraft: Pi Edition on a Raspberry Pi computer. If you're using a Windows PC, just keep reading. If you're using a Mac, flip to "Setting Up Your Mac" on page 11. If you're using a Raspberry Pi, flip to "Setting Up Your Raspberry Pi" on page 18.

NOTE *For information on other platforms and updates to these instructions, visit* https://www.nostarch.com/pythonwithminecraft/.

SETTING UP YOUR WINDOWS PC

You need to install five things so you can control Minecraft with Python:

- Minecraft
- Python 3
- Java
- Minecraft Python API
- Spigot Minecraft Server

In this section, I'll guide you through installing each of these on your computer. Let's start with Minecraft.

INSTALLING MINECRAFT

If you already own Minecraft and have the latest version installed on your PC, skip ahead to "Installing Python" on page 3. If you're not sure whether you have the latest version of Minecraft, follow the steps in this section to install the latest version.

If you don't already own the game, you can buy a copy from the official Minecraft website, *https://minecraft.net/*. You might need to grab a grown-up to help you with that! Remember the username and password you use when you purchase Minecraft—you'll need it to log in later.

After you've purchased Minecraft, follow these steps to install Minecraft on your PC:

1. Go to *https://minecraft.net/download*.
2. Under the Minecraft for Windows section, find the *Minecraft.msi* link and click it to download it. If you're given the option to save or open the file, select **Save File**.
3. Wait for the file to download and then open it. If a dialog pops up asking whether you want to run this file, click **Run**. Don't worry, we know this file is safe!
4. When the Minecraft Setup Wizard opens, click **Next**. Then click **Next** once more. Then click **Install**.
5. You might be asked whether you want to install Minecraft. Of course you do! Click **Yes**. Wait a bit while Minecraft installs. I got a glass of water and a cookie while the game installed.
6. After the installation completes, click **Finish**.

Minecraft should now be installed.

You know what would be a great idea? Playing Minecraft, of course. Take a few minutes to get it up and running:

1. To open Minecraft, click the **Start Menu** (or press the Windows key on your keyboard), find Minecraft in the list of programs, and click the icon.
2. Minecraft will start up and might install updates.
3. The login window will open next. Enter the username and password you used when you purchased Minecraft and click **Log In**.
4. Click **Play**. Minecraft will download a couple more updates before opening.
5. Finally, click **Single Player ▶ Create New World**. Name your world whatever you want and click **Create New World**. The world will generate, and you can play to your heart's content.

Have some fun! If you've never played Minecraft before, try playing around for a while, until it gets dark in your Minecraft world. Watch out for monsters! Note that when you use Minecraft with Python, you'll be using a multiplayer game world, which will be different from this world. We'll get to that in "Running Spigot and Creating a Game" on page 7.

Back to work! It's time to install Python. To free your cursor from Minecraft, just press ESC on your keyboard. Close Minecraft before continuing the rest of the installation.

INSTALLING PYTHON

Python is the programming language you'll learn in this book. Let's install it now.

1. Go to *http://www.python.org/downloads/*.
2. Click the button labeled **Download Python 3.5.0**. (This is the latest version of Python 3 at the time of this writing, but you might see a later version. Install the most recent version.)
3. Python will begin to download. If you're asked to choose between saving or opening the file, select **Save File**.
4. When the installer has downloaded, click it. If a dialog pops up asking whether you want to run the file, click **Run**.
5. When the installer opens, select the *Add Python 3.5 to Path* checkbox, as shown at the bottom of Figure 1-1. Then click **Install Now**.

Figure 1-1: Make sure you select Add Python 3.5 to Path.

6. A dialog might ask whether you want to allow the program to install software on the computer. Click **Yes** and then wait for Python to install. I stood up to close the window while it was installing, and the installation had finished when I sat back down.

7. Click **Finish**. Python is now installed.

INSTALLING JAVA

Now that Minecraft and Python are both installed, you'll have to set things up so that they can talk to each other. You'll use a program called Spigot to do that, but in order for Spigot to work, you first need to make sure Java is installed on your computer. Let's do that now.

First, check whether Java is already installed:

1. Click the **Start Menu** (or press the Windows key on your keyboard) and enter cmd in the search box. Open the program called cmd.

2. You'll see a window with a black background and a prompt (mine says C:\Users\Craig>). At the prompt, type **java -version** and press ENTER.

3. If you see a message like the one in Figure 1-2, Java is already installed. Skip ahead to "Installing the Minecraft Python API and Spigot" on page 6.

4. If you get a message that says that Java is not recognized, install it using the following instructions.

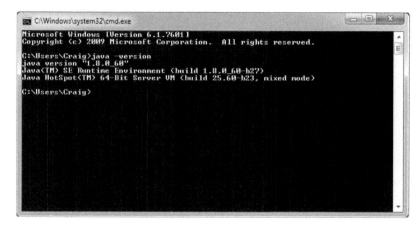

Figure 1-2: After entering the java -version *command, I can see that Java is installed.*

To install Java, follow these steps:

1. Go to *http://www.java.com/en/download/*.

2. Click the **Free Java Download** button. Then click the **Agree and Start Free Download** button.

3. When the installer has downloaded, click it. If a dialog pops up asking whether you want to let the program make changes to your computer, choose **Yes**.

4. When the installer opens, click **Install**.

5. This bit is super important! If a page opens that asks if you want to install another program, such as the Ask Search App, a Yahoo! search bar, or something else, uncheck the box so that this extra program will not install. That's just another program that you don't need.

6. You might be asked if you want to set Yahoo! as your homepage. You probably don't. Select **Do not update browser settings** and click **Next**.

7. Wait while Java installs. I wrote a short message to a friend before it installed. Click **Close** when it finishes.

Now let's check whether Java has installed properly:

1. Click the **Start Menu** and enter cmd in the search box. Open the cmd program.

2. In the cmd window, type java -version at the prompt and press ENTER.

3. If you see a message like the one in Figure 1-2, Java installed correctly. If you get an error that says "'Java' is not recognized as an internal or external command, operable program or batch file," Java hasn't installed properly. To fix this, try reinstalling Java and running it again. If you still get this error after reinstalling, go to *http://www.java.com/en/download/help/path.xml* for more information.

That's it! Java is set up and ready to run the Minecraft server! Let's get to that next.

INSTALLING THE MINECRAFT PYTHON API AND SPIGOT

Next you need to install the Minecraft Python API and the Minecraft server on your computer.

API stands for *application programming interface*. It lets programs communicate with applications that other people have created. In this case, the Minecraft Python API allows programs that you write in Python to communicate with Minecraft. For example, you could write a Python program that uses the API to tell Minecraft to make a block in the game or to change the position of the player.

A standard Minecraft single-player game does not support an API. Instead, your programs will interact with a Minecraft *server*, which allows the use of APIs. Minecraft servers are mostly used online so that many people can play together in a single game world. You can also run a server on your own computer and play by yourself. Both multiplayer and single-player Minecraft servers allow you to use an API with Minecraft. In this book, you'll be using a single-player Minecraft server called Spigot on your computer.

Now that you know what an API and a server do, let's get them installed on your computer. I've created a handy download so you can get these set up quickly. Just follow these steps:

1. Go to *https://www.nostarch.com/pythonwithminecraft/* and download the *Minecraft Tools.zip* file for Windows.

2. When the file has downloaded, right-click it and choose **Extract All**. You will be asked where you want to put the extracted files. Click the **Browse** button and go to your *My Documents* folder. Click the **Make a New Folder** button and call the new folder *Minecraft Python*. Select this folder and click **OK**. Click **Extract** to extract the files.

3. Go to the *Minecraft Python* folder in your *My Documents* folder, where you should see the extracted files.

4. Open the *Minecraft Tools* folder. Its contents are shown in Figure 1-3.

5. Double-click the file called *Install_API*. This will open a new window and install the Minecraft Python API. If you get a warning message, click **Run Anyway**.

6. When the installation completes, press any key to finish.

NOTE   *If you get an error message that says pip is not recognized, that means you didn't install Python correctly. Go back to "Installing Python" on page 3 and reinstall Python. Make sure you select the checkbox that says Add Python 3.5 to Path.*

The Minecraft Python API and Minecraft server are now installed. The final step is to run the server. We'll do that in the next section.

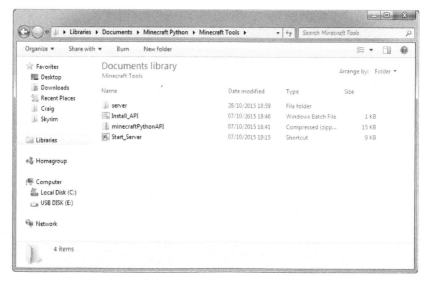

Figure 1-3: The Minecraft Tools *folder*

RUNNING SPIGOT AND CREATING A GAME

When Spigot runs for the first time, it will create a Minecraft world for you. To start Spigot, follow these steps:

1. Go to your *Minecraft Python* folder and open your *Minecraft Tools* folder.

2. In the *Minecraft Tools* folder, double-click the *Start_Server* file. If you get a message asking whether you want to allow access, click **Allow**.

3. Spigot will start your Minecraft server. You'll see a window pop up with a bunch of text in it while Spigot generates the game world for you. When Spigot is done, your screen will look like Figure 1-4. Keep this window open.

```
Start_Server

[19:01:51 INFO]: Structure Info Saving: true
[19:01:51 INFO]: Sending up to 10 chunks per packet
[19:01:51 INFO]: Max TNT Explosions: 100
[19:01:51 INFO]: Tile Max Tick Time: 50ms Entity max Tick Time: 50ms
[19:01:51 INFO]: Zombie Aggressive Towards Villager: true
[19:01:51 INFO]: Item Merge Radius: 2.5
[19:01:51 INFO]: Item Despawn Rate: 6000
[19:01:51 INFO]: Chunks to Grow per Tick: 650
[19:01:51 INFO]: Clear tick list: false
[19:01:51 INFO]: Max Entity Collisions: 8
[19:01:51 INFO]: Custom Map Seeds:  Village: 10387312 Feature: 14357617
[19:01:51 INFO]: Preparing start region for level 0 (Seed: -2823602682222914944)

[19:01:51 INFO]: Preparing start region for level 1 (Seed: -2823602682222914944)

[19:01:52 INFO]: Preparing start region for level 2 (Seed: -2823602682222914944)

[19:01:52 INFO]: [SetSpawn] Enabling SetSpawn v2.1
===[ SetSpawn v2.1 by artur9010 ]===
>Thanks for downloading SetSpawn!
http://dev.bukkit.org/bukkit-plugins/setspawn
=====================================
[19:01:52 INFO]: [RaspberryJuice] Enabling RaspberryJuice v1.7
[19:01:52 INFO]: [RaspberryJuice] ThreadListener Started
[19:01:52 INFO]: Server permissions file permissions.yml is empty, ignoring it
[19:01:52 INFO]: Done (1.336s)! For help, type "help" or "?"
>
```

Figure 1-4: The Spigot server is ready

4. Open Minecraft and click **Multiplayer**.

5. Click the **Add Server** button.

6. In the Server Name box, name your server `Minecraft Python World`, and in the Server Address box, type `localhost`, as shown in Figure 1-5. Then click **Done**.

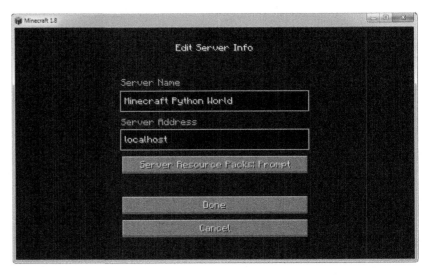

Figure 1-5: Setting up the server

7. Double-click **Minecraft Python World**, and the world created by Spigot will open.

Let's have a quick look at your new Minecraft world on the Spigot server. The world is set up in Creative Mode so you can fly around. Double-tap the spacebar to fly. Holding the spacebar will make you fly higher, and holding SHIFT will lower you toward the ground. If you want to stop flying, just double-tap the spacebar again.

STARTING OVER WITH A NEW WORLD

Creating a brand-new Minecraft world with a server is a little different from creating a new world in single-player mode. Follow these steps to create a new world:

1. Go to the *Minecraft Python* folder. Right-click the *Minecraft Tools* folder and click **Copy**.

2. Right-click anywhere in the *Minecraft Python* folder and click **Paste**. This will create a copy of the *Minecraft Tools* folder with the name *Minecraft Tools - Copy*.

3. Right-click the *Minecraft Tools - Copy* folder and click **Rename**. I named the new folder *New World*, but you can name yours anything you want.

4. Open the *New World* folder (or whatever you named it) and then open the *server* folder.

5. In the *server* folder, select the *world, world_nether,* and *world_the_end* folders, as shown in Figure 1-6. Press DELETE to delete these.

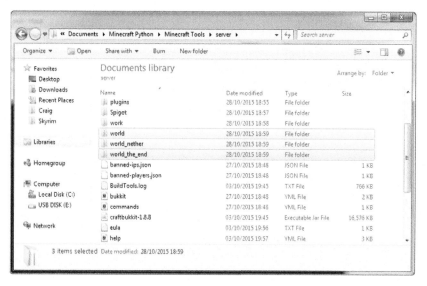

Figure 1-6: I've highlighted the folders that you need to delete.

6. Still in the *server* folder, click the *start* file. (Note that it's important to click this *start* file inside of the *server* folder, not the original *Start_Server* file!) This will start the server again and generate a new world.

7. Now when you open Minecraft and open the Minecraft Python World, you will see a newly generated world.

You can repeat this process to create a new world as many times as you want. If you want to open the old world, you can still run it by clicking the *Start_Server* file in the *Minecraft Tools* folder.

To delete a world and replace it with a new one, just delete the *world, world_nether,* and *world_the_end* folders in the folder of the world you want to replace.

PLAYING OFFLINE

If you don't have access to an Internet connection, you'll get an error when you try to connect to the Minecraft server from your Minecraft game. You can fix this by changing the server's properties. First, make sure you have closed the server window. Then open the *Minecraft Python* folder, then the *Minecraft Tools* folder, and then the *server* folder. Open the *server.properties* file in a text editor, such as Notepad, and change the online-mode setting

(Figure 1-7) from true to false. Save the changes. Then go back to your *Minecraft Tools* folder and double-click *Start_Server* to start the server again. Now you'll be able to play offline.

Figure 1-7: Change the highlighted setting from true *to* false.

SWITCHING TO SURVIVAL MODE

I've set the default game mode for your Minecraft server to Creative Mode. This will make things easier for you when you're writing and running Python programs because you won't have to worry about the player losing health, getting hungry, or being attacked.

But you might want to test some programs in Survival Mode just for fun. It's easy to switch the server from Creative Mode to Survival Mode and back.

To switch the server from Creative Mode to Survival Mode, follow these steps:

1. Open the *Minecraft Tools* folder. Inside this folder open the *server* folder.
2. Find the *server.properties* file and open it with a text editor, such as Notepad.
3. In the file, find the line that says gamemode=1 and change it to gamemode=0, as shown in Figure 1-8.

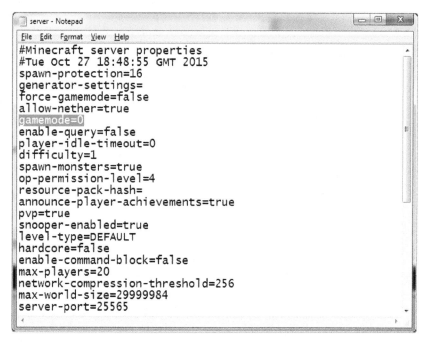

Figure 1-8: I've switched to Survival Mode by setting gamemode to 0.

4. Save the file and close it.

5. Start the server by clicking the *Start_Server* file in the *Minecraft Tools* folder. When you join the Minecraft Python World game, it will now be in Survival Mode.

You can change back to Creative Mode at any time. Just repeat these steps, but in step 3, change gamemode=0 to gamemode=1 in the *server.properties* file.

Now you're set up on your PC! Next let's meet IDLE, which is where you'll be writing your code. Flip to "Getting to Know IDLE" on page 20.

SETTING UP YOUR MAC

You need to install five things so you can control Minecraft with Python:

- Minecraft
- Python 3
- Java Development Kit
- Minecraft Python API
- Spigot Minecraft Server

In this section, I'll guide you through installing each of these on your computer. Let's start with Minecraft.

INSTALLING MINECRAFT

If you already own Minecraft and have the latest version installed on your Mac, skip ahead to "Installing Python" on page 13. If you're not sure whether you have the latest version of Minecraft, follow the steps in this section to install the latest version.

If you don't already own the game, you can buy a copy from the official Minecraft website, *https://minecraft.net/*. You might need to grab a grown-up to help you with that! Remember the username and password you use when you purchase Minecraft—you'll need it to log in later.

After you've purchased Minecraft, follow these steps to install Minecraft on your Mac:

1. Go to *htttps://minecraft.net/download*.

2. Under the Minecraft for Mac OS X section, find the *Minecraft.dmg* link and click it to download it. (If the Minecraft for Mac OS X section isn't visible, click **Show all platforms**.)

3. Wait for the file to download (I looked out the window for a moment) and then open it. When the window pops up, drag the Minecraft icon to the *Applications* folder as shown in Figure 1-9.

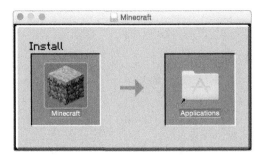

Figure 1-9: Drag the Minecraft icon into the Applications folder to install it.

Minecraft should now be installed.

You know what would be a great idea? Playing Minecraft, of course. Take a few minutes to get it up and running:

1. To open Minecraft, click the Finder icon on the Dock to open the file browser.

2. In the sidebar, click **Applications**.

3. Find Minecraft in the *Applications* folder as shown in Figure 1-10. Double-click it and select **Open**.

4. You might be asked whether you want to open Minecraft, because it was downloaded from the Internet. Click **Open**.

5. Minecraft will start up and might install updates.

6. The login window will open next. Enter the username and password you used when you purchased Minecraft and click **Log In**.

Figure 1-10: Find Minecraft in the Applications folder.

7. Click **Play**. Minecraft will download a couple more updates, then open.

8. Finally, click **Single Player ▸ Create New World**. Name your world whatever you want and click **Create New World**. The world will generate, and you can play to your heart's content.

Have some fun! If you've never played Minecraft before, try playing around for a while, until it gets dark in your Minecraft world. Watch out for monsters! Note that when you use Minecraft with Python, you'll be using a multiplayer game world, which will be different from this world. We'll get to that in "Running Spigot and Creating a Game" on page 16.

Back to work! It's time to install Python. To free your cursor from Minecraft, just press ESC on your keyboard. Close Minecraft before continuing the rest of the installation.

INSTALLING PYTHON

Python is the programming language you'll learn in this book. Let's install it now.

1. Go to *https://www.python.org/downloads/mac-osx/*.

2. Click the link that says **Latest Python 3 Release - Python 3.5.0**. (This is the latest version of Python 3 at the time of this writing, but you might see a later version. Install the most recent version.) Python will begin to download.

3. When the installer has downloaded, click it.

4. When the installer opens, click **Continue** three times. You'll be asked to agree to the terms of the software license agreement. Click **Agree**.

5. Click **Install** and then wait for Python to install. I checked the weather forecast while I waited.

6. Click **Close**. Python is now installed.

INSTALLING JAVA

Now that Minecraft and Python are both installed, you'll have to set things up so that they can talk to each other. You'll use a program called Spigot to do that, but in order for Spigot to work, you first need to install the latest Java Development Kit (JDK) on your computer. Let's do that now:

1. Go to *http://www.oracle.com/technetwork/java/javase/downloads/index.html* and click the **Java Download** button.
2. Select **Accept License Agreement** and then click **Mac OSX x64**.
3. When the installer has downloaded, click it.
4. When the installer opens, double-click the **Install** icon.
5. When asked for your password, enter it.
6. Wait for Java to install. Click **Close** when it finishes.

Now let's test whether the JDK has installed properly:

1. Click **System Preferences**.
2. You should see a Java icon under System Preferences, as shown in Figure 1-11.

Figure 1-11: Java is installed.

That's it! Java is set up and ready to run the Minecraft sever! Let's get to that next.

INSTALLING THE MINECRAFT PYTHON API AND SPIGOT

Next you need to install the Minecraft Python API and the Minecraft server on your computer.

API stands for *application programming interface*. It lets programs communicate with applications that other people have created. In this case, the Minecraft Python API allows programs that you write in Python to communicate with Minecraft. For example, you could write a Python program that uses the API to tell Minecraft to make a block in the game or to change the position of the player.

A standard Minecraft single-player game does not support an API. Instead, your programs will interact with a Minecraft *server*, which allows the use of APIs. Minecraft servers are mostly used online so that many people can play together in a single game world. You can also run a server on your own computer and play by yourself. Both multiplayer and single-player Minecraft servers allow you to use an API with Minecraft. In this book, you'll be using a single-player Minecraft server called Spigot on your computer.

Now that you know what an API and a server do, let's get them installed on your computer. I've created a handy download so you can get these set up quickly. Just follow these steps:

1. Go to *https://www.nostarch.com/pythonwithminecraft/* and download the *MinecraftTools Mac.zip* file.
2. When the file has downloaded, open the *Downloads* folder and click **Show in Finder**.
3. In Finder, CONTROL-click on the file and select **Copy MinecraftTools Mac.zip**.
4. Go to your *Documents* folder. CONTROL-click in the folder and select **New Folder**. Call the new folder *MinecraftPython*. Make sure you don't include a space in the name of the folder.
5. Open the *MinecraftPython* folder. CONTROL-click in the folder and select **Paste Item**. The *MinecraftTools Mac.zip* file will be copied here.
6. CONTROL-click and choose **Open With ▸ Archive Utility**. When Archive Utility has opened the zip file, you'll have a new folder called *MinecraftTools*.
7. Open the *MinecraftTools* folder. Its contents are shown in Figure 1-12.
8. CONTROL-click the file called *Install_API.command* and select **Open**. This will open a new window. Enter your password to install the Minecraft Python API.

NOTE   *If you get an error that says* Install_API.command *can't be opened because it is from an unidentified developer, click* **System Preferences***, and then click* **Security and Privacy***. You will see a message that says "Install_API.command was not opened because it is from an unidentified developer." Click* **Open Anyway***. Then the window should pop up.*

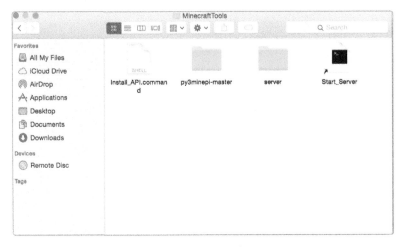

Figure 1-12: The contents of the MinecraftTools *folder*

9. When the installation completes, close the window.

The Minecraft Python API and Minecraft server are now installed. The final step is to run the server. We'll do that next.

RUNNING SPIGOT AND CREATING A GAME

When Spigot runs for the first time, it will create a Minecraft world for you. To start Spigot, follow these steps:

1. Go to your *MinecraftPython* folder and open your *MinecraftTools* folder.
2. In the *MinecraftTools* folder, CONTROL-click the *Start_Server* file and select **Open**. If you get an error message, go to **System Preferences** and then to **Security and Privacy** and click **Open Anyway**.
3. Spigot will start your Minecraft server. You'll see a window pop up with a bunch of text in it while Spigot generates the game world for you. When it's done, make sure you keep this window open.
4. Open Minecraft and click **Multiplayer**.
5. Click the **Add Server** button.
6. In the Server Name box, name your server `Minecraft Python World`, and in the Server Address box, type `localhost`, as shown in Figure 1-13. Then click **Done**.
7. Double-click **Minecraft Python World**, and the world created by Spigot will open.

Let's have quick look at your new Minecraft world on the Spigot server. The world is set up in Creative Mode so you can fly around. Double-tap the spacebar to fly. Holding the spacebar will make you fly higher, and holding SHIFT will lower you toward the ground. If you want to stop flying, just double-tap the spacebar again.

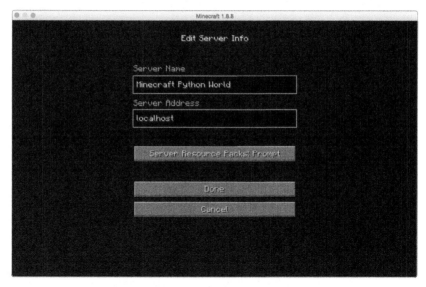

Figure 1-13: Add the server so that you can access it easily in the future.

STARTING OVER WITH A NEW WORLD

Creating a brand-new Minecraft world with a server is a little different from creating a new world in single-player mode. Follow these steps to create a new world:

1. Go to the *MinecraftPython* folder. CONTROL-click the *MinecraftTools* folder and click **Copy**.

2. CONTROL-click anywhere in the folder and click **Paste**. This will create a copy of the *MinecraftTools* folder with the name *MinecraftTools copy*.

3. CONTROL-click the *MinecraftTools copy* folder and click **Rename**. I named the new folder *New World*, but you can name yours anything you want.

4. Open the *New World* folder (or whatever you named it) and then open the *server* folder.

5. In the *server* folder, select the *world*, *world_nether*, and *world_the_end* folders. Press SHIFT-DELETE to delete these.

6. Go back to the *New World* folder and click the *Start_Server* file. This will start the server again and generate a new world.

7. Now when you open Minecraft and open the Minecraft Python World you will see a newly generated world.

You can repeat this process to create a new world as many times as you want. If you want to open the old world, you can still run it by clicking the *Start_Server* file in the *MinecraftTools* folder instead of the *New World* folder.

To delete a world and replace it with a new one, just delete the *world*, *world_nether*, and *world_the_end* folders in the folder of the world you want to replace.

PLAYING OFFLINE

If you don't have access to an Internet connection, you'll get an error when you try to connect to the Minecraft server from your Minecraft game. You can fix this by changing the server's properties. First, make sure you have closed the server window. Then open the *MinecraftPython* folder, then the *MinecraftTools* folder, and then the *server* folder. Open the *server.properties* file in a text editor, such as TextEdit, and change the online-mode setting from true to false (see Figure 1-7 on page 10). Save the changes. Then go back to your *MinecraftTools* folder and click *Start_Server* to start the server again. Now you'll be able to play offline.

SWITCHING TO SURVIVAL MODE

I've set the default game mode for your Minecraft server to Creative Mode. This will make things easier for you when you're writing and running Python programs because you won't have to worry about the player losing health, getting hungry, or being attacked.

But you might want to test some programs in Survival Mode just for fun. It's easy to switch the server from Creative Mode to Survival Mode and back.

To switch the server from Creative Mode to Survival Mode, follow these steps:

1. Open the *MinecraftTools* folder. Inside this folder open the *server* folder.

2. Find the *server.properties* file and open it with a text editor, such as TextEdit.

3. In the file, find the line that says gamemode=1 and change it to gamemode=0 (see Figure 1-8 on page 11).

4. Save the file and close it.

5. Start the server by clicking the *Start_Server* file in the *MinecraftTools* folder. When you join the Minecraft Python World game, it will now be in Survival Mode.

You can change back to Creative Mode at any time. Just repeat these steps, but in step 3, change gamemode=0 to gamemode=1 in the *server.properties* file.

Now you're set up on your Mac! Next let's meet IDLE, which is where you'll be writing your code. Flip to "Getting to Know IDLE" on page 20.

SETTING UP YOUR RASPBERRY PI

Log in to your Raspberry Pi and start the desktop with the startx command. (If you're using the most recent version of the Raspberry Pi operating system, you won't need to enter this command.)

Depending on your Raspberry Pi, you might have two or three different versions of Python installed. For this book, you'll use the most recent version of Python, Python 3.

By default, the Raspberry Pi computer comes installed with a simplified version of Minecraft called Minecraft: Pi Edition. Everything you need to get started programming your Minecraft world with Python is already installed. If you're new to using a Raspberry Pi, you can find instructions for getting started on the official website, *http://www.raspberrypi.org/*.

If you're using an older SD card image (created before August 2014), you might find that Minecraft is not installed. It's easy to install if it isn't already there. First you'll need to connect to the Internet with your Raspberry Pi. You can find a guide for connecting your Raspberry Pi to the Internet at *http://www.raspberrypi.org/*.

Once you're connected to the Internet, follow these steps:

1. On the desktop, double-click **LXTerminal**.

2. Once LXTerminal is open, enter this command:

```
$ sudo apt-get update
```

3. Once the update has finished, enter this command:

```
$ sudo apt-get install minecraft-pi
```

4. Wait until the installation is complete. Minecraft is now installed.

There are some limitations to Minecraft on the Raspberry Pi compared to the desktop edition. The game world is a lot smaller, and a lot of blocks and other features (such as Survival Mode) are missing, but you'll still be able to write and run all the awesome programs in this book.

Before we move on, let's create a folder where you can store your Python programs. On the taskbar, click the file browser icon. Open the *Documents* folder, and then right-click in the background of the file browser and select **Create New...▸ Folder**. Name the folder *Minecraft Python* and click **OK**.

NOTE *If you're using an original Raspberry Pi, you'll find that some of the programs in this book run slowly due to limitations of the Raspberry Pi. The Raspberry Pi 2 will have fewer problems with speed.*

To open Minecraft, click the start menu in the top-left corner of the desktop. (If you're using an older version of the Raspberry Pi operating system, the start menu will be in the bottom-left corner.) Go to **Games** and click **Minecraft**. Minecraft will open. The first time you open Minecraft, you'll have to click **Create World**.

As a general rule, don't resize the window, as you might encounter some problems.

Sometimes when you open other windows or dialogs (such as confirmation that you want to save a file in Python), they'll hide behind the Minecraft window. Just minimize Minecraft when you want to use other windows. If you're having any issues, try restarting your Raspberry Pi after installing Minecraft.

GETTING TO KNOW IDLE

Now that you have everything installed and set up, let's check out IDLE, the software you'll be using to write and run your Python programs. Your Python installation includes IDLE, so you don't need to install it separately. Let's open IDLE now!

Windows Open the Start Menu and enter **IDLE** in the search box.

Mac Open the *Applications* folder and click the IDLE icon.

Raspberry Pi On the desktop, double-click the IDLE icon labeled Python 3.

An IDLE window will open, as shown in Figure 1-14. This window is called the Python shell. The Python shell is so awesome that it blew my mind when I learned how to program with Python!

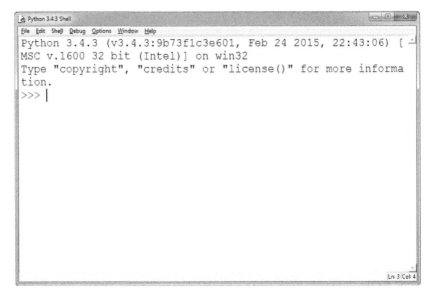

Figure 1-14: An IDLE window that is used for writing Python programs

GETTING TO KNOW THE PYTHON SHELL

The Python shell allows you to write and run programs one line at a time. You can write a line of code, instantly run it and see what happens, and then write another line. This is great because you can play around and test your code easily.

In the window you should see three chevrons (>>>) at the beginning of the line. This is called the *command prompt*. The command prompt is the Python shell telling you that it's ready for you to give it a command. Let's start with a really basic command: getting Python to add two numbers.

Click in the Python shell, next to the command prompt, and type **2 + 2**. Note that you don't have to type the command prompt itself (>>>). You should have something that looks like this:

```
>>> 2 + 2
```

After you type this command, press ENTER. The Python shell will output the result. In this case it's 4:

```
>>> 2 + 2
4
```

You can also use the shell with text. Type this code into the Python shell and press ENTER:

```
>>> "W" + "o" * 5
Wooooo
```

As you can see, this code outputs the word Wooooo. The number at the end of the command determines how many *o*'s there are in the word. By changing this number, you can change how long the word is. Try changing it to 20 (or any other number that you want):

```
>>> "W" + "o" * 20
Wooooooooooooooooooooo
```

Wooooooooooooooooooooo! The Python shell can be a lot of fun.

Notice that IDLE colors the code. This is called *syntax highlighting*, and it makes the different parts of the code easier to see. All of the code in this book is the same color as it is in IDLE so the colors will match when you write your programs.

Next let's look at IDLE's text editor.

SAY HELLO TO IDLE'S TEXT EDITOR

When it comes to writing longer programs, you can't use the shell. IDLE's text editor is the solution! Unlike the shell, it doesn't run a line of code immediately after you enter it. Instead, it runs the whole program when you tell it to.

In IDLE, click **File** on the menu bar and select **New File**. A new window will open that looks like the one in Figure 1-15. This is the text editor.

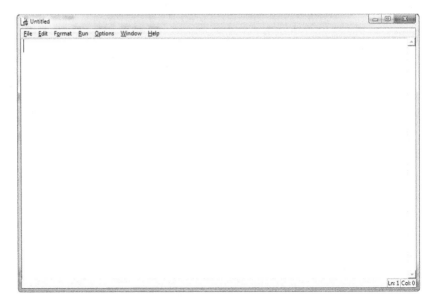

Figure 1-15: IDLE's text editor

"Hey!" I hear you say. "The text editor looks just like IDLE's Python shell." Well, yes it does, but there is one really big difference. The new window doesn't have a command prompt (>>>) at the beginning of each line.

Let's see what that means. On the first line of the text editor, type this code and press ENTER:

```
print(2 + 2)
```

Did you expect something to happen? Pressing ENTER doesn't run the code here—it just creates a new line. Because the text editor doesn't run code when you press ENTER, you can write as many lines as you want before running them. Let's add a few more lines. This is what your file should look like when you're done:

```
print(2 + 2)
print("W" + "o" * 20)
print("PYTHON!")
print("<3s")
print("Minecraft")
```

Before you run your Python code from IDLE's text editor, you need to save it. To save the program, click **File**, then **Save As**. Create a folder in your *Minecraft Python* folder called *Setting Up*. Save this program as *pythonLovesMinecraft.py* in the *Setting Up* folder.

Now let's run it. Go to **Run** on the menu and click **Run Module**. The shell window will open and your program will run in it. The output is shown in Figure 1-16.

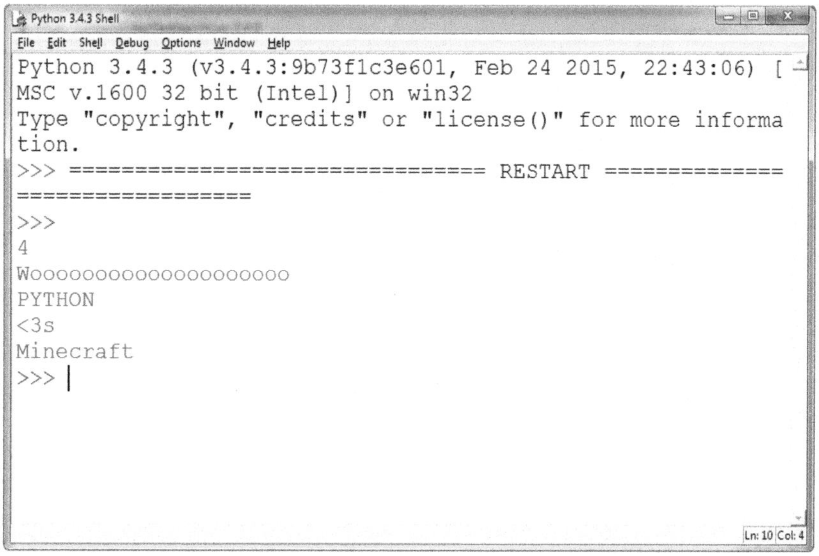

Figure 1-16: The output of the Python program

Unlike in the shell, commands run from the text editor will not automatically output their results. This is why you use print() to output the results of your code. Don't worry too much about the details now—you'll learn all about this later in the book.

Whenever you run programs from IDLE's text editor, the shell will open to run the program. Even though you write the program in a separate window, IDLE always uses the shell to run your program.

WHEN TO USE THE PYTHON SHELL AND WHEN TO USE THE TEXT EDITOR

Now that you've seen the difference between IDLE's Python shell and IDLE's text editor, you might be wondering when it's better to use one over the other. As a general rule, I use the Python shell when I only want to test a few lines and I don't intend to reuse them. As you follow along with this book, I recommend that you run the short examples using the Python shell.

I use the text editor for programs that have quite a few lines of code or that I want to reuse. All of the missions in this book use the text editor so you can save your progress, but you can always play around in the shell whenever you want to try something out quickly.

THE PROMPTS USED IN THIS BOOK

Throughout this book, whenever you see a piece of code that is written in IDLE's Python shell, it will begin with the command prompt (>>>) like this:

```
>>> print("Wooooo Minecraft")
```

I recommend that you copy the code into IDLE as you read so that you can familiarize yourself with it. Any output from the shell will be written on the next line:

```
>>> print("Wooooo Minecraft")
Wooooo Minecraft
```

Code that's written in the text editor *won't* begin with the command prompt, like so:

```
print("Adventures")
```

The output for the code won't automatically display on your computer. To show you what the output should look like when you run it, I'll either explain it or display it in a new box. For example, running the code above should output:

```
Adventures
```

To make it easier for you to follow the explanations of the code in the book, I've included markers to point out what I'm talking about. Whenever you see one in the code, there'll be a corresponding explanation in the text, and vice versa. The markers look like this:

❶ ❷ ❸ ❹ ❺ ❻

TESTING YOUR MINECRAFT PYTHON SETUP

Let's make sure you have all of the software installed correctly. To do this, we'll take a quick dive into a very basic Python program that will interact with Minecraft.

First things first: if you're using a PC or a Mac, you need to open three pieces of software. Follow these steps:

1. Open Spigot by going to your *Minecraft Tools* folder and clicking *Start_Server.*
2. Open Minecraft and connect to the Spigot server by selecting **Minecraft Python World** from the multiplayer menu.
3. Hit ESC on your keyboard to free your cursor from the Minecraft window, and then open a Python shell in IDLE.

You'll need to have these three pieces of software open whenever you write programs that interact with Minecraft.

If you're using a Raspberry Pi, open IDLE and Minecraft.

Now enter this line into your shell. Make sure that you enter lowercase and uppercase letters to match exactly!

```
>>> from mcpi.minecraft import Minecraft
```

Press ENTER so you're on the next line in the shell. Then enter this line:

```
>>> mc = Minecraft.create()
```

At this point, if you see an error message that looks something like Figure 1-17, there's something wrong.

```
Python 3.4.3 Shell                                              _ □ ✕
File  Edit  Shell  Debug  Options  Window  Help
Python 3.4.3 (v3.4.3:9b73f1c3e601, Feb 24 2015, 22:43:06)
[MSC v.1600 32 bit (Intel)] on win32
Type "copyright", "credits" or "license()" for more infor
mation.
>>> from mcpi.minecraft import Minecraft
>>> mc = Minecraft.create()
Traceback (most recent call last):
  File "<pyshell#1>", line 1, in <module>
    mc = Minecraft.create()
  File "C:\Python34\lib\site-packages\mcpi\minecraft.py",
line 171, in create
    return Minecraft(Connection(address, port))
  File "C:\Python34\lib\site-packages\mcpi\connection.py"
, line 17, in __init__
    self.socket.connect((address, port))
ConnectionRefusedError: [WinError 10061] No connection co
uld be made because the target machine actively refused i
t
>>>
                                                   Ln: 13 Col: 4
```

Figure 1-17: An error message that means I haven't started Spigot

Check these things in order: Do you have Minecraft open? Is Spigot running? Are you in the multiplayer world? Are you using the correct version of Python (3, not 2)? If the error occurred after you typed the first line, that means you didn't install the API correctly. Go through the steps to install the API again. If the error happened after the second line, you might not have Java or Spigot installed correctly. Try reinstalling these things one at a time.

If you get an error that says `ImportError: No module named 'mcpi'`, you might be using an older version of Python. Make sure you have the latest version installed!

If you don't get an error message, add this line to the program in IDLE:

```
mc.player.setTilePos(0, 120, 0)
```

When you do this, the player will fly high into the air! This code teleports the player to a new position. You'll learn more about this in Chapter 2. Turn the page to get started!

2

TELEPORTING WITH VARIABLES

Are you ready to control your Minecraft world with the power of Python? In this chapter, you'll take a brief tour through the basics of Python. Then you'll put your new skills to the test and create your own teleportation tour of your Minecraft world!

The concepts described in this chapter aren't specific to Minecraft Python, so you'll be able to use them in any Python program that you create.

WHAT IS A PROGRAM?

A *program* is a set of instructions that makes your computer do a specific task or tasks. Imagine a stopwatch app on a mobile phone. The stopwatch program has instructions that tell it what to do when you press start and stop. It also has instructions that display the time on the screen as it's being counted. Some guy or gal programmed that stopwatch to work.

Millions of programs are used every day all around the world. A phone's messaging app is a program, traffic lights are controlled by programs, and even computer games like Minecraft are programs.

In this book, you'll learn the fundamentals of programming and how to write programs to make your ideas come to life in Minecraft.

STORING DATA WITH VARIABLES

Let's start by learning how to store data with variables. *Variables* let you store data to use later in a program. *Data* is any information you might want to record, such as numbers, names, any kind of text, lists of items, and so on. For example, here's a variable called pickaxes that stores the number value 12:

```
>>> pickaxes = 12
```

Variables can store numbers, words, and even complete sentences, such as "Get out of here, Creeper!" You can also change variables, which lets you do some pretty neat things in Minecraft. In fact, shortly you'll use variables to take advantage of the power of teleportation!

To create a variable in Python, you'll use a variable name, an equal sign (=), and a value. Let's say you're about to take off on a grand adventure through many Minecraft biomes; you'll want to bring a lot of food with you. You can represent food as a variable. For example, in the following Python shell, bread is the variable name and 145 is the value:

```
>>> bread = 145
```

The variable's name is always on the left of the equal sign, and the value you want to store is always on the right, as shown in Figure 2-1. This Python code line *declares* the variable bread and *assigns* the value 145 to it.

After you've declared a variable and assigned it a value, you can enter the name of the variable into the Python shell to check what it's holding:

$$\underbrace{\texttt{bread}}_{\text{variable name}} = \underbrace{\texttt{145}}_{\text{value}}$$

Figure 2-1: Parts of a variable declaration. You must be very hungry if you have 145 loaves of bread.

```
>>> bread
145
```

You can use almost any name for a variable, but it's best to use a name that describes the variable's purpose so you'll understand what's going on in your program. Although it's not a rule, you should start variable names with a lowercase letter instead of a capital letter. This is a style that Python programmers follow, and it's good practice for you to follow, too, so others can easily read your code if you ever want to share it.

Although the value of a variable is stored, it is not saved. The value of a variable is stored in the computer's temporary memory, meaning that when the computer is switched off or the program stops running, the value of the variable is no longer stored. Try closing IDLE and then opening it again. When you try to get the value of bread, what happens?

THE STRUCTURE OF PROGRAMMING LANGUAGES

Syntax is the set of rules that describes the grammar and punctuation of a programming language, similar to the grammar and punctuation in a human language. Once you understand Python's syntax, you'll be better able to write programs that a computer can follow; however, if you don't use correct syntax, the computer won't understand what you're telling it to do.

Think of a single instruction in your code as a sentence. To end a sentence in English, you use a period (called a full stop in the United Kingdom). Instead of a period, Python uses a new line to indicate the end of an instruction and the start of the next. Each instruction on a new line is called a *statement*.

For example, say you want to keep track of how many pickaxes, iron ore blocks, and cobblestone blocks you have. In the Python shell, you'd write it like this:

```
>>> pickaxes = 12
>>> iron = 30
>>> cobblestone = 25
```

Figure 2-2 shows what this looks like in the Python shell.

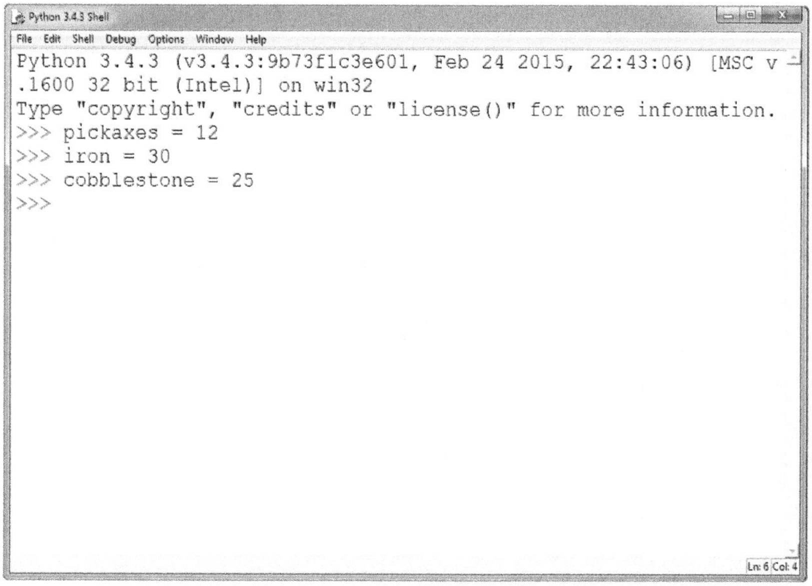

Figure 2-2: Entering code in the Python shell

Notice that each statement is on its own line. Because of the new lines, Python will understand that you want to keep track of three different items. But if you don't put each statement on a new line, Python gets confused and gives you a syntax error:

```
>>> pickaxes = 12 iron = 30 cobblestone = 25
SyntaxError: invalid syntax
```

A *syntax error* is Python's way of telling you it doesn't understand. Python won't be able to follow these instructions because it doesn't know where one statement ends and another begins.

Python also won't know what to do if you start lines with a space:

```
>>>    iron = 30
SyntaxError: unexpected indent
```

If you look closely, you'll see that the code has spaces at the beginning of the line. When you get an unexpected indent syntax error, like the one here, you'll know that your line of code starts with spaces when it shouldn't.

Python is very picky about how you write code. If you get a syntax error when entering the examples in this book, check your work carefully. Most likely, you'll find a small mistake.

SYNTAX RULES FOR VARIABLES

You need to know a few syntax rules for naming variables so Python can understand them:

- Don't include symbols in your variable names, except for underscores (_), or you'll get a syntax error.
- Don't start a variable name with a number, as in 9bread. Using numbers elsewhere in a variable name is fine, as in bread9.
- You don't need to add spaces on either side of the equal sign: your program will run fine without them. But they do make the code easier to read, so it's a good idea to add them.

Variables are very handy. Next, you'll learn how to change the value of variables, and then you'll be ready to teleport your player!

CHANGING THE VALUES OF VARIABLES

You can change the value of a variable at any time in the same way you'd declare a variable. For example, say you meet five Minecraft cats and you want to save this value as a variable. First you declare a variable, cats, and assign the value 5 to it, which would look like this in a Python shell:

```
>>> cats = 5
>>> cats
5
```

Later you meet five more cats and decide you want to update this value. What happens if you change the value of cats to 10?

```
>>> cats = 10
>>> cats
10
```

When you ask Python for the new value of cats, it's no longer 5! Now when you use the cats variable in a program, it will use the new value of 10.

There are many types of data that you can store in variables. *Data types* tell the computer how to work with a particular piece of data. I'll start by discussing one of the types you'll use most often: integers. Later in the chapter, I'll also introduce the floats data type.

INTEGERS

Integers are positive or negative whole numbers. Values such as 10, 32, –6, 194689, and –5 are integers, but 3.14 and 6.025 are not.

You probably use integers every day without even thinking about it, even in Minecraft! For example, you might see 12 cows on a hillside while you're on your way to mine 5 diamonds with 2 fresh apples in your inventory. All those numbers are integers.

Let's say you have five pigs in your Minecraft world and you want to write a program that uses the number of pigs in some way. In Python, you'd declare an integer variable to represent the number of pigs:

```
>>> pigs = 5
```

You can also store negative values in variables. For example, to say the temperature is negative five degrees, you would set a variable like so:

```
>>> temperature = -5
```

To use Python variables and integers with Minecraft, complete the first mission.

MISSION #1: TELEPORT THE PLAYER

In this mission, you'll explore how variables work by teleporting your player to a new location using integers.

As shown in Figure 2-3, your player has a *position* in the Minecraft world that is represented by three *coordinates*: x, y, and z. The letter y represents height, and x and z represent horizontal positions on a flat plane.

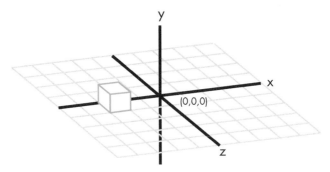

Figure 2-3: 3D coordinates

If you're using the Raspberry Pi version of the game, the player's position is given by three numbers in the top-left corner of the game window, which you can see in Figure 2-4. If you're using the desktop edition of the game, you can see the player's coordinates by pressing F3 and finding the first line in the second block of text on the left, labeled *XYZ*, as shown in Figure 2-5.

Move your player around the game and watch the position numbers change; the coordinates should update in real time as the player walks. Pretty cool, right? But walking long distances takes a long time. Why spend so much time walking when you can change positions instantly using Python? Let's look at how to do this.

Figure 2-4: The player's position displayed in Minecraft: Pi Edition

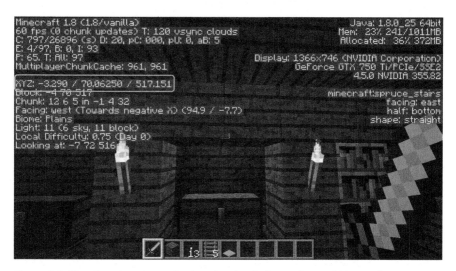

```
Minecraft 1.8 (1.8/vanilla)                    Java: 1.8.0_25 64bit
60 fps (0 chunk updates) T: 120 vsync clouds   Mem:  23% 241/1011MB
C: 797/26896 (s) D: 20, pC: 000, pU: 0, aB: 5  Allocated:  36% 372MB
E: 4/97, B: 0, I: 93
F: 65, T: All: 97                              Display: 1366x746 (NVIDIA Corporation)
MultiplayerChunkCache: 961, 961                        GeForce GTX 750 Ti/PCIe/SSE2
                                                       4.5.0 NVIDIA 355.82
XYZ: -3.290 / 70.06250 / 517.151
Block: -4 70 517                                       minecraft:spruce_stairs
Chunk: 12 6 5 in -1 4 32                                       facing: east
Facing: west (Towards negative X) (94.9 / -7.7)               half: bottom
Biome: Plains                                                 shape: straight
Light: 11 (6 sky, 11 block)
Local Difficulty: 0.75 (Day 0)
Looking at: -7 72 516
```

Figure 2-5: The player's position displayed in the desktop edition of Minecraft

Switch on your computer or Raspberry Pi and follow these steps:

1. Open IDLE and click **File ▶ New File** (or **New Window** on some computers). You can see the empty text editor window in Figure 2-6. If you're using a Raspberry Pi or have more than one version of Python installed on your computer, make sure you use Python 3, not Python 2.7.

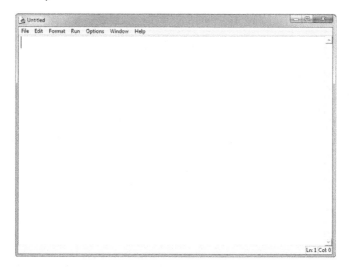

Figure 2-6: A new text editor window in IDLE

2. When the new window appears, click **File ▸ Save As**.

3. Create a new folder called *variables* inside the *Minecraft Python* folder that you created in Chapter 1.

4. Open the *variables* folder, name your file *teleport.py*, and click **Save**.

Now that you're working in IDLE's text editor, add the following two lines of code at the top of your program:

```
from mcpi.minecraft import Minecraft
mc = Minecraft.create()
```

These lines connect your program to Minecraft; you'll use them in every program that interacts with Minecraft. Next, create three integer variables called x, y, and z.

```
x = 10
y = 110
z = 12
```

These variables represent the position that you want to teleport your player to. For now, set these variables to 10, 110, and 12, as shown here.

Then enter the following line of code, which will transport the player:

```
mc.player.setTilePos(x, y, z)
```

The setTilePos() part of the program is a *function*, which is a prewritten and reusable piece of code. The setTilePos(x, y, z) function tells Minecraft to change the player's position using the three variables you just set. The values inside the parentheses are called *arguments*. You *passed* the variables you just created to the function as arguments so the function can use the values of x, y, and z when it runs.

WARNING *If you're using a Raspberry Pi, don't use values larger than 127 or smaller than –127 for the x and z variables. The Minecraft Pi world is small, and numbers outside this range will crash the game.*

Listing 2-1 contains the full code to teleport your player, which you can also see in Figure 2-7:

```
teleport.py  ❶ # Connect to Minecraft
             from mcpi.minecraft import Minecraft
             mc = Minecraft.create()

             # Set x, y, and z variables to represent coordinates
             x = 10
             y = 110
             z = 12
```

```
# Change the player's position
mc.player.setTilePos(x, y, z)
```

Listing 2-1: The finished teleport code

To make this program easier to understand, I've included some *comments* ❶. Comments are useful statements in code that describe what the code does but are ignored by Python. In other words, when you run the program, Python passes commented lines without doing anything. A single-line comment begins with a hash mark (#). My comments describe what each part of *teleport.py* does. It's a good habit to write comments in your code so you can remember what the parts of your program do when you return to them later.

Figure 2-7 shows the completed program written in IDLE's text editor.

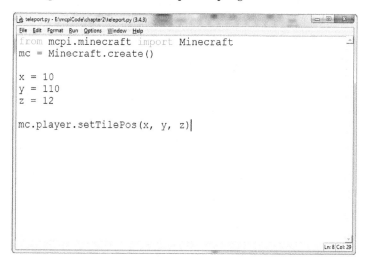

Figure 2-7: The completed program in IDLE's text editor

Now let's run the program! Follow these steps:

1. Open Minecraft by clicking the desktop icon.

2. If you're using a Raspberry Pi, click **Start Game** and **Create a New World**. If you're using the desktop edition of Minecraft, open the game world using the instructions in "Running Spigot and Creating a Game" on page 7 for Windows and on page 16 for Mac.

3. After the world has been generated, press the ESC key (or TAB if you're using a Raspberry Pi) to release the mouse. You can now move the mouse outside of the Minecraft window or double-click the Minecraft window to reselect the game. Figure 2-8 shows the IDLE and Minecraft windows on my computer.

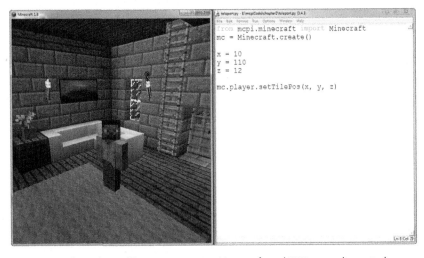

Figure 2-8: This is how I like to arrange my Minecraft and IDLE text editor windows.

4. Click the IDLE text editor window that has your *teleport.py* program.

5. Click **Run ▸ Run Module** or press F5. If you haven't saved the program, IDLE will always ask if you want to save before running. Click **OK** to save the program. If you click Cancel, the program won't run.

NOTE *When you're running programs from IDLE on a Raspberry Pi, a dialog asking you to save your program might appear and hide itself behind the Minecraft window. If you think IDLE has frozen, it might be that the dialog is hiding. Just minimize the Minecraft window and click OK in the IDLE dialog. After clicking OK, maximize the Minecraft window.*

Well done! Your program should now run, and after a few seconds, your player should be teleported to coordinates (10, 110, 12), as shown in Figure 2-9. Your world isn't the same as mine, so you'll see some differences when you run it on your computer.

BONUS OBJECTIVE: JUMP AROUND

Do you think you've got the hang of teleportation? Try replacing x, y, and z with other integers to see where your player ends up! Try negative values, too!

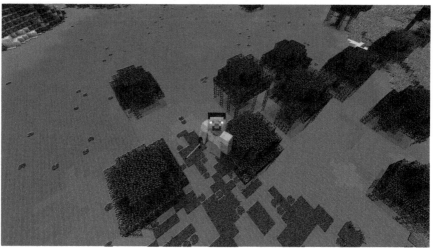

Figure 2-9: I've teleported from my house to position (10, 110, 12), which is above a swamp. Look out below!

FLOATS

Not all numbers are whole numbers. Decimal points are used to represent values that can't be described with whole numbers. For example, you might have half (0.5) of an apple. Numbers that use decimal points are called *floating point numbers*, or *floats*. This is another data type that Python uses. Floating point numbers are used instead of integers when you want to be more precise. Floats can also represent whole numbers (as in 3.0), but integers can't represent numbers with decimal places.

You might have noticed that your player's position coordinates (as shown in Figures 2-4 and 2-5) include decimals, which means they're floats!

In Python, you declare a float variable in the same way that you declare an integer variable. For example, to set the variable x to 1.34, you'd write this:

```
>>> x = 1.34
```

To create a negative float, put a minus sign (-) before the value:

```
>>> x = -1.34
```

In the next mission, you'll gain even more control over your teleportation powers by using floats to teleport the player to precise locations.

MISSION #2: GO EXACTLY WHERE YOU WANT

You learned how to set the player's position using integers, but you can set the player's position more accurately if you use floats. In this mission, we'll revise the program from Mission #1 to teleport the player using a float value:

1. In IDLE, open the *teleport.py* program (page 34) by clicking **File ▶ Open** and selecting the file from your *variables* folder.
2. Save a copy of the program as *teleportPrecise.py* in your *variables* folder.
3. In the *teleportPrecise.py* file, change the x, y, and z variables to use floats instead of integers. That is, change the values of x, y, and z from 10, 110, and 12 to 10.0, 110.0, and 12.0.
4. Change the last line of code to mc.player.setPos(x, y, z) by removing the word Tile.
5. Save the program.
6. Open a Minecraft world and run the code.

The final result should look like this:

teleportPrecise .py

```
# Connect to Minecraft
from mcpi.minecraft import Minecraft
mc = Minecraft.create()

# Set x, y, and z variables to represent coordinates
x = 10.0
y = 110.0
z = 12.0

# Change the player's position
mc.player.setPos(x, y, z)
```

Notice the difference between `mc.player.setPos(x, y, z)`, used here, and `mc.player.setTilePos(x, y, z)`, used in Listing 2-1. The `setTilePos()` function uses integers to tell the game the position of the block that you want to teleport to. The `setPos()` function is a little different—it uses floats to tell the game the position of the block as well as the precise position *on* that block that you want to teleport to. Using my program, I teleported to the top of my tower, as shown in Figure 2-10.

Figure 2-10: I've teleported myself to the top of my tower, using floats to be very precise.

BONUS OBJECTIVE: TELEPORT ACCURATELY

Change the values of the x, y, and z variables using a mixture of positive and negative floats and run the program. Then, change the decimal values slightly from your new ones. What happens?

SLOWING DOWN TELEPORTATION USING THE TIME MODULE

Python runs your code as fast as possible. But you can slow down the action by making your programs wait a certain number of seconds before continuing.

To use time in your programs, you need the `time` module, which contains a set of prewritten functions relating to time. To use the `time` module, add the following line of code to the top of your programs:

```
import time
```

Order is very important when you're using the time module and the sleep() function, which is part of the time module. The sleep() function will make a program wait a specified number of seconds before continuing. You must always import the time module before you use the sleep() function. If you don't, Python won't be able to find the sleep() function and will be so confused that it will stop your program from running. This is why it's best to import any module you use at the top of your code. All of your import statements will be grouped together at the top of the program. For example, I usually include the lines of code to connect to Minecraft first, and then add the import time statement on the third line.

Here is an example of how to use the sleep() function:

```
time.sleep(5)
```

This line of code pauses your program for five seconds. You can use any number, including integers and floats, as the following example shows:

```
time.sleep(0.2)
```

When your program reaches this line of code, it will wait 0.2 seconds. Now that you can control the flow of time, you're ready for the next mission!

MISSION #3: TELEPORTATION TOUR

The beauty of teleportation in Minecraft is that you can send your player anywhere. Using all the skills you've learned so far, you'll send your player on an automated tour of your entire Minecraft world!

In this mission, you'll practice changing the values of variables by modifying the code from Mission #1 (page 31) to teleport the player to several locations across the map. The player will teleport to one location, wait a few seconds, and then teleport to another location.

1. In IDLE, open the *teleport.py* program (page 34) by clicking **File ▸ Open** and selecting the file from your *variables* folder.

2. Save a copy of the program as *tour.py* in your *variables* folder.

3. Just after the code that connects your program to Minecraft, add import time.

4. At the end of the program, add time.sleep(10).

5. Copy the lines with the x, y, and z variables and the setTilePos() function and paste them at the end of the program, so those lines appear twice.

6. Change the values of both sets of x, y, and z variables to any numbers you want. You can find the coordinates for any position in your game by moving there and writing down the player's coordinates like you did earlier in this chapter.

7. Save the program.

8. Open a Minecraft world and run the code.

The final result should look like this, with new coordinates filled in:

tour.py

```
# Connect to Minecraft
from mcpi.minecraft import Minecraft
mc = Minecraft.create()
import time

# Set x, y, and z variables to represent coordinates
x = # Fill in
y = # Fill in
z = # Fill in

# Change the player's position
mc.player.setTilePos(x, y, z)

# Wait 10 seconds
time.sleep(10)

# Set x, y, and z variables to represent coordinates
x = # Fill in
y = # Fill in
z = # Fill in

# Change the player's position
mc.player.setTilePos(x, y, z)
```

The player should teleport to the first location, wait 10 seconds, and then teleport to the second location, as shown in Figure 2-11.

BONUS OBJECTIVE: MORE TELEPORTATION

Copy the *tour.py* code to move the player as many times as you want. Replace the 10 in the function time.sleep(10) with a different value. You could even use a different number for each sleep() function so your player waits a different amount of time at each location.

Then edit the code so that between teleports, only one of the x, y, and z variables changes. You don't have to change every variable every time! Try using floats instead of integers, too.

Figure 2-11: I've set the coordinates in my program to teleport to my house and then to teleport to the desert.

DEBUGGING

Everyone makes mistakes; often, even the best programmers don't get their code right the first time. Writing a program that works is just one skill that a good programmer needs. Fixing programs when they don't work is another essential skill. This process is called *debugging*, and each problem in a misbehaving program is called a *bug*. In this section, you'll learn tips and tricks to fix all your future programs.

Bugs can completely stop a program from running, or they can make the program behave in an unexpected way. When a program doesn't run, Python will show you an error message, such as the one in Figure 2-12.

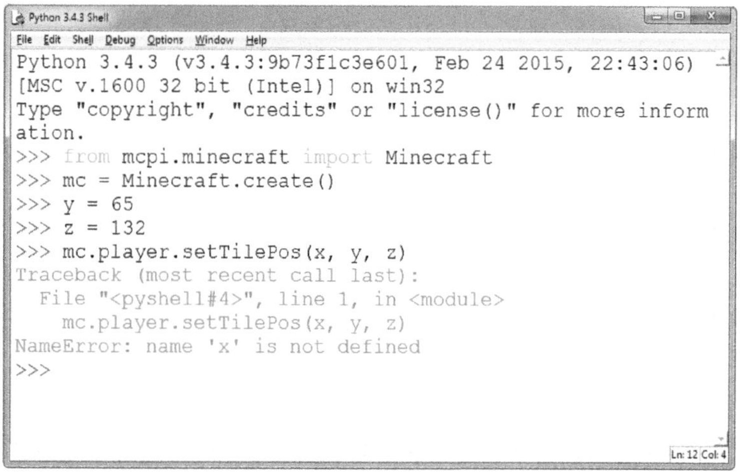

Figure 2-12: Python gives me an error message because I didn't stick to Python's syntax.

In Figure 2-12 you can see that I've entered some code in the Python shell, and it has returned an error message. A lot of information is displayed in the error message, but based on the last line (`NameError: name 'x' is not defined`) I can tell that something is wrong with my x variable. Specifically, the x variable has not been defined. To fix this, I need to add an extra line of code that defines the x variable, like so:

```
>>> x = 10
```

This line will fix the error message, but it doesn't mean all errors will be fixed.

Bugs that allow the program to run but cause it to behave strangely won't show an error message, but you'll know something is wrong when your program produces an unexpected result. For example, if you forget to write a line of code in your teleportation programs, such as `setTilePos()`, the program will run without any errors, but the player won't change position. That's not a very useful teleportation program!

WARNING *Typos are among the most common causes of bugs. Spelling something in a way the computer doesn't expect can stop your program from running. Be careful, and make sure your spelling and capitalization are correct!*

MISSION #4: FIX THE BUGGY TELEPORTATION

In this mission, you'll debug two programs. The first program, Listing 2-2, is similar to *teleport.py* (page 34), but this version has five mistakes. Open a new file in the IDLE text editor, copy Listing 2-2 into it, and save it as *teleportBug1.py*.

```
from mcpi.minceraft inport Minecraft
# mc = Minecraft.create()

x = 10
  y = 11
z = 12
```

Listing 2-2: A broken version of the teleport program

To debug this program, complete the following steps:

1. Run *teleportBug1.py*.
2. When you get an error message, read the last line for a hint about what's wrong.
3. Correct the bug and run the code again.
4. Keep correcting the bugs until the program teleports the player to a new location.

HINT   *Don't forget to double-check that you're actually calling the* setTilePos() *function!*

Let's try debugging another program. The version of *teleport.py* in Listing 2-3 runs, but for some reason, the player doesn't teleport to the specified position. Copy Listing 2-3 into an IDLE file and save it as *teleportBug2.py*.

```
from mcpi.minecraft import Minecraft
mc = Minecraft.create()

x = 10
y = 110
z = -12

mc.player.setPos(x, z, y)
```

Listing 2-3: The teleport program with bugs

Unlike with *teleportBug1.py*, you won't get any error messages when you run the program. To fix this program, you'll need to read the code until you find the mistake. The program should teleport the player to position (10, 110, –12). Run the program and check the coordinates that the player has teleported to. This might help you debug the program and identify the problem with it.

When you've squashed all the bugs in these two programs, add a comment to each to explain what the problems were. Jotting down problems you encounter in debugging can help you remember to watch out for similar bugs in the future.

WHAT YOU LEARNED

Congratulations! You've written your first Python programs to control a Minecraft player through the power of variables and functions. You explored two data types (integers and floats), controlled time, and debugged broken programs. You also learned two useful functions specific to the Minecraft Python API : `setPos()` and `setTilePos()`.

In Chapter 3, you'll master the art of speed building in Minecraft, using mathematical operations and functions that set blocks!

3

BUILDING QUICKLY AND TRAVELING FAR WITH MATH

In Chapter 2, you learned how to create a variable and change its value. In this chapter, you'll learn how to use math in Python to generate any block you want and quickly build complex structures in your Minecraft world. You'll even give yourself superpowers to make the player super jump!

EXPRESSIONS AND STATEMENTS

When you're having a conversation with someone, you want them to understand what you're telling them. You use short phrases, such as "three diamonds" or "behind a tree," to give information to the person you're talking to. However, the phrases don't make sense on their own unless they're combined into sentences, such as "I found three diamonds behind a tree."

Python programming has concepts similar to phrases and sentences, which are called expressions and statements.

You can combine values, variables, and operators to create small pieces of code called *expressions*, like 2 + 2. Expressions can be combined into *statements*, which you learned about in Chapter 2. Statements are single lines or short blocks of code that do something in a program, such as zombies = 2 + 2. In this example, 2 + 2 is an expression and is part of the statement zombies = 2 + 2.

For longer programs that use a text editor instead of the Python shell, be sure to write entire statements. For example, the Python shell and a program written in a text editor will treat the expression 2 + 2 entirely differently. When you're using the Python shell in IDLE, Python will output 4 as the result of 2 + 2, as shown here:

```
>>> 2 + 2
4
```

However, when you're using a text editor, Python won't do anything with the expression because it's not part of a complete statement. To turn this expression into a complete statement, you could assign its value to a variable, like this:

```
zombies = 2 + 2
```

Then print that variable to see its value:

```
print(zombies)
```

When you run this code, it will print 4.

Again, when writing programs in the text editor, it's very important that you use full statements, not just expressions.

OPERATORS

In math, *operators* are used to alter and combine numbers. For example, the addition operator lets you add two (or more) numbers, and the subtraction operator is used to subtract one number from another.

Python uses all the basic math operators that you already know—addition, subtraction, multiplication, and division—as well as more advanced operators, like exponents. Let's start with addition.

ADDITION

In Python, addition looks like you would normally write it using the plus sign (+). For example, if you have two flowers and you pick two more, you could describe that with a statement using addition:

```
>>> flowers = 2 + 2
```

Python works out the result of the expression on the right side of the equal sign and then assigns it to the variable on the left. In this case, the result of the expression on the right is 4. For the rest of the time that this particular code is in use, the variable flowers will have a value of 4.

You can use addition in Minecraft to build things in the blink of an eye. Are you ready for your next mission? Let's get started!

MISSION #5: STACK BLOCKS

You can use the setBlock() function to create and place a block in Minecraft. Just like setPos() and setTilePos(), setBlock() takes x-, y-, and z-coordinates as arguments, but it also needs a fourth value: the block type. This value identifies the kind of block you want to place in the game.

Whether it's grass, lava, melon, or any other block, each type is represented by a specific integer. For example, grass is 2, empty air is 0, water is 8, and melon is 103. For a full list of blocks and their integer values, see "Block ID Cheat Sheet" on page 285.

To use setBlock(), pass values for the x-, y-, and z-coordinates and the integer representing the block type to the function, separated by commas. For example, let's place a melon block (type 103) at coordinates (6, 5, 28):

```
from mcpi.minecraft import Minecraft
mc = Minecraft.create()
mc.setBlock(6, 5, 28, 103)
```

After the first two familiar lines that you'll see in all Minecraft Python programs, just call setBlock() with all the values you want to use. You can also use variables instead of numbers to get the same effect, as shown in Listing 3-1.

blockStack.py
```
from mcpi.minecraft import Minecraft
mc = Minecraft.create()
x = 6
y = 5
z = 28
blockType = 103
mc.setBlock(x, y, z, blockType)
```

Listing 3-1: A program to create a melon block

First, create variables to represent the block coordinates (x, y, and z) and type (blockType). Then, pass all the variables to the setBlock() function, and the Minecraft Python API works its magic. Now you can use those variables again anywhere in your program, and if you decide to change their values later, you only have to change them in one place.

When you combine this code with math operators, you can do some pretty cool things. Let's create a stack of blocks.

Create a new folder called *math* within the *Minecraft Python* folder. Open IDLE and create a blank program using IDLE's text editor. Save this file as *blockStack.py* in the *math* folder. Copy the code from Listing 3-1 into your editor and add the two lines from Listing 3-2 to stack another melon block on top of the one you just set.

blockStack.py

```
❶ y = y + 1
❷ mc.setBlock(x, y, z, blockType)
```

Listing 3-2: Extra code to stack a second melon block on top of the first melon

You're adding 1 to the value of y ❶, and you're using the setBlock() function to create another new block ❷. By increasing the value of y by 1, the second block is placed higher on the y-axis than the first block, so the second block is stacked on top of the first one.

From here, your mission is to add two more blocks to the stack. Try modifying your *blockStack.py* program so it stacks four blocks instead of two! When you run your program, a stack of four melon blocks should appear, as shown in Figure 3-1.

Figure 3-1: I've made a stack of melon blocks.

HINT *To add a second block on top of the first, we increased the y variable by 1 and then used the setBlock() function again. What do you think would happen if you reused these two statements at the end of your program? What if you used them three times? Would this be a solution for creating a stack of four blocks?*

MISSION #6: SUPER JUMP

In Chapter 2, you learned how to change the player's location. Let's take that skill one step further and send the player high into the air using the power of addition. First, find out where the player is by calling getTilePos(), as shown in Listing 3-3.

superJump.py

```
from mcpi.minecraft import Minecraft
mc = Minecraft.create()

position = mc.player.getTilePos()
x = position.x
y = position.y
z = position.z
```

Listing 3-3: Code to find the player's position

The dot between the position variable and the x, y, and z is called *dot notation*. Dot notation is used by certain variables and functions, such as all of the functions you use in the Minecraft Python API (for example, mc.setTilePos()). You'll learn more about dot notation in Chapters 11 and 12.

Once you have the player's position, you can set the x, y, and z variables to the player's current coordinates, which are represented by position.x, position.y, and position.z. You can then teleport the player anywhere you want in relation to the current coordinates, as shown in Listing 3-4.

superJump.py

```
x = x + 5
mc.player.setTilePos(x, y, z)
```

Listing 3-4: Code to move the player's x position up by 5 blocks

Here, I've transported the player 5 blocks along the x-axis, but this isn't that special: you can move the player around horizontally any time you want in Minecraft. Let's give the player a super jump instead!

Your mission is to make the player jump 10 blocks into the air above their current position. You should be able to do this using the code in Listings 3-3 and 3-4 but with some slight differences. Copy the code in Listings 3-3 and 3-4 into IDLE, save it as *superJump.py*, and change the y variable in a similar way to how I changed the x variable. When you run the program, the player should jump into the air, as in Figure 3-2.

Figure 3-2: Here's the super jump in action!

SUBTRACTION

Python handles subtraction similarly to how it handles addition. Let's say you're out exploring a cave, a spider attacks you, and you lose some health:

```
health = 20
health = health - 2
```

The value of health in the statement is now 18. Just as with the addition operation, Python works out the result of the operation on the right of the equal sign and sets the variable to that value.

Let's have some fun with subtraction in Minecraft!

MISSION #7: CHANGE THE BLOCKS UNDER YOU

Have you ever wanted to set a trap for someone in Minecraft? Imagine the ground beneath the player suddenly changing to lava when they least expect it. You can use Python to make your wish come true. Using subtraction, you can place blocks below the player's current position. In fact, it takes only a few lines of code to place any block you want directly below the player!

In this mission, you'll change the block underneath the player to lava using getTilePos() and setBlock(). But this is a dangerous mission, so be careful when testing it: if you don't move the player to a new position quickly enough, they might fall into the lava!

The program in Listing 3-5 creates a block at the player's current position. Copy this code into a new file in IDLE and save it as *blockBelow.py*. Then, using your knowledge of the subtraction operator, change the code so it places a lava block directly below the player's feet, as shown in Figure 3-3.

```
from mcpi.minecraft import Minecraft
mc = Minecraft.create()
pos = mc.player.getTilePos()
x = pos.x
y = pos.y
z = pos.z
blockType = 10
mc.setBlock(x, y, z, blockType)
```

Listing 3-5: This code places a block at the player's current location.

Notice that I've named the variable that stores the player's position pos. I chose this name because I use this variable a lot, it's easy to understand what the name means, and it's shorter and faster to type than position.

The y-coordinate determines how high or low a block is. Your mission is to figure out how to change the y variable to place a block below the player.

Figure 3-3: After the block below me changed, I fell into the lava.

BONUS OBJECTIVE: BLOCKS ALL AROUND YOU

You've learned how to place blocks below the player. Can you work out how to place a block above the player? Once you've figured out how to do this, try to place several blocks around the player at once. Then you'll be able to start creating buildings around the player!

Try combining this program with the one from Mission #6 (page 51). Can you work out how to make the player jump into the air and then place a block immediately below them so they don't fall? Feeling evil? You could write a program that has the player fall from a great height into a pool of lava.

USING MATH OPERATORS IN ARGUMENTS

When you use a function, such as setBlock() or setTilePos(), you give the function arguments, which specify the values you want the function to use when it runs.

So far, you've been introduced to the addition and subtraction operators. You can use these operators inside a function's parentheses to set the values of arguments. Let's revisit the stacking blocks in Mission #5 (page 49). We can use the addition operator inside the parentheses of the setBlock() function, as shown in Listing 3-6, and it will add two values together within the parentheses without the need for an extra statement.

blockStack1.py

```
from mcpi.minecraft import Minecraft
mc = Minecraft.create()

x = 6
y = 5
z = 28
blockType = 103
mc.setBlock(x, y, z, blockType)
❶ mc.setBlock(x, y + 1, z, blockType)
```

Listing 3-6: The block stacking program with an operator in the arguments

Listing 3-6 is the almost same as the stacking blocks program. However, it uses the addition operator in the setBlock() function's parentheses instead of in a separate statement. The last line uses y + 1 as an argument in the function ❶. Although the value of this argument is 6 (5 + 1), the value of the y variable is still 5. The argument lets you add to the y variable without actually changing its value, which is useful if you want to use y again somewhere else in your code.

You can also add two variables together and use them as a single argument. Listing 3-7 is the same as Listing 3-6, but an extra variable named up determines the distance the new block will be placed on the y-axis.

blockStack2.py

```
from mcpi.minecraft import Minecraft
mc = Minecraft.create()

x = 6
y = 5
z = 28
blockType = 103
up = 1
mc.setBlock(x, y, z, blockType)
❶ mc.setBlock(x, y + up, z, blockType)
```

Listing 3-7: Another version of the stacking program that uses an addition operator in the arguments

On the last line, the y and up variables are added together ❶. As in Listing 3-6, this makes the setBlock() function's second argument 6. Variables are useful because if you want to place the new block two blocks higher on the y-axis, all you have to do is change your code and set up to 2. You can see the effect of all three versions (Listings 3-1 and 3-2, 3-6, and 3-7) of the program in Figure 3-4.

Figure 3-4: The three versions of the program have the same effect, even though they are different.

MISSION #8: SPEED BUILDING

Usually, you spend your first day in Minecraft building a shelter. With what you've learned so far, you can build a simple house and spend your first night in style! The program in this mission will help you quickly generate a building's walls, ceiling, and floor. Instead of spending lots of time placing every block by hand, you can construct the basic structure of your building in a few lines of code.

You've used setBlock() to create a single block, but setBlock() has a friend called setBlocks(), which creates several blocks in the shape of a cuboid. A *cuboid* is a 3D rectangle. A cuboid's length, width, and height can all be different values.

The setBlocks() function lets you create many blocks in a large area. To use setBlocks(), just pass it two sets of coordinates and the block type. The first set of coordinates identifies where you want one corner of the cuboid, and the second set specifies where you want the opposite corner. Figure 3-5 shows you the corners of the cuboid, labeled with their coordinates.

Let's create the cuboid in Figure 3-5. As you can see in Listing 3-8,

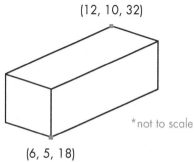

Figure 3-5: A cuboid and the coordinates used to set its dimensions

mine is made of cobblestone, but use any block type you like. Well, you can use anything except for lava, water, or air—those would give you a pretty strange house!

building.py

```
from mcpi.minecraft import Minecraft
mc = Minecraft.create()
❶ pos = mc.player.getPos()
x = pos.x
y = pos.y
z = pos.z
width = 10
height = 5
length = 6
❷ blockType = 4
❸ air = 0
mc.setBlocks(x, y, z, x + width, y + height, z + length, blockType)
```

Listing 3-8: Code that builds a cuboid of blocks

Notice that I've used getPos() ❶ instead of getTilePos(). The getPos() function is the same as the getTilePos() function, but it returns the coordinates as three floats instead of three integers.

The width, height, and length of this cuboid are 10, 5, and 6 respectively, and I've used a block ID of 4 to generate cobblestone ❷. You can see the finished building in Figure 3-6.

Figure 3-6: The building that the program creates

However, the house has a slight problem: it's completely solid! After I ran the program, I punched a hole in the side of the building so you can see that it's solid in the center. This cuboid is a great start, though, and now you'll be in charge of hollowing it out so the player can actually go inside.

Your mission is to change the program to create a building with walls, a ceiling, and a floor at the player's position. To accomplish this, you'll create a cuboid made of air inside the solid cuboid you just made. The two cuboids together should produce an empty box. You can see the result of the finished program in Figure 3-7. I've created a hole in the side so you can see the hollow center.

Figure 3-7: When your program is finished, it should create a hollow cuboid. A cuboid is perfect for creating buildings quickly!

Listing 3-8 already includes a variable called air ❸, which you can use to set the blocks inside the building to air. Copy Listing 3-8 into IDLE, save it as *building.py*, and adapt it to create a second cuboid made of air. You'll need to add an extra setBlocks() function on the last line to create this air cuboid. The air cuboid should be one block inside the walls all the way around, which is what you need to figure out how to do using addition and subtraction. Be patient: if your first try doesn't work, try something else!

HINT *To create the air cuboid one block inside the walls, you can use the addition and subtraction operators. Create the air cuboid using setBlocks() and increase the first x, y, and z arguments by 1. Then subtract 1 from the x + width, y + height, and z + length arguments.*

BONUS OBJECTIVE: BUILD ALL KINDS OF THINGS

You can reuse the code you wrote to create the building whenever you want. What if you want to construct a different-sized building? Can you work out how to change the width, height, and length of the building?

With just a few changes, your program can also have many other uses. Can you work out how to use it to generate a swimming pool? Hint: You'll need to change the block type of the inner cuboid to water (block ID 8) and remove the top of the outer cuboid so the player can get in the pool.

MULTIPLICATION

In Python code, multiplication looks slightly different from what you're probably used to seeing. Instead of writing an × to multiply two numbers, you use an asterisk (*). But other than the symbol, multiplication works the same as usual. The expression 2 * 2 equals 4, just like 2 × 2.

Imagine there are four trees outside your Minecraft house, and suddenly the number of trees doubles. You can represent this calculation in Python like this:

```
trees = 4
trees = trees * 2
```

The value of trees in this example is 8, which is 4 multiplied by 2.

DIVISION

In Python, division is represented by a forward slash (/) instead of the ÷ symbol.

The division operator divides one value by another. Just put the number that you want to divide on the left side of the forward slash (/) and the number you want to divide by on the right.

Let's say eight skeletons are outside your Minecraft fortress, but half of them walk away. To find out how many are left, you would divide 8 by 2. Here's how you'd represent this using a division operator in Python:

```
skeletons = 8
skeletons = skeletons / 2
```

Now just 4 skeletons are outside your fortress. Phew! Let's try out these two operators in Minecraft.

MISSION #9: SPECTACULAR SPIRES

One strength of variables is that you can change the value of a single variable, and its value will change everywhere the variable appears in the program. You can make a program do totally different things just by changing a single variable using math operators, like multiplication and division.

In this mission, you'll discover how to use division and multiplication to build a very tall, thin tower, also called a *spire*.

Figure 3-8 shows what the spire will look like when the program is finished.

Figure 3-8: A spire created from stone blocks

The program will use a single variable to set the spire's height. Using multiplication and division, you'll set different spire heights.

In Listing 3-9, I've started the program that creates the spire, but I haven't used the height variable or math operators to set the height of each part.

spire.py
```
from mcpi.minecraft import Minecraft
mc = Minecraft.create()

pos = mc.player.getTilePos()
x = pos.x
y = pos.y
z = pos.z

height = 2
blockType = 1

# Spire sides: should be same as height
sideHeight = height
mc.setBlocks(x + 1, y, z + 1, x + 3, y + sideHeight - 1, z + 3, blockType)

# Spire point: should be two times the height
❶ pointHeight = 4
mc.setBlocks(x + 2, y, z + 2, x + 2, y + pointHeight - 1, z + 2, blockType)

# Spire base: should be half the height
❷ baseHeight = 1
mc.setBlocks(x, y, z, x + 4, y + baseHeight - 1, z + 4, blockType)
```

Listing 3-9: The spire-building program

Copy Listing 3-9 into a new file in IDLE and save it as *spire.py* in the *math* folder. This program will create a spire, but changing the height variable and rerunning the program won't affect the height of all parts of the spire.

To fix this program so all parts of the spire's height change when you change the height variable, you need to change the pointHeight ❶ and baseHeight ❷ variables to include expressions that use the height variable and multiplication or division operators. You want pointHeight to be twice the size of height and baseHeight to be half the size of height. For example, if I wanted the spire point to be three times the height of the spire sides, I would change the code to pointHeight = height * 3 and baseHeight = height / 2.

After you've made these changes, when you change the height variable, all the spire's parts will change size.

You don't need to change any other parts of the program.

You can test the program by changing the original height variable and rerunning it. If you change the height variable to 3, your spire will look like Figure 3-9.

Figure 3-9: You can make the spire taller just by changing the height variable.

Because you use the height variable to set the values for pointHeight and baseHeight, it's very easy to change the spire. Play around with this code by changing the original height variable to a few different numbers. Rerun the program each time to see what happens!

EXPONENTS

You can use an *exponent* to show that a number should be multiplied by itself a certain number of times. For example, 3^4 (three to the power of four) is a short way of saying 3 * 3 * 3 * 3.

In Python, ** is the exponential operator. The number you want to multiply (the *base*) goes on the left of the operator, and the number of times you want to multiply it by itself (the *exponent*) goes on the right.

Say you want to start a Minecraft farm. You need to till four plots of land. You want each plot of land to be four blocks by four blocks so you can grow lots of wheat. Mathematically, you can write this as 4 * 4 * 4, or 4^3. Here's the code to work out how much wheat you're growing:

```
wheat = 4 ** 3
```

Your answer should be 64 individual plots of wheat, because 4 * 4 is 16 and 16 * 4 is 64.

PARENTHESES AND ORDER OF OPERATIONS

When you use several math operators in one expression, you need to be careful how you arrange them. Different operators have different *priority*. When you're using multiple operators, division and multiplication are evaluated first from left to right, and then addition and subtraction are calculated. Let's look at how this expression is evaluated:

```
mooshroom = 5 * 2 - 1 + 4 / 2
```

Because multiplication and division always happen before addition and subtraction, Python starts on the left by multiplying 5 by 2 to get 10, and then divides 4 by 2 to get 2. That gives us 10 – 1 + 2. Next, Python starts back on the left by subtracting 1 from 10, and then adds 2 to that, setting mooshroom to 11.

But you can control the order of operations by using parentheses. Expressions with operators in parentheses will evaluate the operations in parentheses before anything else. Let's look at how parentheses change the order of operations. To start, here's a statement that doesn't use any parentheses:

```
zombiePigmen = 6 * 3 - 2
```

Written this way, zombiePigmen ends up with a value of 16, because 6 times 3 is 18, and 18 minus 2 is 16. However, with parentheses, the result changes:

```
zombiePigmen = 6 * (3 - 2)
```

zombiePigmen now has a value of 6! Instead of following the usual order, first Python subtracts 2 from 3, which results in 1, and then multiplies 6 by 1 to get 6.

When you want a calculation to happen in a certain order, use parentheses to tell Python what to do first. This gives you even more control over Python.

HANDY MATH TRICKS

In the following sections, I'll teach you two more math skills to level up your Python programming, and then we'll combine what you've learned so far in one more mission.

SHORTHAND OPERATORS

Quite often, you'll want to use an operator on a variable and then store the result in the same variable. For example, you might want to add five sheep to your existing herd:

```
sheep = 6
sheep = sheep + 5
```

But typing sheep = sheep + 5 will probably get tiresome after a while. Don't worry; there's a shorter way! Python has *shorthand operators* that let you use a math operator on a variable and reassign the result to the same variable. Here are the four shorthand operators:

- Addition (+=)
- Subtraction (-=)
- Multiplication (*=)
- Division (/=)

For example, you can rewrite the sheep example using the addition shorthand operator:

```
sheep = 6
sheep += 5
```

The value of sheep equals 11, just like before.

PLAYING WITH RANDOM NUMBERS

Using random numbers is one way to add some mystery and fun to your programs. You never know what you'll end up with! Many real-world board games rely on random numbers: think about how many games you've played where you had to roll the dice to see how many spaces could move. A dice roll is a classic example of random numbers in action.

Python can generate random numbers for you easily, so let's simulate the roll of a die. The number generated should be between 1 and 6:

```
❶ import random
❷ diceValue = random.randint(1, 6)
```

When you want to create random numbers, make sure you include import random ❶ at the start of your program. The randint() ❷ function generates an integer value that the program can use just like any other number. The numbers you place inside the parentheses as arguments tell randint() to generate values between the first number and the second number. In this example, the number generated can have a value of 1, 2, 3, 4, 5, or 6.

You can use randint() to add a random number to the value of a variable, and you can even generate negative numbers. Let's see how!

```
import random
score = 0
score += random.randint(0, 99)
points = random.randint(-99, 99)
```

The lowest number that Python can generate to add to score is 0, and the highest is 99. On the other hand, because of the negative argument, points might get set to a number as low as –99!

MISSION #10: SUPER JUMP SOMEWHERE NEW!

In this chapter's last mission, you'll make the player jump a random distance on the x-, y-, and z-axes by storing the player's current position and then adding a random number to each of the three coordinates. Use the random numbers between –10 and 10 to change the x and z values, and make sure the random values for y are between 0 and 10.

To get started, copy Listing 3-10 into a new file in IDLE and save it as *randomJump.py*.

randomJump
.py

```
from mcpi.minecraft import Minecraft
mc = Minecraft.create()
import random

pos = mc.player.getPos()
x = pos.x
y = pos.y
z = pos.z

❶ x = x + random.randint(-10, 10)
mc.player.setPos(x, y, z)
```

Listing 3-10: The incomplete random jump program

The random number generation code for the y and z variables is missing, and it's up to you to add it. Once you do, the player will have the ability to jump anywhere, as I did in Figure 3-10. Let the randomness take you to new and exciting places!

At the moment, the code doesn't use shorthand operators to change the values of the variables. Try changing the addition expression at ❶ to use shorthand instead.

Figure 3-10: I jumped in a random direction and ended up on top of this tree. Where did you end up?

BONUS OBJECTIVE: RANDOM BLOCKS TELEPORTATION

Let's make the *randomJump.py* program even more random! After the player jumps to a random position, place a random block below them. You could also adapt the teleportation tour program from Mission #1 (see *teleport.py* on page 34) to make the player teleport to a random position each time. If you accidentally teleport somewhere and get stuck, you can always rerun *teleport.py*, which should teleport you to somewhere safe.

WHAT YOU LEARNED

In this chapter, you learned how to do math in Python. You'll use addition, subtraction, multiplication, and division frequently in the Python programs in the rest of this book and in the programs that you create in the future. You've also learned how to generate random numbers and created some very useful programs in Minecraft along the way. Great job!

In Chapter 4, you'll learn about the string data type in Python, which is used to contain letters, symbols, and numbers. Strings are very useful in Minecraft, because you can use them to post messages to Minecraft's chat. You'll also explore strings to manipulate Minecraft's chat and do other cool things.

4

CHATTING WITH STRINGS

In Chapters 2 and 3, you worked with integers and floats, which are both number types. In this chapter, you'll use another data type called *strings*. You can use strings to work with letters and symbols as well as numbers.

Strings help you display data to people using your programs—an important part of programming. Using strings, you can to tell Python to *output* data to the screen, which displays and communicates information to the user.

With Minecraft you can use strings in various places, such as posting messages to the chat, which is a way of communicating with other players when you are in multiplayer mode. Although posting messages is a standard feature in other versions of Minecraft, it is a hidden feature in the Raspberry Pi version. But you can access this feature through the power of programming. You'll be able to share secret information with your friends and brag about your treasures!

You'll also learn about functions in this chapter. If you are eagle-eyed, you'll notice that you've seen some functions already. setPos(), setTilePos(), setBlock(), setBlocks(), getPos(), and getTilePos() are all *functions*—reusable blocks of code that make it easier for you to complete tasks. Pretty cool, huh?

In this chapter's missions, you'll build on the knowledge you've learned so far. You'll print messages to the Minecraft chat using strings and practice inputting data to create objects in your Minecraft world.

WHAT ARE STRINGS?

A *string* data type includes any amount of text, from a single letter or symbol—like "a" or "&"—to a large block of text. Each letter, number, or symbol in a string is called a *character*. When you want to include letters, symbols, words, sentences, or a combination of these things in your program, you use strings.

With the string data type, you can store letters, numbers, and symbols. All strings are enclosed in quotation marks. For example, this is a string:

```
"Look out! There's a zombie behind you!"
```

The following is also a string:

```
'Welcome to my secret base!'
```

Did you catch the slight difference in the way these examples are written? When writing a string, you can use either single or double quotation marks: ' or ". Be careful not to mix quotation marks! If you start a string with a single quote, you must end it with a single quote. If you start with a double quote, end with a double quote. There is a good reason for including both of these options in the Python programming language; for example, if you want to use an apostrophe in your string, you can safely include it if you enclose your string in double quotes.

THE PRINT() FUNCTION

Displaying text and other information to the user is important for user interaction; otherwise, the user won't know what's going on in your programs. The information you display to the user is called *output*. To output data to the user's screen, you use the print() function.

To output a message, pass a string to the print() function as an argument:

```
>>> print("String")
```

This tells Python that you want to display the word String to the user. So to print chocolate to the Python shell, you write:

```
>>> print("chocolate")
```

And that output would be:

```
chocolate
```

You can also use print() to print the values of variables. For example, if you have a variable called name that stores a name as a string, and you want to display it to the screen, you can do this:

```
>>> name = "Steve the Miner"
```

After you store the string "Steve the Miner" in name, you can simply write print(name) to display this output:

```
>>> print(name)
Steve the Miner
```

Now that you know the basics of strings, complete the mission to say hello to your Minecraft world!

MISSION #11: HELLO, MINECRAFT WORLD

If you want to chat with other players in Minecraft Pi, the Minecraft Python API lets you send messages to the chat using the postToChat() function. The postToChat() function takes a string as an argument and posts that string to the Minecraft chat window. For example, Listing 4-1 posts "Hello, Minecraft World" to the chat.

message.py
```
from mcpi.minecraft import Minecraft
mc = Minecraft.create()
mc.postToChat("Hello, Minecraft World")
```

Listing 4-1: Use Python to send a greeting over Minecraft chat.

Recall that an argument is information that you pass to a function when you call the function. The function needs this information in order to do its job. For example, in the previous chapter, we needed to pass numbers to our functions to define what we wanted them to do. In this case, postToChat() needs a string, such as "Hello, Minecraft World".

The postToChat() function is similar to the print() function. Both can show strings on the screen, and both can take a variable that stores a string as an argument. The difference is that the print() function outputs strings to the Python shell while postToChat() displays the output in the Minecraft chat.

Copy the code from Listing 4-1 and save it as *message.py* in a new folder called *strings*. When you run the program, you should see the message posted to chat, as shown in Figure 4-1.

Figure 4-1: My message was posted in the chat.

Try passing a different string to postToChat() to make it display a different chat message.

BONUS OBJECTIVE: WHERE ARE YOU?

You can post all sorts of information to the chat using the mc.postToChat() function. Try displaying the player's current x position or the block type they're standing on. Recall that the mc.player.getTilePos() function gets the player's current position and the mc.getBlock() function tells you the block type at certain coordinates.

THE INPUT() FUNCTION

So far, all of your variables have been set in your programs, or *hardcoded*. To change the value of a variable, you'd have to edit the program. It would be handy to be able to change these variables while the program is running or accept *user input* from the player.

One way of adding this kind of interactivity to your program is by using the input() function. It prints a string to the console (to tell the user what kind of information they should enter) and then waits for the user to type a response. Try entering this code into the Python shell to see what happens:

```
>>> input("What is your name? ")
```

You'll see the string that you passed to input(), and you'll be able to type in a response.

What is your name?

When you enter a response, you should see something like this:

What is your name? Craig
'Craig'

Neat! But if you want to use this input somewhere in your program, you'll have to save it to a variable. Unlike the Python shell, programs created in the text editor do not automatically output the results of statements. For example:

```
>>> name = input("What is your name? ")
What is your name? Craig
```

Notice how this time after you type in your name and press ENTER, the program doesn't automatically display your input. To see the saved input, just pass the variable name as an argument to the print() function:

```
>>> print(name)
Craig
```

Awesome! Now you've stored your input in a variable and printed the variable's value. This is very handy because it lets you get input from the user to use anywhere in your program. Let's use this technique to write chat messages to the Minecraft chat!

MISSION #12: WRITE YOUR OWN CHAT MESSAGE

Let's make the chat more interactive! You can use the Python shell to write a message in Minecraft chat, as you did in Mission #11. In this mission, we'll write a slightly different program that saves the string you want to post to the chat in a variable named message.

Listing 4-2 will get you started. Copy it into a new file in IDLE and save it as *messageInput.py* in your *strings* folder.

messageInput .py
```
from mcpi.minecraft import Minecraft
mc = Minecraft.create()
❶ message = "This is the default message."
❷ mc.postToChat(message)
```

Listing 4-2: How to output strings to Minecraft's chat

The program stores the message you want to output to chat in the variable message ❶. In this case, the variable is a string that says "This is the default message." Then the program passes message to the postToChat() function ❷, which outputs the string to the Minecraft chat.

In this program, the string is hardcoded, meaning it will be the same every time the program runs. But with a single change, you can make it print whatever the user writes! In other words, you can write your own custom messages every time you run the program. You'll create your very own chat program.

To make the program accept input, replace the string `"This is the default message."` ❶ with the `input()` function. Give the `input()` function an argument, such as `"Enter your message: "`. Remember to put this string inside the `input()` function's parentheses! After you've made the changes to the program, run it. You should see a prompt in the Python shell displaying `"Enter your message: "`. Enter your message and press ENTER. The message displays in the shell and in the Minecraft chat, as shown in Figure 4-2.

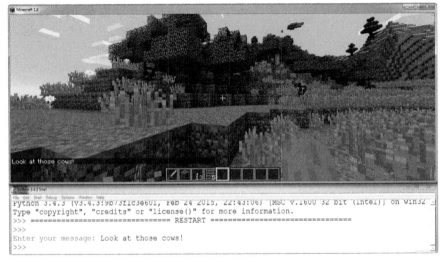

Figure 4-2: When I enter a message in the IDLE shell, it's posted to Minecraft's chat.

Now your program lets you write a message to display to chat, instead of you having to write the message in your program. See how much easier it is to chat using input?

BONUS OBJECTIVE: MORE MESSAGES

The program asks for one message, but can you figure out how to make it ask for one message, wait a few seconds (using the `sleep()` function), and then ask for a second message?

JOINING STRINGS

Often, you'll need to print a combination of strings. This is called joining, or *concatenating*, strings, and Python makes it easy.

In Chapter 3 we used the addition operator (+) to add numbers, but you can also use it to concatenate strings. For example:

```
firstName = "Charles"
lastName = "Christopher"
print(firstName + lastName)
```

The output of `print()` will be "CharlesChristopher". If you want a space character between the values, you can add a space by using the addition operator like this:

```
print(firstName + " " + lastName)
```

Python often provides multiple ways to achieve the same result. In this case, you could use a comma to create the space instead:

```
print(firstName, lastName)
```

Both of these statements will output "Charles Christopher". You can concatenate hardcoded strings with variables that happen to be strings too. Just write the value like you would write any other string:

```
print("His name is " + firstName + " " + lastName)
```

This will output "His name is Charles Christopher".

Putting together blocks of text is useful, but sometimes you'll want to join strings to another data type, like an integer. Python will not let you concatenate a string with an integer; in this case, you need to tell Python to first convert the integer to a string. Let's try it.

CONVERTING NUMBERS TO STRINGS

Converting one variable type to another is handy. For example, imagine you store the number of golden apples you have, which is an integer, in a variable called `myGoldenApples`. You want to brag to your friends about how many golden apples you have, because they're rare and you like to brag. You could print a message like "My not-so-secret golden apple stash: ", followed by the value stored in `myGoldenApples`. But before you can include the value of `myGoldenApples` in the printed message, you have to tell Python to change the integer in `myGoldenApples` to a string.

The `str()` function converts non-string data types, like integers and floats, into strings. To convert to a string, put the value you want to convert inside the parentheses of the `str()` function.

Let's go back to your golden apple stash. Say you've set `myGoldenApples` to 2, and you want Python to treat that 2 as a string instead of an integer. Here's how you'd print your message:

```
print("My not-so-secret golden apple stash: " + str(myGoldenApples))
```

This statement outputs the string `"My not-so-secret golden apple stash: 2"`.

You can convert floats to strings as well. Say you ate half a golden apple, and now `myGoldenApples` stores 1.5 apples. `str(myGoldenApples)` works the same on the 1.5 as it did on the 2. It converts 1.5 to a string so you can include it in your message.

After you've converted numbers to strings, you can concatenate them however you like. Let's have some fun turning numbers into strings and concatenating them!

CONCATENATING INTEGERS AND FLOATS

If you want to concatenate two pieces of data, they must be strings. But the plus sign is used for both addition and concatenation, so if you're concatenating integers, floats, and other numbers, Python will try to add them instead. You must change number values to strings in order to join them using concatenation.

To join two numbers instead of adding them, just use the str() method:

```
print(str(19) + str(84))
```

Because you told Python to treat the numbers 19 and 84 as strings and concatenate them, this statement outputs `1984` instead of `103`, the sum of 19 and 84.

You can use concatenation as many times as you want within a statement. For example:

```
print("The year is " + str(19) + str(84))
```

This line of code outputs `The year is 1984`.

Now that you have a bit of practice using concatenation, let's put your new skills to the test in the next mission!

MISSION #13: ADD USERNAMES TO CHAT

When you're playing a game with more than two people, it can be confusing to figure out who is writing a message in Minecraft chat. The obvious solution is to include the user's name at the start of their message. In this mission, you'll modify the program from Mission #12 to include a username for all messages sent to chat.

Open *messageInput.py* in IDLE and save it as a new file called *userChat.py* in the *strings* folder. Then add code to take in the user's name as input before taking in their message. The message posted to chat should be in the following format: "Anna: I need TNT." You'll need to use concatenation to accomplish this mission.

In the program, find this line of code:

```
message = input("Enter your message: ")
```

On the line above it, you need to add another variable called username and set its value to input("Please enter a username: "). After you've added the username variable, find this line:

```
mc.postToChat(message)
```

Using concatenation, join the username and message strings inside the postToChat() function. Add ": " between the two strings so the output has a colon and a space between the username variable and the message variable. Figure 4-3 shows what the output of the finished program should look like.

Figure 4-3: Now when I post to chat using my program, it displays my username.

Save your updated program and run it. In the Python shell you will be asked to enter a username. Type your name and press ENTER. Then you'll be prompted to write a message, so do that as well. Your username and message should be displayed in Minecraft chat.

BONUS OBJECTIVE: A USER WITHOUT A NAME

What happens if you leave the username blank and press ENTER? Why do you think this is?

CONVERTING STRINGS TO INTEGERS WITH INT()

Like the str() function, which converts non-string data types into strings, the int() function converts non-integer data types into integers.

The int() function is useful when used with the input() function. The input() function returns the user input as a string, but you'll often want to use this input in math operations. To do that, you'll first have to convert the input to an integer type using int().

Here's how it works. Suppose we have already assigned an integer value to a variable called cansOfTunaPerCat, and we want a program that tells us how much tuna gets eaten, depending on the number of cats the user has. Here's an example of a program we could write:

```
cansOfTunaPerCat = 4
cats = input("How many cats do you have? ")
cats = int(cats)
dailyTunaEaten = cats * cansOfTunaPerCat
```

You can do the same thing in a single line by putting one function inside the other:

```
cats = int(input("How many cats do you have? "))
dailyTunaEaten = cats * cansOfTunaPerCat
```

Now that you know how to convert input into an integer, you can use it to input block types into Minecraft programs.

MISSION #14: CREATE A BLOCK WITH INPUT

There are tons of block types in Minecraft. Although you can choose lots of blocks in creative mode, many others cannot be used. However, the Python API for Minecraft gives you access to all of the block types and lets you set them using the setBlocks() function.

You've used the setBlocks() function before, but you had to hardcode the block type into your program. This means you couldn't change it while your program was running. Now you can use the input() function. By writing a program that accepts input, every time you run the program you can choose the type of block you want to create. You could create a wool block the first time you run the program, then create iron ore the second time.

In this mission, you'll write a program that lets your user decide which kind of block they want to set. Copy Listing 4-3 into a new file and save it as *blockInput.py* in your *strings* folder.

blockInput.py
```
from mcpi.minecraft import Minecraft
mc = Minecraft.create()
❶ blockType = # Add input() function here
pos = mc.player.getTilePos()
```

```
x = pos.x
y = pos.y
z = pos.z
mc.setBlock(x, y, z, blockType)
```

Listing 4-3: Code to set a block at the player's position

This program sets a block at the player's current position. Change it so the blockType variable is set using the input() function ❶. I suggest including a question or other text prompt so the user knows to type a block number, not some other kind of input. If you don't include a prompt, IDLE will just wait on a blank line until the user enters something, and you want to make it clear that the program needs a number from the user.

Recall that input() returns your input as a string, and in order for it to input the value as an integer, you need to use the int() function. The expression to collect input for the block type should look like this:

```
blockType = int(input("Enter a block type: "))
```

Save your modified program, run it, and enter any block number you like. Figure 4-4 shows the result of the program.

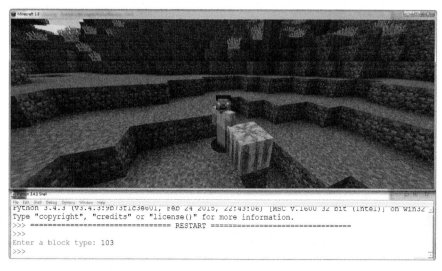

Figure 4-4: I can now create whichever block I want!

BOUNCE BACK FROM ERRORS

Python uses *exception handling* to make sure your program can recover from errors and continue running when they occur. For example, exception handling is one way to manage incorrect user input.

Say your program requested an integer, but the user entered a string. Normally, the program would display an error message, which is also called *throwing an exception*, and then stop running.

With exception handling, you can manage that error yourself: you can keep the program running smoothly, display a useful error message to the user—such as "Please enter a number instead"—and give them a chance to fix their problem without restarting the program.

A try-except statement is one tool you can use to handle errors. It is particularly good for providing useful feedback to the user when they enter incorrect input, and it can prevent your program from stopping when an error occurs.

The statement is made up of two parts: the try and the except. The first part, try, is the code you want to run if no errors occur. This code might take input or print a string. The except part of the statement will run only if an error occurs in the try part.

Imagine a bit of code that asks you how many pairs of sunglasses you own (I own three pairs):

```
try:
❶    noOfSunglasses = int(input("How many sunglasses do you own? "))
except:
❷    print("Invalid input: please enter a number")
```

This program requires a number. If you enter letters or symbols, it will print "Invalid input: please enter a number". The error occurs because the int() function can only convert strings that contain only integers ❶. If you enter a number, the code will work, but if you enter something that isn't a number, like many sunglasses, this input will cause an error in the int() function.

By the way, did you notice anything different about this bit of code? It is our first time using a statement that calls for *indentation*, which is when you type several spaces *before* typing any text. I'll discuss indentation more when I cover if statements in Chapter 6 and for loops in Chapters 7 and 9. For now, just make sure you type your code exactly as it appears in this book.

Usually when an error occurs, Python shows a message that is difficult to understand and doesn't clearly tell the user how to fix the problem. But with try-except, you can stop Python's error messages from being displayed to the user when they enter the wrong type of data; instead, you can give the user simple, helpful instructions on what to do. Sometimes the user will just press ENTER instead of entering input. Normally, this creates an error, but with the code inside the try-except statement ❶, the string "Invalid input: please enter a number" will be printed instead ❷.

You can put almost any code inside a try-except statement, even other try-except statements. Try it out in the next mission!

MISSION #15: ONLY NUMBERS ALLOWED

Remember the program you wrote in Mission #14? When you entered an integer value, the program worked exactly as it was supposed to and created a block. But if you entered a string, the program would stop working and show an error, as shown in Figure 4-5.

Figure 4-5: cake is not a number, so the program did not create a block.

This error message makes sense when you're used to Python. But what if someone who had never used Python before tried to enter a string instead of an integer? They'd get an error message they wouldn't understand. Your mission is to use error handling to write a message that's easy to understand.

Open the program *blockInput.py* that you created in Mission #14. Save the program as *blockInputFix.py* in the *strings* folder.

You'll change the program so it uses a try-except statement when it asks for a block number. Find the last line of code in the program. It should look like this:

```
mc.setBlock(x, y, z, blockType)
```

Add a try statement on the line above this one and add four spaces at the start of the line before the `mc.setBlock()` function. Next, on the line above `setBlock()`, add this code to get an input from the user: `blockType = int(input("Enter a block type: "))`.

Then, on the line just after the `setBlock()` function, write an except statement. Inside the except statement add a line of code that posts a message to the Minecraft chat to say that the block type must be a number;

for example, `"You didn't enter a number! Enter a number next time."`. Here's what the changed code should look like (notice the four spaces, or indentation, at the start of lines ❶ and ❷):

```
try:
❶    blockType = int(input("Enter a block type: "))
     mc.setBlock(x, y, z, blockType)
except:
❷    mc.postToChat("You did not enter a number! Enter a number next time.")
```

The `int()` function expects to convert the input entered by the user into an integer ❶. Because we've added the try-except statement to the program, if the user enters input that contains something that isn't a number (such as letters or symbols), an error will occur. Instead of displaying the normal Python error message, the program will output a string to the chat asking the user to enter only a number ❷. You might want to change the chat message so it's a bit more polite!

When you're finished entering a friendlier error message, save the *blockInputFix.py* file, and run it to admire your handiwork. The result should look something like Figure 4-6.

Figure 4-6: The error message shown in the chat is much easier to understand.

MISSION #16: SPRINT RECORD

This chapter's final mission combines everything you've learned about variables (Chapter 2) and math operators (Chapter 3) with posting messages to the chat. Your task is to create a record keeper: the program will work out how far the player travels in 10 seconds and display the results in the chat.

Remember that you can use the following code to make your programs wait, or sleep, a certain number of seconds:

```
import time      # Place this somewhere near the top of your program
time.sleep(30)   # Makes the program wait 30 seconds
```

Use this sleep() example and type in the following code to get started with this new program:

sprint.py
```
import time
from mcpi.minecraft import Minecraft
mc = Minecraft.create()

❶ pos1 = mc.player.getTilePos()
x1 = pos1.x
y1 = pos1.y
z1 = pos1.z

time.sleep(10)

❷ pos2 = mc.player.getTilePos()
x2 = pos2.x
y2 = pos2.y
z2 = pos2.z

# Compare the difference between the starting position and ending position
❸ xDistance = x2 - x1
yDistance =
zDistance =

# Post the results to the chat
❹ mc.postToChat("")
```

Let's break down this code. The program gets the player's starting position ❶, waits 10 seconds, and then gets the player's finishing position at ❷. To finish the program, you need to work out the difference between the starting and finishing positions. To do this, set the values of the yDistance and zDistance variables, which start at ❸. To help you out, I've included the value of the xDistance variable, which should be x2 - x1. The values of the yDistance and zDistance variables should be similar to this, but use different variables instead of x1 and x2.

On the last line, output the results to the Minecraft chat ❹. The results should be in the following format: "The player has moved x: 10, y: 6, and z: -3". Use strings, concatenation, and the values of xDistance, yDistance, and zDistance variables to do this.

Save this program in the *strings* folder as *sprint.py* and run it. Figure 4-7 shows the result of the program.

Figure 4-7: The distance I traveled is displayed when the program finishes.

If you have the program running but you're finding it difficult to switch between the command line and Minecraft fast enough, try adding a three-second countdown before step 2. Post this countdown to the chat.

BONUS OBJECTIVE: AS THE CROW FLIES

At this point, the program displays the distance traveled along each axis separately: the x direction, the y direction, and the z direction. How would you create and display the distance traveled as a single integer, that is, as the crow flies? Hint: You'll need to use trigonometry, specifically the Pythagorean theorem. If you're not sure how to do this now, don't worry; you'll see a similar program with code to calculate the distance traveled as a single integer in Mission #40 (page 141).

WHAT YOU LEARNED

Congratulations! You've learned a lot in this chapter. You created strings, displayed strings using print statements, and joined them using concatenation. You wrote programs that accept user input, changed the data types of values, and handled exceptions. Along the way, you applied your Python knowledge to make your Minecraft chat more lively.

In Chapter 5, you'll learn how to control the flow of the program and tell your programs how to make decisions.

5

FIGURING OUT WHAT'S TRUE AND FALSE WITH BOOLEANS

You ask yes-or-no questions all the time: Is it raining? Is my hair too long? Once you know whether the answer is yes or no, you can decide what to do next: bring an umbrella, or not; trim your hair, or not. In all these situations, what you do depends on whether the answer to the question is yes or no. Deciding what to do based on the answer to a question is also important in programming. In this chapter, you'll learn how to ask questions in Python.

In programming, the questions you ask are usually about comparing values. Is one value equal to another? Is a value bigger or smaller than another? The yes-or-no question is called a *condition*, and the answer isn't *yes* or *no* but True or False. Say you ask the question "Do I have more gold blocks than my friend?" or, in other words, "Is my gold stash greater than my friend's gold stash?" To make that question into a condition that Python can understand, we have to phrase it as a statement (such as "My gold stash is greater than my friend's") that can be true or false.

Testing whether a condition is true or false is so useful in Python that there's a special data type just for storing the values True and False. So far you've seen a few other data types: integer, float, and string data types. The data type that stores True and False values is the *Boolean* data type. Booleans can only be True or False. When you use Python to ask questions, the result is either True or False. When a condition is true or false, programmers say that it *evaluates to* True or *evaluates to* False.

In this chapter you'll use Booleans, comparison operators, and logical operators to test different conditions involving values. Then you'll be ready for Chapter 6, where you'll use the answers to questions to make decisions about what to do next in a program.

BOOLEAN BASICS

A Boolean is a bit like a light switch: it is either True (on) or False (off). In Python, you can declare a Boolean variable like this to represent that the light is on:

```
light = True
```

Here you assign the value True to the variable light. To turn the light off, you could assign the value False to light:

```
light = False
```

Always capitalize the first letter of True and False. If you don't, Python won't recognize the value as a Boolean and will throw an exception instead of evaluating your calculation!

In the next mission, you'll use Booleans to stop the player from smashing blocks in the game world.

MISSION #17: STOP SMASHING BLOCKS!

In Minecraft, it's easy to smash blocks, which is great when you want to mine for resources. But it's annoying to spend ages building a really cool structure and then accidentally smash and destroy it! In this mission, you'll make your Minecraft world indestructible.

By using setting("world_immutable", True) you can make blocks *immutable*, which means they can't be changed. The setting() line of code is a function like the setTilePos() and setPos() functions you've seen. Listing 5-1 shows how to make the world immutable.

immutableOn
.py

```
from mcpi.minecraft import Minecraft
mc = Minecraft.create()

mc.setting("world_immutable", True)
```

Listing 5-1: Code that stops blocks from being broken

The setting() function has options that you can set to True to turn them on. One of the options is "world_immutable". To turn a setting() option on, you write True after the name of the setting inside the parentheses.

Type Listing 5-1 into IDLE and save it as *immutableOn.py* in a new folder called *booleans*. When you run it, you shouldn't be able to smash most blocks, as shown in Figure 5-1. But what happens when you *do* want to break blocks again? Copy your program into a new file and change it to allow the player to smash blocks. (Hint: Use a Boolean!) Save the new file as *immutableOff.py* in the *booleans* folder.

Figure 5-1: No matter how hard I try, the block won't break!

CONCATENATING BOOLEANS

Like integers and floats, Booleans must be converted to strings before they can be concatenated. For example, you concatenate Booleans and strings when you want to output Booleans using the print() function. To do this, use the str() function:

```
>>> agree = True
>>> print("I agree: " + str(agree))
I agree: True
```

The agree variable stores a Boolean. It is converted to a string on the second line with str(agree), concatenated to the "I agree: " string, and printed.

COMPARATORS

You are very good at comparing values. You know that 5 is greater than 2, 8 and 8 are the same number, and 6 and 12 are not the same number. A computer is also good at comparing values; you just need to tell it exactly which kind of comparison you want by typing in a symbol called a *comparator*. For example, do you want it to check if one value is bigger than the other, or do you want it to check if it's smaller?

Comparators (or *comparison operators*) in Python let you compare data. Python uses six comparators:

- Equal to (==)
- Not equal to (!=)
- Less than (<)
- Less than or equal to (<=)
- Greater than (>)
- Greater than or equal to (>=)

Each comparator returns a Boolean value (True or False) that states whether the condition has been met. Let's look at these comparators and explore how to use them!

EQUAL TO

When you want to find out whether two values are the same, you can use the equal to comparator (==). When the values are the same, the comparison returns the Boolean value True. When the values are different, the comparison returns False.

For example, let's assign the value of two variables and then use the equal to operator to compare them:

```
>>> length = 2
>>> width = 2
>>> length == width
True
```

The result is True because the values of the length and width variables are the same.

But if they are different, the result is False:

```
>>> length = 4
>>> width = 1
>>> length == width
False
```

You can use the equal to comparator on all variable types: strings, integers, floats, and Booleans.

Notice how I used == to compare length and width instead of =, which is used to set a variable. Python uses the == operator to tell the difference between a comparison (asking whether two values are equal) and setting a variable (making a variable equal some value). Try to remember this difference to avoid bugs in your code. Don't worry; even I make the mistake of using = instead of == once in a while!

MISSION #18: AM I SWIMMING?

Now you'll use comparators to make a program that states whether or not you're standing in water. The results will be posted to Minecraft chat.

To find out the block type at certain coordinates, you'll use the getBlock() function. This function takes coordinates as three arguments and returns the block type as an integer. For example:

```
blockType = mc.getBlock(10, 18, 13)
```

Here, I stored the result of mc.getBlock(10, 18, 13) in a variable called blockType. If the block type at coordinates (10, 18, 13) is melon (block value 103), the blockType variable will hold a value of 103.

Let's put the getBlock() function to work. Listing 5-2 checks whether the player is standing on dry land.

swimming.py
```
from mcpi.minecraft import Minecraft
mc = Minecraft.create()

pos = mc.player.getPos()
x = pos.x
y = pos.y
z = pos.z

blockType = mc.getBlock(x, y, z)
mc.postToChat(blockType == 0)
```

Listing 5-2: This code checks the block type where the player's legs are.

Here, I get the three coordinates of the player's position and pass those coordinates as arguments to getBlock(). I store the result of mc.getBlock(x, y, z) in blockType. The expression blockType == 0 checks whether the block is air; if it is air, you know you're just standing somewhere in your Minecraft world, the expression is True, and True is posted to chat. If it's not air, False is posted to chat, so you must be underwater or maybe drowning in sand!

Copy Listing 5-2 and save it as *swimming.py* in the *Chapter 5* directory. Then change the code so it checks whether the player is standing in water (block type 9) and run it.

Try standing in water and running the program. Make sure that when the player is in water, the chat displays True. When the player isn't in water, the chat should display False.

The output of the program should look like Figure 5-2.

NOTE *At this point, you will not be able to run this program continuously. You must run the program every time you want to check the block below the player. This applies to all the other missions in this chapter as well.*

Figure 5-2: Although I can see that I am standing in water, Python kindly confirms this.

BONUS OBJECTIVE: I'M FLYING!

With a couple of changes to the code, you can check whether the block *below* you is air. This would tell you that you're flying or jumping. How would you do this?

NOT EQUAL TO

The not equal to comparator is the opposite of the equal to comparator. Instead of checking whether two values are the same, it checks whether they are different. When the two values are different, the comparison evaluates to True. When they are the same, it evaluates to False.

Say you want to make sure that an object is a rectangle but not a square. Because a non-square rectangle has a different length and width, you could write a comparison to check that the length and width are not equal:

```
>>> width = 3
>>> length = 2
>>> width != length
True
```

The width != length expression asks whether the values of width and length are different.

The result of this comparison is True because the width variable and the length variable have different values.

But if these values are the same, the comparison returns `False`:

```
>>> width = 3
>>> length = 3
>>> width != length
False
```

The not equal to comparator also works with strings, integers, floats, and Booleans, just like the equal to comparator.

MISSION #19: AM I STANDING IN SOMETHING OTHER THAN AIR?

Let's say you want to check whether you're standing in something other than air, such as water, lava, dirt, gravel, or any other type of block. In Mission #18, you checked whether the block at your current position was air, and you worked out how to check whether you were standing in water. You could copy and paste the program many times, changing it slightly each time to check for lava, dirt, gravel, and so on, one by one. But that would be very boring. Instead, use the not equal to comparator to check whether you're underground, trapped in sand, at the bottom of the ocean, or even drowning in lava!

Open the program from Mission #18 (*swimming.py*) and save it as *notAir.py* in the *booleans* folder. Delete the last line of the program and replace it with Listing 5-3.

notAir.py ❶ `notAir = blockType == 0`
`mc.postToChat("The player is not standing in air: " + str(notAir))`

Listing 5-3: Changes to the swimming program

The last line of this code will print whether you're not standing in air. The result of the comparison is stored in the `notAir` variable ❶. When the comparison evaluates to `True`, the value of the `notAir` variable will be `True`, and when the comparison evaluates to `False`, the value of the `notAir` variable will be `False`.

But the comparison on the first line isn't quite right ❶. It currently checks whether the `blockType` is equal to air using the equal to comparator (`==`). Instead it should check whether the `blockType` variable is not equal to air using the not equal to comparator (`!=`). Change the first line to use the not equal to comparator instead of the equal to comparator. This will check whether the block at the player's current position is not equal to air.

When you run the program, make sure it works when you're standing in air and when you're underwater, in lava, in gravel, in sand, or teleported into the ground. The message posted to the chat when the condition is `True` is shown in Figure 5-3.

The player is not standing in air: True

Figure 5-3: Just taking a nice, relaxing swim in some water, which is not air.

GREATER THAN AND LESS THAN

When you need to figure out whether one value is bigger than another, you use the greater than comparator. The greater than comparator will return True when the value on the left is greater than the value on the right. If the value on the left is less than or the same as the value on the right, the comparison will return False.

Say we have a minecart that can't lift more than 99 blocks of obsidian. As long our minecart's lifting limit is greater than the number of obsidian blocks it's trying to lift, the blocks can be lifted:

```
>>> limit = 100
>>> obsidian = 99
>>> limit > obsidian
True
```

Brilliant! Our minecart can carry any number of obsidian blocks that is less than 100, and 99 is less than 100, so limit > obsidian evaluates to True. But what if someone adds another block of obsidian to the pile?

```
>>> limit = 100
>>> obsidian = 100
>>> canLift = limit > obsidian
False
```

Oh no, now the limit has been reached! The result is now False: 100 is not greater than 100; it's the same. Our minecart can't lift the obsidian.

The less than comparator works the same way.

A van driving under a bridge needs to know whether it's small enough to fit under it:

```
>>> vanHeight = 8
>>> bridgeHeight = 12
>>> vanHeight < bridgeHeight
True
```

In this case, the van will fit because it's smaller than the bridge height: 8 is less than 12. Later in its journey, the same van might encounter another bridge that is too low to drive under:

```
>>> vanHeight = 8
>>> bridgeHeight = 7
>>> vanHeight < bridgeHeight
False
```

Because 8 is not less than 7, the result is False.

GREATER THAN OR EQUAL TO AND LESS THAN OR EQUAL TO

Like the greater than comparator, the greater than or equal to comparator determines whether one value is greater than another. Unlike the greater than comparator, it will also evaluate to True if the values are the same.

Let's say I'm giving stickers to all the people who came to see my amazing program presentation. I need to check whether I have enough stickers for everyone:

```
>>> stickers = 30
>>> people = 30
>>> stickers >= people
True
```

I have enough stickers: 30 is the same as 30, so stickers >= people evaluates to True. But say one of my friends thinks the stickers look cool and wants one. Now, 31 people want stickers:

```
>>> stickers = 30
>>> people = 31
>>> stickers >= people
False
```

I don't have enough stickers: 30 is not greater than or equal to 31. It looks like my friend can't have a sticker.

By now, you're ready to tackle almost any comparison. While you're at IDLE, try out the less than or equal to comparator (<=) to see how it works, too.

The greater than, greater than or equal to, less than, and less than or equal to comparators don't work with strings, although they do work with integers, floats, and Booleans.

MISSION #20: AM I ABOVE THE GROUND?

The y-coordinate of a player in Minecraft shows how high they are in the game. Blocks are also stored using coordinates, which allows you to get the block types at specific coordinates using getBlock() and to create blocks at specific coordinates using setBlocks().

To get the highest block in Minecraft, you can use the getHeight() function. The function takes an x- and z-coordinate and returns the y-coordinate for the highest block at that position, as shown in Listing 5-4.

aboveGround
.py

```
from mcpi.minecraft import Minecraft
mc = Minecraft.create()
pos = mc.player.getTilePos()
x = pos.x
y = pos.y
z = pos.z
highestBlockY = mc.getHeight(x, z)
mc.postToChat(highestBlockY)
```

Listing 5-4: Code to find the y-coordinate of the highest block at the player's current location

This program gets the current position of the player, gets the y-coordinate for the highest block at the player's position, and then posts this value to Minecraft chat.

By combining this program with a greater than or equal to comparator, you can check whether or not the player is above the ground. Let's do that now.

Copy the program in Listing 5-4 and save it as *aboveGround.py*. Change the program to check whether the player's y-coordinate is greater than the highestBlockY variable. Then, add code to post the result to chat in the format of "The player is above the ground: True/False".

HINT *Remember that you can store the result of a comparison in a variable. For example, if I wanted to check whether y is greater than or equal to 10 and store the answer in a variable called highEnough, I would use the following statement: highEnough = y >= 10.*

Run the program when you've made these changes. The output for the program's False outcomes are shown in Figure 5-4.

The player is above ground: False

Figure 5-4: Now I'm in a cave, so Python is very much correct that I'm not above ground.

MISSION #21: AM I CLOSE TO HOME?

As you wander around the Minecraft world, you might get lost and forget where your home is. You could wander for hours only to discover you were close to home when you first lost your way.

With a single line of code, you can check how far you are from any coordinates in the game. For example, you could use the coordinates of your house and your current position to calculate how far away you are. By adding a comparator, you can also check whether or not you are within a certain number of blocks from your house. We'll say you're close to home if you're only 40 blocks away.

Let's write a Python program to check this for you! The code for this mission should check how far you are from your house, as shown in Listing 5-5.

farFromHome
.py

```
from mcpi.minecraft import Minecraft
mc = Minecraft.create()
import math
❶ homeX = 10
homeZ = 10
pos = mc.player.getTilePos()
x = pos.x
z = pos.z
❷ distance = math.sqrt((homeX - x) ** 2 + (homeZ - z) ** 2)
❸ mc.postToChat(distance)
```

Listing 5-5: Code that outputs the distance to your house

This code assumes your house is at the coordinates x = 10 and z = 10, which are set with the homeX and homeZ variables ❶. In this case, we don't need to know about the y-coordinate. I use the getTilePos() function to get the player's position and set the x and z values.

To calculate the `distance` variable, we use a formula called the *Pythagorean theorem*. It calculates the length of a side of a right triangle, and you can use it in Minecraft to work out the distance between two points. You may have seen this formula written in math class as $a^2 + b^2 = c^2$, where a and b are the two legs of a right triangle, and c is the hypotenuse of the triangle, as shown in Figure 5-5. At ❷, we're solving for c, which is represented by the variable `distance`.

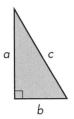

Save Listing 5-5 as *farFromHome.py* in the *booleans* folder.

To finish the program, use a less than or equal to comparator to check whether the value of the `distance` variable is less than or equal to 40 and post the result to chat in the format of `"Your house is nearby: True/ False"` ❸. Use concatenation to combine the string with the result of the comparison. Update the contents of the `postToChat()` ❸ function to output the string.

Figure 5-5: A right triangle

Test the program. When you are within 40 blocks of your house, you should receive a `True` message; when you aren't within 40 blocks, you should see a `False` message. Figure 5-6 shows the program in operation.

Figure 5-6: I'm definitely within 40 blocks of my house. In fact, there's the front door!

LOGICAL OPERATORS

Combining two or more comparators is often necessary in programs. You might want to determine whether two conditions are `True`: for example, you might want a car that is red *and* costs less than $10,000.

To combine two or more comparators, you use *logical operators*. Like comparators, you can use logical operators anywhere that you would use a Boolean value. Logical operators are also called *Boolean operators*. You'll learn about three kinds of logical operators: `and`, `or`, and `not`.

AND

Use the and operator when you want to check whether two comparisons are both True. For an expression with an and operator to be True, both comparisons must be True. If either comparison is False, the statement will return False.

Say I want to find out whether a person is older than 18 and owns a car. I might write the following program:

```
>>> age = 21
>>> ownsCar = True
>>> age > 18❶ and ownsCar == True❷
True
```

Here, we're combining two comparators at ❶ and ❷ with and. Because the age of the person is greater than 18 (age > 18 evaluates to True) and they own a car (ownsCar == True), the entire expression age > 18 and ownsCar == True evaluates to True.

If one of these comparisons was False, the statement would evaluate to False. Say the person doesn't own a car but is older than 18:

```
>>> age = 25
>>> ownsCar = False
>>> age > 18 and ownsCar == True
False
```

Here, age > 18 evaluates to True and ownsCar == True evaluates to False, making the entire expression False.

Table 5-1 summarizes the results of all of the possible Boolean combinations and results when using the and operator.

Table 5-1: The Different Combinations of True and False with the and Operator

Comparison A	Comparison B	A and B
TRUE	TRUE	TRUE
TRUE	FALSE	FALSE
FALSE	TRUE	FALSE
FALSE	FALSE	FALSE

MISSION #22: AM I ENTIRELY UNDERWATER?

In Mission #18 (page 85), you checked whether the player was swimming. The program returned True or False depending on whether the block at the player's current position was equal to water. That told you whether the player's legs were underwater, but it would give the same result whether or not the player's head was underwater. How would you check whether both the player's legs and head were underwater?

With a few simple changes to include an and operator, the *swimming.py* program can check whether the player's legs and head are underwater. Open *swimming.py* and save it as *underwater.py*.

Make the following changes so the program checks whether the player is entirely underwater:

1. Add a second variable that checks the block type at the player's y position + 1. This variable stores the block type at the player's head. Call this variable blockType2.
2. Check whether blockType is equal to water and whether blockType2 is equal to water.
3. Post the result of the comparison to chat with this message: "The player is underwater: True/False".

HINT *To check whether blockType and blockType2 are equal to water, you can use the and operator. First, you check whether blockType is equal to water with the expression blockType == 9. Second, you check whether blockType2 is equal to water with the expression blockType2 == 9. To combine the two, you put an and operator in the middle, like this: blockType == 9 and blockType2 == 9.*

When you run the program, make sure you test that it works in all three cases (when the player is above the water, when only the player's legs are in the water, and when they're entirely under the water). Figure 5-7 shows an example of the program working.

Figure 5-7: The player is under the water, running along the seafloor.

OR

The or operator works differently than and. When either or both comparisons are True, the or expression will return True. As long as one comparison is True, the expression will still be True. But if neither comparison is True, the expression will evaluate to False.

Let's say I want to adopt a cat that is either black or orange in color. I could use the following code to get user input, and then see if the value of the string is either "black" or "orange":

```
catColor = input("What color is the cat?")
myCatNow = catColor == "black" or catColor == "orange"
print("Adopt this cat: " + str(myCatNow))
```

As long as the catColor is either "black" or "orange", I'll adopt it. But if it's a different color, like "gray", myCatNow would be False and I wouldn't adopt the cat.

Table 5-2 contains all of the possible combinations and results of using the or operator with Booleans.

Table 5-2: The Different Combinations of True and False with the or Operator

Comparison A	Comparison B	A or B
TRUE	TRUE	TRUE
TRUE	FALSE	TRUE
FALSE	TRUE	TRUE
FALSE	FALSE	FALSE

MISSION #23: AM I IN A TREE?

The programs you've created so far in this chapter have displayed True or False depending on whether the player is standing on or in a particular block type. But what if you wanted to check whether the player is in a tree? How would you do this? Because trees are made of wood and leaves, you'd have to check whether the player is standing on wood *or* leaves.

Let's write a program. Open *swimming.py* again and save it as a new program called *inTree.py*.

Change the program so it checks the type of block that is one block below the player. You'll want to use the or operator to check whether the block below the player is leaves (block type 18) or wood (block type 11), then post the result to chat.

Recall that you can check the block below the player using y = y - 1.

NOTE *Although trees and leaves both come in different colors, all trees share the same block ID, and all leaves share the same block ID. (The only exceptions are Acacia and Dark Oak wood and leaves, which are a different block type. For now, let's just ignore Acacia and Dark Oak.) The color is set using a second value, which you'll learn about in a later chapter.*

When you run the program, you should see the same output as in Figure 5-8.

Figure 5-8: I'm in a tree.

NOT

The not operator is quite a bit different from the and and or operators. It's used on a single Boolean value or comparison and simply changes its value to the opposite.

In other words, not changes True to False and False to True:

```
>>> not True
False
>>> not False
True
```

The not operator is handy when you start combining it with other logical operators. Let's assign the value of timeForBed if you're not hungry and you are sleepy.

```
>>> hungry = False
>>> sleepy = True
>>> timeForBed = not hungry and sleepy
>>> print(timeForBed)
True
```

The not operator only applies to the Boolean it is in front of. Here it reverses the value of the hungry variable and leaves the sleepy variable alone. Because we set hungry to False earlier, writing not hungry now changes the value to True. The value of sleepy is True. Both values are now True, so timeForBed is True.

MISSION #24: IS THIS BLOCK NOT A MELON?

You're hungry and want to know whether you have food at home. Your favorite food is melon, which you always store in the same space in your house. But you can't remember if you have any melon left, and you need to decide whether to get food on your way home.

Thankfully, you're learning Python! With a bit of brain power, you can write a Python program to check whether you have a melon at home.

In this mission, you'll create a program that says whether or not you need to find food before you return to your Minecraft house. The program will check whether there is a melon at certain coordinates. The coordinates you'll check are up to you—they could be in your house, on your farm, or anywhere you might decide to keep some melon. Placing a melon at these coordinates is also up to you.

Copy Listing 5-6 and save it as *notAMelon.py*.

notAMelon.py
```
from mcpi.minecraft import Minecraft
mc = Minecraft.create()

x = 10
y = 11
z = 12
❶ melon = 103
❷ block = mc.getBlock(x, y, z)

❸ noMelon =   # Check the block is not a melon

❹ mc.postToChat("You need to get some food: " + str(noMelon))
```

Listing 5-6: The start of the code to check whether there is a melon at a specific location

The code is meant to check whether the block at a specific position is a melon block. I've included a variable called melon that stores the block ID of a melon (103) ❶, and I've called the getBlock() method and stored the result in a variable called block ❷. To complete this program, you need to finish the line at ❸ that checks whether the melon variable is not equal to the block variable. The result should be stored in the noMelon variable so that it can be output to the Minecraft chat on the last line ❹.

You can write the check ❸ to see if the melon and block variables are not equal in two ways: you can use the not equal to comparator or the not logical operator. Although the program will work either way, try using the not logical operator for this program.

Run the program when you've made the changes. The result should look something like Figure 5-9.

Figure 5-9: There's a melon on my farm, so I don't need to find some other food.

BONUS OBJECTIVE: A WELL-STOCKED LARDER

Change the block type that the program checks for. You could check if corn is growing on your farm or if someone's stolen your front door.

LOGICAL OPERATOR ORDER

You can combine as many logical operators as you want in a single statement. For example, here's a pretty fancy combination using and, or, and not:

```
>>> True and not False or False
True
```

This code evaluates to True. Are you surprised? In this example, the not False part of the statement is evaluated first to True. This is equivalent to:

```
>>> True and True or False
True
```

The and is then evaluated, and True and True evaluates to True, which is equivalent to:

```
>>> True or False
True
```

Finally, the or is evaluated, so True or False becomes True.

When Python evaluates logical operators, it uses a certain order. If you get the order wrong, you might get a result you weren't expecting! Here's what Python evaluates first, second, and third:

1. not

2. and

3. or

Practice creating statements with logical operators in IDLE and see if you can guess the result of each.

IS MY NUMBER BETWEEN TWO OTHERS?

Often, you'll want to check whether a value is less than one value and greater than another. Let's imagine you wanted to make sure that you had between 10 and 20 wolves, because you love wolves and want more than 10, but 20 or more might cause problems as you'd run out of food. You could test for this condition by using an and operator:

```
wolves = input("Enter the number of wolves: ")
enoughWolves = wolves > 10 and wolves < 20
print("Enough wolves: " + str(enoughWolves))
```

But you could also do it another way. Instead of using the and operator, write the variable once in the middle of two comparisons:

```
wolves = input("Enter the number of wolves: ")
enoughWolves = 10 < wolves < 20
print("Enough wolves: " + str(enoughWolves))
```

If you run either of these programs and enter a number between 10 and 20 but not equal to either, then enoughWolves will be True. You can do the same using the greater than or equal to operators (>=) and the less than or equal to operators (<=):

```
wolves = input("Enter the number of wolves: ")
enoughWolves = 10 <= wolves <= 20
print("Enough wolves: " + str(enoughWolves))
```

In this case, entering 10 or 20 would also give enoughWolves a value of True.

MISSION #25: AM I IN THE HOUSE?

With Python code, you can make cool actions happen when you walk onto a certain area on the map. You could make a secret door open when the player walks onto a specific block, or you could trap them in a box when they walk over a trap. In this mission, I'll show you how to detect if someone is in your Minecraft house.

In Mission #8 (page 55), you created a program that automatically builds the walls, ceiling, and floor of a building. You saved the program as *building.py* in the *math* folder. Open this program.

Read the code in the *building.py* program and make a note of the values of the width, height, and length variables (by default the values were 10, 5, and 6, respectively). Also, write down the coordinates that you are currently standing at. Run the building program to build a house.

Now that you've created a building, we can write a program like Listing 5-7 that checks whether the player is standing inside it.

insideHouse .py

```
from mcpi.minecraft import Minecraft
mc = minecraft.create()
❶ buildX =
  buildY =
  buildZ =
❷ width = 10
  height = 5
  length = 6

  pos = mc.player.getTilePos()
  x = pos.x
  y = pos.y
  z = pos.z

❸ inside = buildX < x < buildX + width and
```

Listing 5-7: The start of the program to check whether the player is inside their house

Listing 5-7 is supposed to check that the player's x-coordinate is within the building created by *building.py*, but the program isn't finished! Your job is to make sure the program also checks the y- and z-coordinates against the coordinates of the house that you built with the *building.py* program.

Copy Listing 5-7 into a new file and save it as *insideHouse.py*. You'll complete the program so it checks whether the player is inside the building.

To complete the program, do the following:

1. Add the coordinates of the building (these are the coordinates you were standing at when you ran the *building.py* program) ❶.
2. Correct the width, height, and length variables if they are different from the ones used in your *building.py* program ❷.
3. Complete the comparison for the inside variable so it checks whether the player's coordinates are inside the building. The first part, to check whether the x position is in the house, has been done for you ❸. You need to add the comparisons for the y and z positions. The expressions are similar to the one that I've included for the x position (buildX < x < buildX + width).
4. Post the value of the inside variable to the chat.
5. When you've made the changes, save and run the program. You should see output similar to Figure 5-10.

Figure 5-10: I'm in my bedroom, which is indeed inside my house.

WHAT YOU LEARNED

In this chapter, you used Booleans, comparators, and logical operators to answer questions in your programs. In Chapter 6, you'll write programs that make decisions based on the answers to these questions. You'll check whether a condition is true or not, and you'll tell the program to run some code if the condition is true or run different code if it's false. In Chapter 7, your programs will keep running a piece of code as long as a condition is true and stop if the condition becomes false. This is the real power of Booleans and comparators. They help you control which code gets run in your program and exactly when the code gets run.

6

MAKING MINI-GAMES WITH IF STATEMENTS

In Chapter 5, you learned how to ask questions in Python. You used comparison operators (like ==, !=, >, <, and so on) and logical operators (and, or, not) to find out whether a condition or set of conditions evaluated to True or False. In this chapter, you'll use the answers to these questions—the results of the conditions you test—to decide what code to run.

You make decisions based on conditions every day. Is it nighttime? If so, you wear your diamond armor and bring a sword to fight off monsters. If not, you might leave all your gear in your secret base. Are you hungry? If that's true, you eat some bread or an apple. If not, you might go off on a grand adventure to work up an appetite. Just as you make decisions in everyday life, your programs need to do different tasks depending on a condition.

We'll use a bit of Python code to help your programs make decisions. if statements tell your program whether or not to run a particular piece of code. An if statement means "*If* this condition is true, run this code." For example, you could check whether the player is standing in a forbidden room and turn the floor to lava if they are. Or, you could check whether they placed a certain block at a certain location and open a hidden door if they did. Using conditions and if statements, you can begin to make your own mini-games in Minecraft.

USING IF STATEMENTS

Being able to control the execution of your program is a very powerful ability; in fact, it's crucial to coding! Programmers sometimes call this concept *flow control*. The easiest way to add this kind of control is by using the simple if statement, which runs code when a condition is True.

An if statement has three parts:

- The if operator
- A condition to test
- A body of code to run if the condition is True

Let's look at an if statement in action. The following code will print "That's a lot of zombies." only if there are more than 20 zombies. Otherwise, it won't do anything.

```
zombies = int(input("Enter the number of zombies: "))
if zombies > 20:
    print("That's a lot of zombies.")
```

Here, zombies > 20 is the condition we're testing, and print("That's a lot of zombies.") is the body of the if statement; it's the code that runs if zombies > 20 is True. The colon (:) at the end of the if line tells Python that the next line will start the body of the if statement. The indentation tells Python which lines of code make up this body. *Indentation* means there is extra space at the beginning of a line of text. In Python you indent lines by four spaces. If we wanted to add more lines of code to run inside the if statement, we would put the same number of spaces in front of all of them, indenting them just like print("That's a lot of zombies.").

Try running this code a few times, testing each condition, and see what happens. For example, try entering a number that is less than 20, the number 20, and a number that is greater than 20. Here is what happens if you enter 22:

```
Enter the number of zombies: 22
That's a lot of zombies.
```

Okay, the result makes sense. Let's run it another time and see what happens when the condition isn't met.

```
Enter the number of zombies: 5
```

Notice that nothing happens if the condition is False. The body of the if statement is entirely ignored. An if statement will execute the code in its body only if the condition is True. When the if statement is finished, the program continues on the line after the if statement.

Let's look at another example to better understand how this works. The following code uses an if statement to check whether a password is correct:

```
password = "cats"
attempt = input("Please enter the password: ")
if attempt == password:
    print("Password is correct")
print("Program finished")
```

The expression after the if statement is the condition: attempt == password. The indented line after if attempt == password: is the if statement's body: print("Password is correct").

The code will print "Password is correct" only if the value stored in the attempt variable is the same as the value in the password variable. If they are not the same, it will not print anything. The last line will run and print "Program finished" whether or not the body of the if statement runs.

Now let's try something a little more explosive.

MISSION #26: BLAST A CRATER

You've already learned how to make the player teleport and jump high. Now you'll make the blocks around the player disappear.

When the program runs, the blocks above, below, and around the player will turn into air. This power is very destructive, so be careful when you use it. To be safe, the program will ask the user whether they are sure they want to destroy the blocks, and it will only do so if the user's answer is yes.

Listing 6-1 creates a crater around the player by deleting all the blocks above, below, and around them. Then it posts "Boom!" to chat. Save this program as *crater.py* in a new folder called *ifStatements*.

```
crater.py    from mcpi.minecraft import Minecraft
             mc = Minecraft.create()

             answer = input("Create a crater? Y/N ")

      ❶ # Add an if statement here

             pos = mc.player.getPos()
      ❷ mc.setBlocks(pos.x + 1, pos.y + 1, pos.z + 1, pos.x - 1, pos.y - 1, pos.z - 1, 0)
             mc.postToChat("Boom!")
```

Listing 6-1: This code creates a crater, no matter what the user enters.

The answer variable uses the input() function to ask the user whether they want to create a crater. At the moment, however, the code will create a crater no matter what the user enters—Y, N, something else, or nothing.

To complete this program, you'll need to add an `if` statement to check whether the user has input Y in response to the question. You can add that logic to the game at ❶. Remember that the user's response is stored in the answer variable, so your `if` statement should check the answer variable. After you add your `if` statement, the program should only run the last three lines of code when the player inputs Y. To do this, you must indent these lines by four spaces.

Keep in mind that the very last argument of the `setBlocks()` function should be the block type you want to set. Here, the last argument is 0, the block type for air. In other words, the crater is created using `setBlocks()` to set the blocks to air ❷, making it look like all the blocks around the player have been destroyed. By adding and subtracting 1 to the values of `pos.x`, `pos.y`, and `pos.z`, the code places air blocks around the player's position as a 3 by 3 cube. This is the crater.

After you've made the changes to the program, save it and run it. The question `Create a Crater? Y/N` will appear in the Python shell. Enter either Y or N. Make sure the Y is a capital letter, or the program won't work properly.

When the user enters Y, a crater will appear, as shown in Figure 6-1.

Figure 6-1: Boom! There's a crater around me.

BONUS OBJECTIVE: BUILD A HOUSE

What else can you make this program do? Try changing the program to build a house around the player instead of creating a crater.

ELSE STATEMENTS

Now we'll look at a more advanced statement to use if we want to run a *different* piece of code when the if condition is False. That's where the else statement comes in.

An else statement works together with an if statement. First you write an if statement to run some code if the condition is True. After the if, you write an else statement to run other code when the condition evaluates to False. It's like you're saying, "If the condition is true, do this. Otherwise, do something else."

The following program will print "Ahhhh! Zombies!" if more than 20 zombies are in a room; otherwise, it will print "You know, you zombies aren't so bad."

```
zombies = int(input("Enter the number of zombies: "))
if zombies > 20:
    print("Ahhhh! Zombies!")
else:
    print("You know, you zombies aren't so bad.")
```

Like the if statement, the else statement uses a colon and indentation to indicate which code belongs to the body of the else statement. But the else statement can't be used by itself; an if must come before it. The else statement does not have its own condition; the body of the else statement runs only if the if statement's condition (zombies > 20 in this example) is not True.

Going back to the earlier password example, we can add an else statement to print a message when the password is incorrect, like this:

```
password = "cats"
attempt = input("Please enter the password: ")
if attempt == password:
    print("Password is correct.")
else:
    print("Password is incorrect.")
```

When the value of attempt matches the value of password, the condition will be True. The program runs the code that prints "Password is correct."

When attempt does not match password, the condition will be False. The program runs the code that prints "Password is incorrect."

What if an else statement is used without an if statement? For example, if a program had just these two lines:

```
else:
    print("Nothing happened.")
```

Python wouldn't understand what was going on, and you'd get an error.

In Mission #17 (page 82), you made a program that stopped the player from smashing blocks by making the world immutable using `mc.setting("world_immutable", True)`. The program helped you protect your precious creations from accidents or vandals. But even though it was useful, the program wasn't very flexible. Turning it off required a second program, which is pretty inconvenient!

Using an `if` statement, an `else` statement, and console input, you can make a program that turns immutable on and off. Your program will ask whether you want the blocks to be immutable and then set immutable to `True` or `False` depending on your response.

Open IDLE and create a new file. Save the file as *immutableChoice.py* in the *ifStatements* folder. Follow these instructions to complete the program:

1. The program needs to ask the user whether they want to make the blocks immutable:

```
"Do you want blocks to be immutable? Y/N"
```

   Add this string as an argument inside `input()` and store the input in a variable called `answer`.

2. The program checks whether the value stored in the `answer` variable is `"Y"`. If it is, it runs the following code:

```
mc.setting("world_immutable", True)
mc.postToChat("World is immutable")
```

   Copy this code and put it in an `if` statement so it runs only if the value of the `answer` variable is equal to `"Y"`. Don't forget to indent!

3. The program runs the following code if the `answer` variable is not `"Y"`.

```
mc.setting("world_immutable", False)
mc.postToChat("World is mutable")
```

   Copy this code and put it in an indented `else` statement.

Save and run the program. When it asks whether or not you want to make the blocks immutable, type Y or N and press ENTER. Test the program. When you choose to make blocks immutable, they shouldn't break; otherwise, they should be breakable.

Figure 6-2 shows the output message and question in the shell.

You'll get the same result if you enter `"N"` as you will if you enter nonsensical input like `"banana"`. Why do you think this happens?

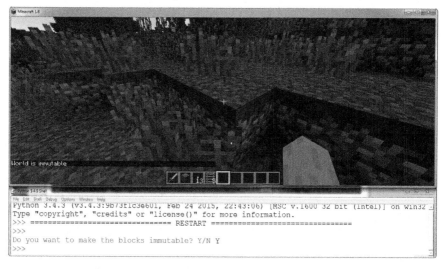

Figure 6-2: I can choose to make the world immutable, and now I can't destroy any of the blocks.

ELIF STATEMENTS

Using an if statement and an else statement, your program was able to run some code if a condition was True and different code if the condition was False. But what if you want more than two blocks of code to run?

To do this, you can use an else-if statement, or elif in Python. First you write an if statement, then you write an elif statement, and then you write an else statement. When you use these statements together, you're saying, "If a condition is True, run this code. Otherwise, if a second, different condition is True, run some other code. Finally, if neither of those two conditions is True, run some other code."

Let's take a look at it. Say you're deciding what flavor to buy at the ice cream shop. You might say, "If there's any chocolate ice cream left, I'll get that. If there isn't chocolate, but there's strawberry, I'll get strawberry. If there isn't chocolate or strawberry, I'll get vanilla."

In a program, this decision process looks like this:

```
hasChocolate = False
hasStrawberry = True
```

```
if hasChocolate:
    print("Hooray! I'm getting chocolate.")
elif hasStrawberry:
    print("I'm getting the second best flavor, strawberry.")
else:
    print("Vanilla is OK too, I guess.")
```

The first two lines just set the stage for the scenario: we'll assume that today, the ice cream shop doesn't have any chocolate left but does have strawberry. So we set hasChocolate to False and hasStrawberry to True.

Next is the logic of the decision process: an if statement prints "Hooray! I'm getting chocolate." if hasChocolate is True. But in this example, it's False, so that message isn't printed. Instead, the program goes on to the elif statement and tests whether hasStrawberry is True. Because it is, the code in the body of the elif statement runs and prints "I'm getting the second best flavor, strawberry."

As you can see, this elif statement has its own condition and body. The elif statement executes only when the condition of the if statement is False and the condition of the elif statement is True.

Finally, the else statement after the elif statement executes when the if statement's condition is False and the elif statement's condition is also False. In this example, the else statement's code would run if both hasChocolate and hasStrawberry were False, printing "Vanilla is OK too, I guess."

For another example, let's go back to the program that printed "Ahhhh! Zombies!" if more than 20 zombies were in a room. We can add an elif statement to test another condition when the if statement's condition is False:

```
zombies = int(input("Enter the number of zombies: "))
if zombies > 20:
    print("Ahhhh! Zombies!")
elif zombies == 0:
    print("No zombies here! Phew!")
else:
    print("You know, you zombies aren't so bad.")
```

We add an elif statement to compare zombies and 0. If zombies == 0 is True, the code in the elif statement's body prints "No zombies here! Phew!" If this elif statement's condition is False, the code moves on to the else statement and prints "You know, you zombies aren't so bad."

MISSION #28: OFFER A GIFT

Let's create a program that checks whether a certain block has a gift placed on it and outputs different responses to chat depending on what the gift is.

The program will allow you to place one of two different gifts. One gift is a diamond block, and because not everyone has that many diamond blocks, the other is a tree sapling.

Listing 6-2 checks whether a block at position 10, 11, 12 is a diamond block or a tree sapling or if there's no gift. However, the program is not complete.

gift.py

```
from mcpi.minecraft import Minecraft
mc = Minecraft.create()
x = 10
y = 11
z = 12
gift = mc.getBlock(x, y, z)

# if gift is a diamond block
❶ if

# else if gift is a sapling
❷ elif

else:
    mc.postToChat("Bring a gift to " + str(x) + ", " + str(y) + ", " + str(z))
```

Listing 6-2: The start of the code that checks whether you've delivered a gift

Create a new file in IDLE and save it as *gift.py* in the *ifStatements* folder. Copy Listing 6-2 into the file. The code that gets the block type has been done for you. The block type is stored in the gift variable. The else statement will run if neither a diamond block nor a tree sapling has been placed, and it will post a message to chat instructing the player to bring a gift to these coordinates. You can change the coordinates in the x, y, and z variables to any location you like.

To complete the program, follow these steps:

1. Complete the if statement at ❶ so it checks whether the gift variable contains the value for a diamond block (57). If it does, make it post this message to chat: "Thanks for the diamond."

2. Add an elif statement under the second comment at ❷ that checks whether the gift variable contains the value for a tree sapling (6). If it does, make it post this message to chat: "I guess tree saplings are as good as diamonds..."

After making the changes, save and run the program. Try putting a diamond block at the coordinates and see what happens. Do the same with a tree sapling, and also try leaving nothing at the coordinates. Don't forget that the sapling needs to be planted in a dirt or grass block! Do you get the correct response in each situation? You'll need to rerun the program each time to check that it works. Figure 6-3 shows my working program.

Figure 6-3: I've placed a tree sapling as a gift.

CHAINING TOGETHER ELIF STATEMENTS

There is no limit to the number of elif statements that you can include with an if statement. You can have one elif statement or 100 elif statements. Python just evaluates them one after the other.

Here's an example using the "number of zombies" program:

```
zombies = int(input("Enter the number of zombies: "))
if zombies > 20:
    print("Ahhhh! Zombies!")
❶ elif zombies > 10:
    print("There's just half a Minecraft zombie apocalypse.")
elif zombies == 0:
    print("No zombies here! Phew!")
else:
    print("You know, you zombies aren't so bad.")
```

Here we've added a new elif statement at ❶, right after the if statement, to check if more than 10 zombies are in the room. If there are, it prints "There's just half a Minecraft zombie apocalypse."; otherwise, the code moves on to the next elif.

The order of the if and elif statements is very important. If you put them in the wrong order, some of the code may never be reached, and your program will not run as expected.

For example, if we swap the if statement's condition with the first elif statement's condition, we run into a problem:

```
zombies = int(input("Enter the number of zombies: "))
if zombies > 10:
    print("There's just half a Minecraft zombie apocalypse.")
elif zombies > 20:
    print("Ahhhh! Zombies!")
elif zombies == 0:
    print("No zombies here! Phew!")
else:
    print("You know, you zombies aren't so bad.")
```

Why is this wrong? Let's look at what happens when zombies is, say, 22. Because 22 is greater than 10, the first if statement's condition, zombies > 10, is True, and the if statement's code runs. Once this happens, none of the other elif and else statements will run. The program never reaches elif zombies > 20 because it already ran the body of the if statement. This is a bug.

If you ever get unexpected results from your if statements, always double-check that your if and elif statements are in the correct order.

MISSION #29: TELEPORT TO THE RIGHT PLACE

When if and elif statements are in the wrong order, code you expect to run will not run, and code you don't expect to run will run. This can cause weird bugs in your programs. To fix the program, you need to put the conditions in the right order. Let's give this a try.

Listing 6-3 won't work. It's supposed to teleport the player to different locations depending on how many points the user enters. The points match up to the correct locations, but it looks like the conditions are not in the right order.

The more points a player has, the better the location. Here's the code. The conditions are set using setPos() for each location transport.

teleportScore
.py

```
from mcpi.minecraft import Minecraft
mc = Minecraft.create()

points = int(input("Enter your points: "))
if points > 2:
    mc.player.setPos(112, 10, 112)
elif points <= 2:
    mc.player.setPos(0, 12, 20)
elif points > 4:
    mc.player.setPos(60, 20, 32)
```

```
elif points > 6:
    mc.player.setPos(32, 18, -38)
else:
    mc.postToChat("I don't know what to do with that information.")
```

Listing 6-3: Depending on your points, you will teleport to a different location.

There's a separate condition for greater than 6 points, greater than 4 points, greater than 2 points, and then 2 or fewer points.

The last line, inside the else statement, won't run unless the user inputs something totally weird, like a string of text instead of their points, or enters nothing at all.

Create a new file in IDLE and save it as *teleportScore.py* in the *ifStatements* folder. Change the program so the conditions are in the correct order and all the locations can be reached. Test the program with different numbers of points to make sure the code for each teleport destination can run. Figure 6-4 shows the program not working.

Figure 6-4: I didn't expect to end up here!

Because the program doesn't work at the moment, when I enter 5, it teleports me to the location for more than 2 points, even though I should go to the location for more than 4 points.

BONUS OBJECTIVE: BEAM ME UP, SCOTTY

Create a program that allows you to input a location you want to teleport to as a string, such as "castle". Use if statements and elif statements to choose which location you want to teleport to. For example, "sea fortress" will teleport you to one location and "tree house" will teleport you to another.

NESTED IF STATEMENTS

Say you have an if statement, and if its condition is True, you want to test another condition (and run some code if this second condition is True). For example, if you're trying to make the entrance to your home base extra secret, you might write some code that checks whether you're standing on a switch. If that's true, another line of code checks whether you're holding the secret item that will unlock the door. How would you do that?

You can put one if statement inside the body of another if statement. This is known as a *nested* if statement.

Listing 6-4 is an example of a nested if statement. A simple cash machine checks whether you have enough money and then asks you to confirm your withdrawal if you do. If you confirm, the program performs the withdrawal.

```
withdraw = int(input("How much do you want to withdraw? "))
balance = 1000

❶ if balance >= withdraw:
    confirm = input("Are you sure? ")
❷   if confirm == "Yes":
        print("Here is your money.")
else:
    print("Sorry, you don't have enough money.")
```

Listing 6-4: An imaginary cash machine written with Python

Notice that the second if statement is indented inside the first if statement. If the outer if statement's condition ❶ is True, you have enough money in your account, and the line confirm = input("Are you sure? ") runs. Then, if the inner if statement's condition ❷ is True, the code prints "Here is your money."

MISSION #30: OPEN A SECRET PASSAGE

In this mission, you'll expand on the previous example a bit. You'll create a building with a secret passage that opens only when a diamond block is placed on a pedestal. When any other type of block is placed on the pedestal, the floor will turn to lava!

First, build a building. To do this quickly, find the *building.py* program (page 56) in the *math* folder and run it. Don't add a door to the building. Outside, where you want to code the entrance to the building, place a single block to represent the pedestal. When you place a diamond block on top of the pedestal, the code will open a secret entrance in the side of the building. Listing 6-5 provides some skeleton code that you can use to get started.

secretDoor.py
```
from mcpi.minecraft import Minecraft
mc = Minecraft.create()

x = 10
y = 11
z = 12
```

```
gift = mc.getBlock(x, y, z)
if gift != 0:
    # Add your code here
else:
    mc.postToChat("Place an offering on the pedestal.")
```

Listing 6-5: The start of the code to open a secret door when you place a gift on a pedestal

Create a new file in IDLE and save it as *secretDoor.py* in the *ifStatements* folder. Change the coordinates in this program to match the location where your diamond block key will need to be placed in your Minecraft world.

Copy Listing 6-5 and add code for these tasks:

- If a diamond block (57) is on the pedestal, open a secret passage to the secret room. (Hint: To create an opening in the building, try setting the blocks to air.)
- When a block that is not diamond is on the pedestal, make the floor under the player turn to lava (10).

You'll need to use a nested if statement to complete this program.

Because this is a more complex program, you should build and test it in stages. When you've added a feature, run the program and make sure that part works before moving on. Debugging small code pieces is easier than fixing lengthy code pieces. Figure 6-5 shows the secret passage opening.

Figure 6-5: The secret passage to the temple is now open.

BONUS OBJECTIVE: ESCALATOR

What else could you make by changing the *secretDoor.py* program? Could you make an automatic door that detects when the player is next to it or an escalator that automatically moves the player up some stairs when they stand at the bottom?

USING IF STATEMENTS TO TEST A RANGE OF VALUES

As you learned in Chapter 5, you can determine whether one value is between two other values in Python. Because a range check evaluates to True or False, you can use a range check as the condition in an if statement, just like you'd use a simple less than/greater than or equal to/not equal to comparison. Any expression that evaluates to True or False can be a condition of an if statement.

Say you've spent all day gathering ingredients to bake some delicious Minecraft cakes. You find enough ingredients to bake 30 cakes, and now you want to sell the cakes. The person buying cakes from you must buy 1 cake but less than 30; otherwise, you won't sell cakes to that person. They can't hog all the cakes!

This code represents the cake situation:

```
  cakes = int(input("Enter the number of cakes to buy: "))
❶ if 0 < cakes < 30:
      print("Here are your " + str(cakes) + " cakes.")
❷ elif cakes == 0:
      print("Don't you want some delicious cake?")
❸ else:
      print("That's too many cakes! Don't be selfish!")
```

If the cakes variable has a value between 0 and 30, such as 15, we print "Here are your 15 cakes." ❶. Otherwise, we print a different message. If cakes has a value of 0, we print "Don't you want some delicious cake?" ❷ and if it's greater than 30, we print "That's too many cakes! Don't be selfish!" ❸.

We can test a more complicated expression by adding a Boolean operator. If I was really weird and didn't want people to buy a quantity of bread between 20 and 30, I could do this using the not operator:

```
bread = int(input("Enter the amount of bread: "))
if not 20 <= bread <= 30:
    print("Here are your " + bread + " breads.")
else:
    print("I don't sell that amount of bread for some reason.")
```

Here I use a not operator and the greater than or equal to comparisons to test a range of values as the first condition. The range check determines whether the amount of bread people want to buy is between 20 and 30. Then, the not flips a True to False and a False to True. So if bread is in the range, the overall expression evaluates to False, and we run the code in the else statement. If bread is not in the range between 20 and 30—say it's 40—the overall expression is True, and we print "Here are your 40 breads."

If someone tries to buy 23 breads, I won't let them. But 17 or 32 is just fine.

MISSION #31: RESTRICT TELEPORT LOCATIONS

Remember the teleport program you created back in Chapter 2? It was called *teleport.py*. In this mission, you'll use range checks and if statements to limit where the player can teleport to. If you're using Minecraft on the Raspberry Pi, there are places outside the game world that don't exist, but your program will still let you teleport to them. If you're using the desktop edition of Minecraft, your world is much bigger, so you don't have the same restrictions as in the Pi edition of the game, but this program is still useful. For example, you could use it in a game of hide-and-seek to limit the area where players can hide.

Listing 6-6 is supposed to get the x-, y-, and z-coordinates from the user's input and teleport them to that position. But the program isn't complete.

teleportLimit.py

```
from mcpi.minecraft import Minecraft
mc = Minecraft.create()
valid = True

x = int(input("Enter x: "))
y = int(input("Enter y: "))
z = int(input("Enter z: "))

if not -127 < x < 127:
    valid = False

# check if y is not between -63 and 63

# check if z is not between -127 and 127

if valid:
    mc.player.setPos(x, y, z)
else:
    mc.postToChat("Please enter a valid location")
```

Listing 6-6: A program to limit the locations that the player can teleport to

In order to restrict where the player can teleport to, we make a variable called valid. This variable will store a True or a False to represent whether or not all the coordinates in the destination are valid. We ask the user to input values for x, y, and z. Then we have an if statement check whether the x variable is not between –127 and 127. If it's not, this x-coordinate is invalid, and the valid variable is set to False.

When the program reaches the final if statement, setPos() will be called only if valid is True. And valid will be True only if all three conditions have been met. Otherwise, the player doesn't get to teleport, and we post a chat message telling the user to enter a valid location.

Create a new file in IDLE and copy Listing 6-6 into it. Save the program as *teleportLimit.py* in the *ifStatements* folder.

Complete the program so it uses if statements and range checks on the y and z variables and sets valid to False if the values are not valid.

When you think you've finished the program, run it. The program should teleport you when you enter values that are within the –127 to 127 range for the x and z variables and within the –63 to 63 range for the y variable. When you enter a value that isn't in these ranges, the program shouldn't teleport you. Figure 6-6 shows how the game should look when the user enters an invalid number.

Figure 6-6: The z variable was too big, so I didn't teleport.

BONUS OBJECTIVE: STAY ABOVE GROUND

One of the problems with the teleport program is that it can teleport you underground, trapping you there. You can make changes to the program to stop the player from teleporting underground. Compare the y-coordinate that the user inputs with the getHeight() function to check that the player will teleport above ground and stop them if they will teleport underground.

BOOLEAN OPERATORS AND IF STATEMENTS

In the previous mission, you used not in your if statements. You can also use and and or. In this case, the if statement will act just like it did with one simple condition: if the overall expression evaluates to True, the body of the statement will run. Here's a program that asks someone if they have cake and whether they want to give us some cake:

```
hasCake = input("Do you have any cake? Y/N")
wouldShare = input("Would you give me some cake? Y/N")
```

```
if hasCake == "Y" and wouldShare == "Y":
    print("Yay!")
else:
    print("Boo!")
```

This code uses the and operator, so Python will only print "Yay!" if the person has cake (hasCake == "Y" is True) and is willing to share it (wouldShare == "Y" is True). If either of these comparisons is not True, the code inside the else statement will print "Boo!"

You can replace and with the or operator to make Python print "Yay!" if the person either has cake or would be willing to share it:

```
hasCake = input("Do you have any cake? Y/N")
wouldShare = input("Would you give me some cake? Y/N")

if hasCake == "Y" or wouldShare == "Y":
    print("Yay!")
else:
    print("Boo!")
```

If either hasCake == "Y" or wouldShare == "Y" is True, the whole expression evaluates to True, and we print "Yay!" The only time we print "Boo!" is if neither condition is True: the person doesn't have cake and wouldn't share it if they did.

Let's try using the not operator with an if statement:

```
wearingShoes = input("Are you wearing shoes? Y/N")
if not wearingShoes == "Y":
    print("You're not wearing shoes.")
```

This program asks the user to enter Y if they are wearing shoes and N if they aren't. It stores the input in wearingShoes. Next is a comparison between wearingShoes and "Y" to see whether they're equal. The not operator reverses the result of a comparison—True becomes False and False becomes True—so if the user entered Y, the comparison starts off True and not makes it False, making the overall expression False. We don't print a message. If the user didn't enter Y, the comparison is False and not makes it True. The overall expression evaluates to True, and we print "You're not wearing shoes."

MISSION #32: TAKE A SHOWER

The best Minecraft houses have a lot of attention to detail. Many people include wooden flooring, fireplaces, and pictures in their houses to make them feel more like home. You'll go one step further and make a working shower.

To get the shower to work, you need to use range checks and Boolean operators. You'll create a shower area, and when the player walks into the shower, the water will switch on. In other words, when the player walks within a range of coordinates, the program should create water blocks above them.

Listing 6-7 provides the basic structure of the program with a few lines of code to help you get started. It's your job to fill in the rest.

shower.py

```
from mcpi.minecraft import Minecraft
mc = Minecraft.create()

❶ shwrX =
  shwrY =
  shwrZ =

❷ width = 5
  height = 5
  length = 5

  pos = mc.player.getTilePos()
  x = pos.x
  y = pos.y
  z = pos.z

❸ if shwrX <= x < shwrX + width and
      mc.setBlocks(shwrX, shwrY + height, shwrZ,
                  shwrX + width, shwrY + height, shwrZ + length, 8)
  else:
      mc.setBlocks(shwrX, shwrY + height, shwrZ,
❹                 shwrX + width, shwrY + height, shwrZ + length, 0)
```

Listing 6-7: The start of the shower program

Copy Listing 6-7 and save it as *shower.py* in the *ifStatements* folder.

To finish the program, add the coordinates for your shower in the shwrX, shwrY, and shwrZ variables ❶. Next, add the size of the shower in the width, height, and length variables ❷. I've included a default value of 5, but you should change this to make your shower the size you want it to be.

Finish the if statement so it checks whether the y and z variables are within the shower area ❸. I've included the check for the x position to help you out (shwrX < x < shwrX + width). The expressions for the y and z positions are similar to this. Hint: You'll want to combine all these checks using and.

The shower is switched on and off using the setBlocks() function ❹. The blocks are set to water (block ID 8) to switch on the shower and air (block ID 0) to switch off the shower.

The setBlocks() functions in the last if/else statement are broken across two lines because their arguments are very long. Python allows you to do this. They could be written on a single line; I wrote them on two lines just to make them easier to read.

Figure 6-7 shows my shower working.

Figure 6-7: Here I am, having a shower.

When you run the program, it will create water above you if you're standing in the shower. The water will not stop until you leave the shower and run the program again. Have fun!

BONUS OBJECTIVE: SAVE WATER

Add a time limit that turns off the shower after a set amount of time.

WHAT YOU LEARNED

Your programs can now make decisions. In this chapter, you learned how to use conditions with if statements, else statements, and elif statements. In Chapter 7, you'll learn about *while loops*. Like if statements, while loops help your program decide what to do and when. But unlike if and else statements—which you use to run some code if a condition is true and different code if it's not true—while loops run code *while* a condition is true and keep running it repeatedly until the condition becomes false.

7

DANCE PARTIES AND FLOWER PARADES WITH WHILE LOOPS

Loops make it easy to repeat code again and again. Instead of copying and pasting the same code, you can use a loop to repeat the code as many times as you want. You'll use loops in this chapter to make your programs repeat without having to rerun them. We'll focus on one type of Python loop known as the while loop.

A SIMPLE WHILE LOOP

You use while loops to repeat blocks of code. Similar to if statements, a while loop will execute the code inside it as long as a condition is True. That is, a condition must be met in order for the body of the statement to run.

The difference between a while loop and an if statement is that the code in the if statement executes only once at the most, whereas the code in the while loop can repeat many times. Programmers call the repeating of code *iteration*. When a loop repeats, you say it *iterates*.

For example, this code uses a while loop to print the numbers 1 to 5:

```
count = 1
while count <= 5:
    print(count)
    count += 1
print("Loop finished")
```

The count variable records the number of times that the loop has repeated. It starts with the value of 1. The condition in the while loop checks whether the count is less than or equal to 5.

NOTE *In Chapter 3 you learned that += is a shorthand operator. You could use the standard addition operator count = count + 1 to do the same thing.*

The first time the loop runs, the value of count is 1, which is less than 5. The condition of the loop is True, and the body of the loop runs. Next, the program prints the value of count to the Python shell, and then it adds 1 to the value of count. The while loop now starts again and checks the condition again, going through each step until the count variable is greater than 5.

Outside the loop is one final line, which prints "Loop finished". Save this program and run it; you should see the following output:

```
1
2
3
4
5
Loop finished
```

Try experimenting a bit with the code. Change the conditions so you list more than 5 numbers or change the amount by which the count variable increases. Here's a refresher on how the code works. The while statement follows these steps:

1. Check whether the condition is True.
2. If the condition is True:
   a. Execute the body of code.
   b. Repeat step 1.
3. If the condition is False:
   a. Ignore the body of code.
4. Continue to the line after the while loop block.

Let's try using a while loop in Minecraft to teleport to lots of new places!

In Mission #3 (page 40), you teleported the player to different positions in the game. Let's rewrite that program using a while loop so you can repeat the teleportation again and again.

By looping some code that will teleport the player to a random location, you can make the program more powerful *and* a lot easier to read. Cool, huh?

The following code will teleport the player to a random location once by picking random values in the game world for the variables x, y, and z. Then it will set the player's position using those variables.

```
import random
from mcpi.minecraft import Minecraft
mc = Minecraft.create()

❶ # Add the count variable here
❷ # Start the while loop here
❸ x = random.randint(-127, 127)   # Indent the code from this line
  y = random.randint(0, 64)
  z = random.randint(-127, 127)

  mc.player.setTilePos(x, y, z)
❹ # Add 1 to the value of the count variable here
```

Right now, however, the code will only teleport the player once. Although that's pretty cool, you can make it totally awesome. Let's write a loop so the code repeats five times, making this quite a whirlwind tour.

To change the code to use a loop, follow these four steps:

1. Create a count variable to control the loop ❶.
2. Add a while loop with a condition based on count ❷.
3. Indent the body of the while statement ❸.
4. Increment the value of count with each loop ❹.

The purpose of the count variable and the count increment is to keep track of the number of times the loop has repeated. I'll talk more about them in the next section. For now, all you need to know is that count lets us control how many times this code repeats.

Listing 7-1 shows the code with the changes added.

random Teleport.py

```
import random
from mcpi.minecraft import Minecraft
mc = Minecraft.create()

count = 0
while count < 5:
    x = random.randint(-127, 127)
    y = random.randint(0, 64)
    z = random.randint(-127, 127)
```

```
mc.player.setTilePos(x, y, z)
count += 1
```

Listing 7-1: Code to randomly teleport the player around the game world

Copy Listing 7-1 into a new file, save it as *randomTeleport.py* in a new folder called *whileLoops*, and run the code. You should see the player zip around the Minecraft world. But the code runs far too quickly! The entire journey is over in less than a second. Let's fix that together.

You'll use the `time` module to slow down the code. Follow these steps:

1. On the first line of the program, add the statement `import time`. This imports Python's `time` module, which contains a set of handy functions related to timing and more.

2. Add the line `time.sleep(10)` at the end of the body of your `while` loop to add a delay of 10 seconds to your program. Make sure you indent this new final line of your program so it's within the `while` loop!

Save the program and run it. Now the player should teleport to a new random location every 10 seconds. Figure 7-1 shows my program running.

Figure 7-1: Every 10 seconds, the program teleports me to a new location.

CONTROLLING LOOPS WITH A COUNT VARIABLE

Count variables are a common way of storing the number of times a program has repeated. You've seen these variables in action a few times now. Let's look at another example:

```
count = 0
while count < 5:
    print(count)
    count += 1
```

The while loop's condition tests that the value of the count variable is less than 5. In the body of the loop, I've changed the value of the count variable to record the number of times the count has repeated. Adding to the value of a count variable is called *incrementing*.

The last line of this code increases the value of the count variable by 1. Each time the code repeats, it will check the new value of the count variable to see whether it is less than 5. When it is equal to or greater than 5, the loop will stop.

If you forget to increment the count variable, you'll end up with an *infinite loop*, which will repeat the loop forever, as shown in the following example:

```
count = 0
while count < 5:
    print(count)
```

The value of count is always 0 because it's never incremented. So, the condition of the loop will always be True, and the loop will repeat *forever*. If you don't believe me, try running the code!

```
0
0
0
0
0
--snip--
```

To break the execution of this infinite program, press CTRL-C. To correct the code, just add the line count += 1 to the loop's body. Now you won't get trapped in an infinite loop. Phew!

Counts don't always have to be incremented by 1. In some situations you may want to increment the count by a different value. In the following example, the count is incremented by 2 every time; the result is that the code prints all the even numbers between 0 and 100:

```
count = 0
while count < 100:
    print(count)
    count += 2
```

You can also count backward using a negative number to *decrement* the value of the count. The following code counts *down* from 100 to 1:

```
count = 100
while count > 0:
    print(count)
    count -= 1
```

The only difference between this example and the previous examples is the condition. Here I've used a greater than comparator (>). As long as the count is greater than 0, the loop continues; when the count reaches 0, the loop stops.

NOTE *The variable used to control a loop isn't always called* count. *You could call it* repeats *or anything else you want. If you look at other people's code, you will see a huge range of different names.*

MISSION #34: THE WATERY CURSE

Let's try something a bit nasty and write a curse for the player that lasts for just a short time. Curses in video games might *debuff* the character in some way, such as slowing them down or making them weaker, often for just a little while.

We'll create a curse program that places a flowing water block at the player's position once a second for 30 seconds. This will make it difficult for the player to move without being pushed around by flowing water.

The following code places a flowing water block at the player's position:

waterCurse.py
```
from mcpi.minecraft import Minecraft
mc = Minecraft.create()

pos = mc.player.getPos()
mc.setBlock(pos.x, pos.y, pos.z, 8)
```

This code will place a water block at the player's current position only once. It is your task to make it repeat. The final code should repeat 30 times, and each iteration of the loop should last 1 second.

Save this code as *waterCurse.py* in the *whileLoops* folder and run it once to make sure it works. You should see a single water block appear at the player's position before the program stops.

Let's talk through what to add next to make this curse last. Use what you learned about while loops and count variables to do the following:

1. Add a count variable to the program.

2. Add a loop to the program to repeat the last two lines of code. The loop should repeat 30 times.

3. Increment the count variable at the end of the loop.

4. Import the time module (on the first line of your program) and then add a 1 second sleep on the last line of the while loop.

Save the program and test it. As you walk around the game world, the program should create one block of water every second for 30 seconds. If you get stuck, go back to the steps in Mission #33 (page 125) for help.

Figure 7-2 shows the curse in action.

Figure 7-2: Oh no! I'm being followed by a small flood.

BONUS OBJECTIVE: A FASTER FLOOD

How would you make the loop repeat twice as fast (every half a second) while still lasting for 30 seconds?

INFINITE WHILE LOOPS

In most cases, it is very important that the Boolean condition in your `while` loop eventually become `False`; otherwise, the loop will iterate forever, and your computer might crash.

But there are times when you may want to program an infinite loop. For example, video games often use an infinite loop to check for user input and manage player movement. Of course, these video games include a Quit button so you can pause or stop the infinite loops when you need to take a break!

A simple way to create an infinite loop is to use a `True` condition when you define a `while` loop, as shown here:

```
while True:
    print("Hello")
```

This code will repeat forever, printing the string `"Hello"` over and over again. Whether or not you meant to create an infinite loop, pressing CTRL-C in the Python shell is a common way to stop it. In IDLE you can select **Shell ▶ Restart Shell** to stop the loop as well.

Note that any code that is placed *after* an infinite `while` loop will never run. In the following example, the last line of code is unreachable due to the infinite `while` loop that comes before it:

```
while True:
    print("Hello")
print("This line is never reached")
```

Although infinite loops can sometimes be tricky, you can also create them to do lots of cool things. Let's try this next!

MISSION #35: FLOWER TRAIL

The program you'll write in this mission is like the one in Mission #34, but instead of placing water blocks, you'll create a trail of flowers behind the player. Flowers are much nicer than floods!

Open the file *waterCurse.py* in the *whileLoops* folder and then save it as *flowerTrail.py*.

To make an infinite trail of flowers appear as the player walks around the game, make the following changes to the program:

1. Change the condition of the `while` loop to `True`.

2. Delete the `count` variable and the increment.

3. Change the block type argument in the `setBlock()` function from 8 to 38.

4. Reduce the value of the argument in the `sleep()` function to 0.2 to make five flowers appear every second.

5. Save the program and run it. Figure 7-3 shows what you should see.

Figure 7-3: Look at all the beautiful flowers!

FANCY CONDITIONS

Because while loops expect a Boolean value for their condition, you can use any of the comparators and Boolean operators that you've learned about so far. For instance, you've already seen that the greater than and less than operators work just like they did in earlier chapters.

But you can control while loops with comparators and Boolean operators in other ways as well. Let's take a look!

We'll start by writing a more interactive condition. The following code creates the continueAnswer variable before the loop starts and checks that the value is equal to "Y". Note that we can't use the word continue as a variable name because it is a reserved word in Python.

```
continueAnswer = "Y"
coins = 0
while continueAnswer == "Y":
    coins = coins + 1
    continueAnswer = input("Continue? Y/N")
print("You have " + str(coins) + " coins")
```

In the last line of the while loop, the program asks for input from the user. If the user presses anything besides "Y" in response, the loop will exit. The user can repeatedly press Y and Y and Y, and each time the value of the coins variable will increase by 1.

Notice that the variable being checked, continueAnswer, is created before the loop starts. If it wasn't, the program would display an error. That's why the variable we use to test the condition must exist before we try to use it, and it must be True when the program reaches the while loop the first time; otherwise, the condition won't be met, and the while loop's body statement will never execute.

MISSION #36: DIVING CONTEST

Let's have some fun with while loops and the equal to (==) comparator. In this mission, you'll create a mini-game in which the player dives underwater for as long as they can. The program will record how many seconds they stay underwater and display their score at the end of the program. To congratulate the player, the program will shower them with flowers if they stay underwater longer than 6 seconds.

Here is some code to get you started:

divingContest
.py

```
from mcpi.minecraft import Minecraft
mc = Minecraft.create()
import time

score = 0
pos = mc.player.getPos()
❶ blockAbove = mc.getBlock(pos.x, pos.y + 2, pos.z)

❷ # Add a while loop here
time.sleep(1)
pos = mc.player.getPos()
❸ blockAbove = mc.getBlock(pos.x, pos.y + 2, pos.z)
❹ score = score + 1
mc.postToChat("Current score: " + str(score))

mc.postToChat("Final score: " + str(score))

❺ if score > 6:
    finalPos = mc.player.getTilePos()
    mc.setBlocks(finalPos.x - 5, finalPos.y + 10, finalPos.z - 5,
                 finalPos.x + 5, finalPos.y + 10, finalPos.z + 5, 38)
```

Save the program as *divingContest.py* in your *whileLoops* folder. The score variable keeps track of how many seconds the player is underwater.

Run the code to see what happens. At the moment, the program isn't complete: it only checks whether the player is underwater once and then finishes.

Before you fix this, let's look at what the rest of the code does. The blockAbove variable stores the type of the block located at the player's head ❶. For example, if the player's head is underwater, this variable will store a value of 8 (which means the block is water). Later in the code, you'll set blockAbove to store the value of the block above the player's head again ❸ so when you create your while loop, it will update blockAbove to the current block above the player's head. At ❹, the program adds 1 point to the total for every second the player is underwater, and at ❺, it uses an if statement to create a shower of flowers above the player if the score is greater than 6.

It's up to you to add a loop to the program that uses the blockAbove variable as a condition at ❷. Make the while loop check whether blockAbove is equal to water (block type 8) or equal to flowing water (block type 9). You can use the following condition in the while loop to check this: while blockAbove == 8 or blockAbove == 9. This checks whether the player is currently underwater and will continue to check whether the player is underwater every time the loop repeats.

To test your program, find some water that's at least three blocks deep and dive into it. The program will run only if you're already underwater. When you run the program, it should start displaying how many seconds you've been underwater. After a while, swim to the surface. The program should display your score and shower you with flowers if you were underwater for 6 seconds or more. Figure 7-4 shows the player underwater and the score being displayed. Figure 7-5 shows the flowers that appear when you win.

Figure 7-4: I'm holding my breath underwater, and the number of seconds I've been underwater is displayed.

Figure 7-5: I won my very own flowery celebration!

BOOLEAN OPERATORS AND WHILE LOOPS

You can use Boolean operators like *and*, *or*, and *not* with a while loop when you want the loop to use more than one condition. For example, the following loop will iterate while the user has not input the correct password and has made three attempts or fewer:

```
password = "cats"
passwordInput = input("Please enter the password: ")
attempts = 0

➊ while password != passwordInput and attempts < 3:
➋     attempts += 1
➌     passwordInput = input("Incorrect. Please enter the password: ")

➍ if password == passwordInput:
       print("Password accepted.")
```

The while loop condition ➊ does two tasks: it checks whether the password is different from the user's input (password != passwordInput) and checks whether the user has tried to enter the password three times or less (attempts < 3). The and operator allows the while loop to check both conditions at the same time. If the condition is False, the loop increments the

attempts variable ❷ and asks the user to reenter the password ❸. The loop
will finish if the user enters the correct password or the attempts variable
is greater than 3. After the loop finishes, the program will output Password
accepted only if the user entered the correct password ❹.

CHECKING A RANGE OF VALUES IN WHILE LOOPS

You can also check for values in a certain range using a while loop. For
example, the following code checks whether the value the user has entered
is between 0 and 10. If it is not, the loop will exit.

```
position = 0
❶ while 0 <= position <= 10:
    position = int(input("Enter your position 0-10: "))
    print(position)
```

If the position variable is greater than 10, the loop won't repeat ❶. The
same will happen if the value is less than 0. This is useful in Minecraft when
you're checking whether the player's position is in a certain area in the
game, as you'll see in the next mission.

MISSION #37: MAKE A DANCE FLOOR

It's time to dance! But before you can bust out some sweet moves, you'll
need a dance floor. The program in this mission will generate a dance
floor that flashes different colors every half second as long as the player
stays on the floor.

The following is the start of the code. It creates a dance floor at the
player's current position and uses an if statement to change colors. But the
code is not complete.

danceFloor.py
```
from mcpi.minecraft import Minecraft
mc = Minecraft.create()
import time

pos = mc.player.getTilePos()
floorX = pos.x - 2
floorY = pos.y - 1
floorZ = pos.z - 2
width = 5
length = 5
block = 41
❶ mc.setBlocks(floorX, floorY, floorZ,
              floorX + width, floorY, floorZ + length, block)

❷ while floorX <= pos.x <= floorX + width and  # Check z is within the floor
❸     if block == 41:
          block = 57
      else:
          block = 41
```

```
mc.setBlocks(floorX, floorY, floorZ,
            floorX + width, floorY, floorZ + length, block)
pos = mc.player.getTilePos()
time.sleep(0.5)
```

Open IDLE, create a new file, and save the program as *danceFloor.py* in the *whileLoops* folder. The code builds the dance floor based on the player's current position ❶ and stores the dance floor's location and size in the floorX, floorY, floorZ, width, and length variables. Inside the while loop, the code uses an if statement to alternate the blocks that the dance floor is made of ❸, making the dance floor look like it's flashing.

To get the program to work properly, you need to change the while loop's condition to check whether the player's z-coordinate is on the dance floor ❷. In other words, check whether pos.z is greater than or equal to floorZ and less than or equal to floorZ plus length. For guidance, look at how I checked whether pos.x is on the dance floor by using (floorX <= pos.x <= floorX + width). Figure 7-6 shows the dance floor in action!

Figure 7-6: I'm showing off my moves on the dance floor.

When you've completed the program, save it and run it. A dance floor should appear below the player and change every half second. Dance around a bit—have some fun! When you're done, leave the dance floor and make sure it stops flashing. It won't switch on again unless you run the program again to create a new dance floor.

BONUS OBJECTIVE: PARTY'S OVER

When the player is finished dancing on the dance floor, make the floor disappear. To do this, change the dance floor to air when the loop finishes.

NESTED IF STATEMENTS AND WHILE LOOPS

You can write more powerful programs by using if statements and nested if statements inside while loops. You may have noticed a nested if statement in the code in Mission #37 (page 135).

In the following example, the nested if statement checks the last word that was printed and decides whether to print the words "mine" and "craft". The loop repeats 50 times.

```
word = "mine"
count = 0
while count < 50:
    print(word)
    if word == "mine":
        word = "craft"
    else:
        word = "mine"
```

The word variable stores the first word that will be printed. The if statement in the loop checks whether the current word is "mine" and, if it is, changes the word to "craft" and prints it on the next iteration of the loop. If the word isn't "mine", it will be changed to "mine". This is an infinite loop, so be sure to use CTRL-C to escape!

You can also nest elif statements and other while loops inside while loops.

The following program asks the user if they want to print all the numbers between one and a million:

```
userAnswer = input("Print the numbers between 1 and 1000000? (yes/no): ")

❶ if userAnswer = "yes":
       count = 1
❷     while count <= 1000000:
           print(count)
           count += 1
```

The if statement checks whether the user's input is yes ❶. If it is, the program runs the loop that is nested in the if statement ❷. If the input is anything else, the program won't run the loop and will finish.

MISSION #38: THE MIDAS TOUCH

Midas is a king of legend. Everything he touched turned to gold. Your mission is to write a program that changes every block below the player to gold—except for air and water, of course, or you'd be in real trouble! Recall that the gold block has a value of 41, still water is 9, and air is 0.

midas.py

```
from mcpi.minecraft import Minecraft
mc = Minecraft.create()

air = 0
water = 9

❶ # Add an infinite while loop here
      pos = mc.player.getTilePos()
      blockBelow = mc.getBlock(pos.x, pos.y - 1, pos.z)

❷     # Add if statement here
          mc.setBlock(pos.x, pos.y - 1, pos.z, 41)
```

Open IDLE and create a new file. Save the file as *midas.py* in the *whileLoops* folder. You need to add a bit more to the program so it can do what you need it to do. First, you'll add an infinite while loop ❶. Remember that an infinite while loop has a condition that is always True. You also need to add an if statement that checks whether the block below the player is not equal to air and not equal to still water ❷. The value of the block below the player is stored in the blockBelow variable, and the values for air and water are stored in the air and water variables.

When you've completed the program, save it and run it. The player should leave a trail of gold behind them. When you jump in water or fly in the air, the blocks below you should not change. Figure 7-7 shows the program in action.

Figure 7-7: Every block I walk on turns to gold.

To exit the infinite loop, go to **Shell ▸ Restart Shell** in your IDLE shell or click in the shell and press CTRL-C.

ENDING A WHILE LOOP WITH BREAK

With while loops, you have complete control over how and when the loop ends. So far you've only used conditions to end loops, but you can also use a break statement. The break statement lets your code immediately exit a while loop. Let's look at this concept!

One way to use break statements is to put them in an if statement nested in the loop. Doing so immediately stops the loop when the if statement's condition is True. The following code continually asks for user input until they type "exit":

```
❶ while True:
❷     userInput = input("Enter a command: ")
❸     if userInput == "exit":
❹         break
      print(userInput)
❺ print("Loop exited")
```

This is an infinite loop because it uses while True ❶. Each time the loop repeats, it asks for the user to enter a command ❷. The program checks whether the input is "exit" ❸ using an if statement. If the input meets the condition, the break statement stops the loop from repeating ❹, and the program continues on the line immediately after the body of the loop, printing "Loop exited" to the Python shell ❺.

MISSION #39: CREATE A PERSISTENT CHAT WITH A LOOP

In Mission #13 (page 72), you created a program that posts the user's message to chat using strings, input, and output. Although this program was useful, it was quite limited because you had to rerun the program every time you wanted to post a new message.

In this mission, you'll improve your chat program using a while loop so users can post as many messages as they want without restarting the program.

Open the *userChat.py* file in the *strings* folder and then save it as *chatLoop.py* in the *whileLoops* folder.

To post a new message every time you want to without rerunning the program, add the following to your code:

1. Add an infinite while loop to the program.
2. Add an if statement to the loop to check whether the user's input is "exit". If the input is "exit", the loop should break.
3. Make sure the userName variable is defined before the start of the loop.

When you've added the changes, save your program and run it. A prompt in the Python shell will ask you to type in a username. Do this and press ENTER. The program will then ask you to enter a message. Type a message and then press ENTER. The program will keep asking you to enter a message until you type exit. Figure 7-8 shows my chat program running.

Figure 7-8: I'm chatting with myself.

BONUS OBJECTIVE: BLOCK CHAT

Expand the chat feature so users can create blocks. For example, if the user enters "wool", the program creates a wool block. You can do this by adding elif statements to your if statement to check user input.

WHILE-ELSE STATEMENTS

Like an if statement, while loops can have secondary conditions triggered by else statements.

The else statement executes when the condition of a while statement is False. Unlike the body of a while statement, the else statement will execute only once, as shown here:

```
message = input("Please enter a message.")

while message != "exit":
    print(message)
    message = input("Please enter a message.")
else:
    print("User has left the chat.")
```

This loop repeats as long as the message entered is not equal to "exit". If the message is "exit", the loop will stop repeating, and the body of the else statement will print "User has left the chat."

If you use a break statement in the while statement, the else isn't executed. The following code is similar to the preceding example but includes a nested if statement and a break statement. When the user types abort instead of exit, the chat loop will exit without printing the "User has left the chat." message to the chat.

```
message = input("Please enter a message.")

while message != "exit":
    print(message)
    message = input("Please enter a message.")
    if message == "abort":
        break
else:
    print("User has left the chat.")
```

The if statement checks whether the message entered is "abort". If this is True, the break statement runs and the loop will exit. Because the break statement was used, the body of the else statement will not run, and "User has left the chat." will not be printed.

MISSION #40: HOT AND COLD

In this mission, we'll create a Hot and Cold game in Minecraft. If you've never played, the idea is that your friend hides an object and you have to find it. Your friend gives you hints based on how far away from the object you are. If you're close, your friend says "Hot," and if you're far away, they'll say "Cold." When you're right next to the object, they'll say "You're on fire!" and if you're very far away, they'll say "Freezing!"

The object of the game is to find and stand on the diamond block that has been placed randomly in the game world. In this version of the game, you'll play by yourself, and the Python program will tell you how far away from the hidden block you are. The game ends when you stand on the diamond block.

Listing 7-2 places a block in a random location.

blockHunter.py

```
from mcpi.minecraft import Minecraft
import math
import time
import random
mc = Minecraft.create()

destX = random.randint(-127, 127)
destZ = random.randint(-127, 127)
❶ destY = mc.getHeight(destX, destZ)

block = 57
❷ mc.setBlock(destX, destY, destZ, block)
mc.postToChat("Block set")

while True:
    pos = mc.player.getPos()
❸   distance = math.sqrt((pos.x - destX) ** 2 + (pos.z - destZ) ** 2)

❹   if distance > 100:
        mc.postToChat("Freezing")
    elif distance > 50:
        mc.postToChat("Cold")
    elif distance > 25:
        mc.postToChat("Warm")
    elif distance > 12:
        mc.postToChat("Boiling")
    elif distance > 6:
        mc.postToChat("On fire!")
    elif distance == 0:
❺       mc.postToChat("Found it")
```

Listing 7-2: The start of the Hot and Cold program

Before randomly placing a block, the program makes sure that the block won't be placed underground. To do so, it uses the getHeight() function ❶, which finds the block that is the highest y-coordinate (that is, on the surface) for any position in the game. Then it places a diamond block at a random position ❷.

The code at ❸ calculates the distance to the diamond block. It uses the sqrt() function, which is in the math module—this is why import math is needed at the beginning of the program. The sqrt() function calculates the square root of a number.

NOTE *Listing 7-2 uses a formula called the* Pythagorean theorem. *The formula uses two sides of a triangle to calculate the length of the third. In this case, I use the distance from the player to the hidden block on the x-axis and the z-axis to calculate the distance to the hidden block in a straight line.*

The message that the program displays depends on how far away you are from the block, which you can find out using an `if` statement and the distance variable ❹. The program displays "Freezing" if you're very far away and "On fire!" if you're very close.

Copy Listing 7-2 into a new file in IDLE and save the program as *blockHunter.py* in the *whileLoops* folder.

At the moment the program works, but it doesn't end when you find the block. To finish the code, you need to add a break statement when the player's distance from the block is 0 ❺.

When you've completed the program, save it and run it. A random block will be generated, and you'll need to find it. The program should stop when you find the block and stand on it. Figure 7-9 shows that I've just found the block.

Figure 7-9: I've found the block, and now I just need to stand on it.

BONUS OBJECTIVE: TIME FOR TIME

The *blockHunter.py* program gives you as long as you need to find the block. Can you think of a way to display how long it takes the player to find the block or even limit the amount of time they have to play the game?

WHAT YOU LEARNED

Well done! You've learned a lot about while loops. You can create while loops and infinite while loops, and you can use loops with conditions and Boolean operators. Using loops, you can now write programs that repeat code, which will save you lots of time so you can focus on mastering Minecraft. In Chapter 8, you'll learn another way to make reusable code using functions.

8

FUNCTIONS GIVE YOU SUPERPOWERS

Functions are reusable blocks of code that perform specific tasks. Say you want to write code that builds a tree in Minecraft. You could rewrite the tree-building code every time you need to use it in your program (or copy and paste it); however, this would be inefficient, especially if you wanted to change it.

Instead of copying and pasting, you could write the tree-building code as a *function*. Recall that we used some functions in earlier chapters: str(), input(), and int(). They're all functions that are built into Python. You've even been using Minecraft functions, such as the getBlocks() and setPos() functions, which come with the Minecraft Python API. In this chapter, you'll create your *own* functions.

You create and use functions for the following reasons:

Reusability Functions save time. Because you don't have to rewrite the same code over and over again, writing a program is faster and easier.

Debugging By containing tasks in groups of code, it is easier to identify where a problem originates and make changes to fix the problem.

Modularity You can develop different functions to use in the same program independently of one another. This makes it easier to share code with other people and reuse functions in other programs.

Scalability Using functions makes it easier to increase the size of a program and the amount of data it processes.

DEFINING YOUR OWN FUNCTIONS

Let's look at how you can use functions in your code. In the following example, I make a function called greeting() that simply prints two lines:

```
def greeting():
    print("Hello")
    print("Nice to meet you")
```

The def keyword, which is an abbreviation for *define*, tells Python you're writing a function. Anytime you want to write a function, you must first write def followed by the function's name. In this example, greeting is the name of the function. Don't forget to add the parentheses and the colon at the end of the first line. The lines that follow the colon are the *body* of the function, which is the code that will run when the function is called.

NOTE *Keep indentation consistent in your code. Always indent the body of the function by using four spaces.*

A function can contain as many statements as you want. It can also include if statements, loops, variables, conditions, math operators, and so on. When you reach the end of the function code, stop indenting lines so Python knows which statements belong to the function and which statements belong to other parts of your code.

You can create as many functions as you want in a program, as long as they have different names.

CALLING A FUNCTION

To use, or *call*, a function, you write the name of the function with any arguments it might require in parentheses. If your function doesn't take any arguments, just write the function's name and a set of empty parentheses.

To call the greeting() function defined earlier, you would use the following code:

```
greeting()
```

You can call the function as many times as you want. Let's call the greeting() function three times:

```
greeting()
greeting()
greeting()
```

When you run the program, it should produce the output of the function three times, like so:

```
Hello
Nice to meet you
Hello
Nice to meet you
Hello
Nice to meet you
```

You must call the function in the body of your code, or the function will not do anything. This is a common mistake. If you run a program that defines some functions and your code doesn't do anything, it might be because you forgot to call the functions you created.

You can also call functions from within another function that you've created. These include built-in Python functions as well as those you've created. You'll see this in action in just a moment.

FUNCTIONS TAKE ARGUMENTS

The parentheses in a function contain its arguments, which are values the function uses. The values are used for specific variables inside the function when it runs. Not every function needs arguments. For example, the greeting() function doesn't take arguments.

But let's say I want to display a greeting to someone using their name. I'll write this as a function so I can reuse the code to greet different people:

```
def fancyGreeting(personName):
    print("Hello, " + personName)

fancyGreeting("Mario")
fancyGreeting("Steve")
```

In this example, function is called twice using different arguments, "Mario" and "Steve". When you run the program, the output looks like this:

```
Hello, Mario
Hello, Steve
```

If you forget to include an argument when you call a function that needs one, you will get an error. Also, if a function needs multiple arguments and you forget to include even one of them, you will get an error. For example, let's try calling the fancyGreeting() function with no arguments, like this:

```
fancyGreeting()
```

The following error message is displayed:

```
Traceback (most recent call last):
  File "<pyshell#2>", line 1, in <module>
    fancyGreeting()
❶ TypeError: fancyGreeting() takes exactly 1 argument (0 given)
```

This is a useful error message because the last line explains what is wrong with the code ❶. The fancyGreeting() function takes one argument, but because it was given no argument, that caused the error.

You can create a function that takes several arguments. For example, the following program contains a function that says hello to someone, waits a number of seconds, and then says goodbye. The function uses an argument for the person's name and the number of seconds the program will wait:

```
import time

❶ def helloAndGoodbye(personName, secsToWait):
      print("Hello, " + personName)
      time.sleep(secsToWait)
      print("Goodbye, " + personName)

❷ helloAndGoodbye("Mario", 10)
  helloAndGoodbye("Steve", 23)
```

Each argument is separated by a comma when the function is defined ❶. Then, when the functions are called, the arguments are passed in the same order in which they were defined ❷.

NOTE *You might encounter the terms* argument *and* parameter *used almost interchangeably. The parameters of a function define the types of arguments it accepts or requires, and the arguments are the values that you pass to the function when you call it. For simplicity, we'll just use the term* argument *in this book.*

MISSION #41: BUILD A FOREST

Your mission is to create a forest of trees in Minecraft. Because a forest is just a bunch of trees, we'll create the forest by making a function that builds one tree and then call that function many times to create a forest.

Listing 8-1 is the basic code you'll be using.

forest.py

```
from mcpi.minecraft import Minecraft
mc = Minecraft.create()

❶ def growTree(x, y, z):
    # Creates a tree at the coordinates given
    # Write your code to make a tree here

pos = mc.player.getTilePos()
x = pos.x
y = pos.y
z = pos.z

❷ growTree(x + 1, y, z)
```

Listing 8-1: The structure of a program that uses functions to create a forest of trees

The growTree() function ❶ created in this code takes arguments for the coordinates where the tree will be built. Your task is to write code in the body of the function that creates a tree at the given coordinates. You'll use the setBlock() and setBlocks() functions to do this.

Copy Listing 8-1 into a new file in IDLE and save it as *forest.py* in a new folder called *functions*.

When you've created something that resembles a tree and it appears onscreen, try writing more calls to the function using different arguments so trees appear at different locations. The first one has been done for you ❷. Try creating at least nine trees in front of the player each time you run your program. Figure 8-1 shows the trees that my program created.

Figure 8-1: I've just grown a beautiful row of trees.

REFACTORING A PROGRAM

Quite often you'll write a program that uses the same block of code several times. Making changes to the program will become tedious when you want to change the same code in different places. You might have done this in programs you've written in the past, but there's a much better way.

You can restructure your programs to use functions. To do this, move the code that is repeated several times into a single function that you can then use as many times as you want in the rest of the code. Because you'll only need to make changes in one place instead of several, you'll save space and the program will be easier to maintain. The process of restructuring your code in this way is called *refactoring*.

For example, the following code asks three people their names and then prints a greeting to each of them:

```
name1 = input("Hello, what is your name?")
print("Pleased to meet you, " + name1)
name2 = input("Hello, what is your name?")
print("Pleased to meet you, " + name2)
name3 = input("Hello, what is your name?")
print("Pleased to meet you, " + name3)
```

The code here repeats the same two statements three times. What if you wanted to change the question or the greeting? It's not much of a problem changing the code for 3 people, but what if you were writing code for 100 people?

The alternative is to write the code as a function and call it three times. Here is the code after refactoring it:

```
def helloFriend():
    name = input("Hello, what is your name?")
    print("Pleased to meet you, " + name)

helloFriend()
helloFriend()
helloFriend()
```

Now when the program runs, it will ask for input and then output a string, and it will do both tasks three times. Here are the input and output:

```
Hello, what is your name? Craig
Pleased to meet you, Craig
Hello, what is your name? Still Craig
```

```
Pleased to meet you, Still Craig
Hello, what is your name? Craig again
Pleased to meet you, Craig again
```

The second version of the code has the same outcome as the first version, but as you can see, it's much easier to read and much easier to change.

MISSION #42: REFACTOR AWAY

Sometimes you'll write a program only to realize afterward that you should have used functions (I do this all the time). Refactoring code to include functions is a very important skill.

In this mission, you'll practice refactoring a program to use a function instead of repeating the same statements several times.

Listing 8-2 places a melon block underneath the player every 10 seconds. We'll rewrite the code to use a function. Currently, the program places three blocks by using the same line of code three times. Figure 8-2 shows the result of the program.

melon
Function.py

```python
from mcpi.minecraft import Minecraft
mc = Minecraft.create()

import time

pos = mc.player.getPos()
x = pos.x
y = pos.y
z = pos.z
mc.setBlock(x, y - 1, z, 103)
time.sleep(10)

pos = mc.player.getPos()
x = pos.x
y = pos.y - 1
z = pos.z
mc.setBlock(x, y, z, 103)
time.sleep(10)

pos = mc.player.getPos()
x = pos.x
y = pos.y - 1
z = pos.z
mc.setBlock(x, y, z, 103)
time.sleep(10)
```

Listing 8-2: Some code that needs refactoring

This code isn't very pretty, is it? Several lines are repeated, which is always a sign that the code needs refactoring with the help of a function definition.

HINT   *Identify which parts of the code repeat to get an idea of what your function should do.*

Figure 8-2: Three delicious melons under the ground

Change the code so it places six blocks in total by calling your function six times. Create a new file and save it as *melonFunction.py* in the *functions* folder. Copy Listing 8-2 into your file and refactor the code to use a function. Call the new function makeMelon().

COMMENTING WITH DOCSTRINGS

Using comments in Python code is a way to explain what code does. When Python runs a program, it ignores everything in a comment, so comments don't affect how the code runs. The main purpose of comments is to explain what your code is supposed to do to others who might look at or use your code. Comments are also useful reminders for yourself in the future.

Because functions are supposed to be reusable, it makes sense to explain their purpose. To write explanations for our functions, we'll use long explanations called *docstrings*. A docstring is a multiline comment that you place at the start of a function to explain its use.

The duplicateWord() function in the following example has a docstring that explains its task:

```
def duplicateString(stringToDbl):
❶    """ Prints a string twice on the same line.
     stringToDbl argument should be a string """
     print(stringToDbl * 2)
```

The docstring should be on the first line of a function ❶. The docstring begins and ends with a set of three quotation marks (""") and can be written across as many lines as necessary.

LINE BREAKS IN ARGUMENTS

To make long lists of arguments easier for programmers to read, Python allows you to place arguments across several lines. For example, the function call in this program has its arguments split across several lines to increase readability:

```
from mcpi.minecraft import Minecraft
mc = Minecraft.create()

pos = mc.player.getPos()
width = 10
height = 12
length = 13
block = 103
mc.setBlocks(pos.x, pos.y, pos.z,
             pos.x + width, pos.y + height, pos.z + length, block)
```

Line breaks in arguments are particularly useful when you want to use math operators on arguments, when you are using long variable names as arguments, or when you have several arguments to provide to a function.

FUNCTION RETURN VALUES

There are two types of functions: those that return a value and those that don't. So far, you've created functions that don't return a value. Let's look at those that do return a value.

Returning a value from a function is very useful, because it allows a function to work with data and then return a value to the main body of the program. For example, imagine you sell cookies. To calculate the price you have to sell each cookie at to make enough profit, you add two gold coins to the amount you paid to make the cookie and then multiply the sum by 10. By using a function that returns a value, you can write this calculation and reuse it in Python.

When making your own functions, you can use the return keyword to return a value from the function. For example, here is the code to calculate your selling price for a cookie:

```
def calculateCookiePrice(cost):
    price = cost + 2
    price = price * 10
    return price
```

To return a value, you just write return followed by the value you want, which in this case is price. To use a function that returns a value, you call it in a place that would expect a value. For example, to set the priceOfCookie variable, call the calculateCookiePrice() function and enter a cost, such as 6:

```
priceOfCookie = calculateCookiePrice(6)   # Value will be 80
```

You can use functions that return values to set the values of variables, and you can use them anywhere that you are expected to put a value, even as an argument for another function.

Functions that do not return a value cannot be used to set the values of variables. Let's take a quick look at the difference.

Because the following function returns a value, it can be used anywhere a value can be used, such as to set a variable or even as an argument in another function call:

```
def numberOfChickens():
    return 5

coop = numberOfChickens()
print(numberOfChickens())
```

Run this code to see its output. You can treat the result from the function like a value and even do math with it. Here I add 4 to the returned value and store it in a variable called extraChickens:

```
extraChickens = 4 + numberOfChickens()   # Value of 9
```

However, the following function doesn't have a return statement, which means you can't use it in place of a value. All you can do is call the function:

```
def chickenNoise():
    print("Cluck")

chickenNoise()
```

Writing this code in the text editor and running it prints "Cluck", although it can't be used in other statements because it doesn't return a value to the program. For example, I could try to concatenate the function with a string, like so:

```
multipleNoises = chickenNoise() + ", Bork"
```

If I ran this program, I would get the following error message:

```
Traceback (most recent call last):
  File "<pyshell#3>", line 1, in <module>
    multipleNoises = chickenNoise + ", Bork"
TypeError: unsupported operand type(s) for +: 'function' and 'str'
```

This error means you can't combine this function with a string, because the function doesn't return a value.

However, if I change the code to return a value instead of just printing it:

```python
def chickenNoise():
    return "Cluck"

multipleNoises = chickenNoise() + ", Bork"
print(multipleNoises)
```

the file would run and display the following output:

```
Cluck, Bork
```

Keep this difference in mind. Remember to include a return statement when you need it and exclude it when your function doesn't need to return a value. The more experienced you become with functions, the easier it will be to decide whether you want your function to return a value.

MISSION #43: BLOCK ID REMINDER

Because Minecraft has so many blocks, it's difficult to remember all the block IDs. I always remember the melon (103) and air (0) values but forget others, so I keep having to build houses out of melons!

To make remembering easier, I want you to create a program for me that returns the values of different blocks. Your program should have many functions that help me remember block IDs. The name of each function should be the same as the name of the block whose value it returns. For example, Listing 8-3 has a function called melon() that returns the value of the melon block (103).

blockIds.py
```python
def melon():
    """ Returns the value of the melon block """
    return 103
```

Listing 8-3: The start of the program that will help me remember block IDs

Create a new file in IDLE and save it as *blockIds.py* in the *functions* folder. Copy Listing 8-3 into the file and add functions to it that return the values of the following blocks (see "Block ID Cheat Sheet" on page 285):

- Water
- Wool
- Lava
- TNT
- Flower
- Diamond block

After you've added your functions, test them by calling the functions to create blocks. Because your new functions return a block's value, you can use them to set the value of a variable to pass into the setBlock() function. The following code will help you get started:

```
from mcpi.minecraft import Minecraft
mc = Minecraft.create()

# Functions go here

block = melon()
pos = mc.player.getTilePos()
mc.setBlock(pos.x, pos.y, pos.z, block)
```

Figure 8-3 shows the result of the completed program with a test for the melon() function. Notice that the placement of any block is hardcoded into this program; it will always place a block at your current location.

Figure 8-3: Now I don't have to remember the block types, all thanks to this handy function.

HINT   *To place a diamond block, TNT, or any other kind of block, you'll first need to define the function that returns the value of the block you want. Then you'll need to call that function in your code, just like I called the* melon() *function in this example.*

BONUS OBJECTIVE: MORE BLOCKS

Add extra functions for any other block types that you want.

USING IF STATEMENTS AND WHILE LOOPS IN FUNCTIONS

In Chapters 6 and 7, you learned about putting if statements inside of other if statements and while loops inside of other while loops. You learned that you can even put if statements within while loops and vice versa! In this section, you'll learn how to put if statements and loops inside functions. This makes your functions very flexible, because you can use them to make decisions and repeat code.

IF STATEMENTS

When you're writing an if statement within a function, the syntax is identical to that of a regular if statement. You just need to remember to indent the if statement by an extra four spaces at the start of every line so Python knows it's part of the function.

The following code takes a number written as a string and returns the number as an integer. For example, the argument "four" returns the value 4:

```python
def wordToNumber(numToConvert):
    """ Converts a number written as a word to an integer """
    if numToConvert == "one":
        numAsInt = 1
    elif numToConvert == "two":
        numAsInt = 2
    elif numToConvert == "three":
        numAsInt = 3
    elif numToConvert == "four":
        numAsInt = 4
    elif numToConver == "five":
        numAsInt = 5

    return numAsInt
```

Let's look at another example. The following function checks whether you've met a person before and uses an appropriate greeting depending on the result:

```python
❶ def chooseGreeting(metBefore):
    """ Chooses a greeting depending on whether you've met someone before.
    metBefore argument should be a Boolean value """
    if metBefore:
❷       print("Nice to see you again")
    else:
❸       print("Nice to meet you")

chooseGreeting(True)
chooseGreeting(False)
```

The `chooseGreeting()` function takes one Boolean argument, called `metBefore` ❶. The `if` statement inside the function then prints output based on the value of the argument. If the value is `True`, the output will be `"Nice to see you again"` ❷, and if it is `False` ❸, the output will be `"Nice to meet you"`.

MISSION #44: WOOL COLOR HELPER

You've used the `setBlock()` and `setBlocks()` methods with arguments to set block coordinates and block type, but these methods also have an optional extra argument that will set the block *state*.

Each block in Minecraft has 16 states, 0 to 15. Wool, for example, has a different color for every state. TNT (block ID 46) won't explode when you smash the block in its default state (state 0), but it is explosive when you smash it in block state 1. Although every block has 16 states, not all of them have different behaviors.

To set a block's state, you provide the `setblock()` or `setblocks()` function with an extra argument. The following code creates a pink block of wool:

```
from mcpi.minecraft import Minecraft
mc = Minecraft.create()

block = 35
state = 6
# Creates a single block of pink wool
mc.setBlock(10, 3, -4, block, state)

# Creates a cuboid of pink wool
mc.setBlocks(11, 3, -4, 20, 6, -8, block, state)
```

Wool (block ID 35) has many uses in Minecraft due to its different colors, but it's difficult to remember the different block states. Fortunately, you don't need to memorize the different block states when you can use a program to remind you.

Let's make a program that contains the wool block's states. The program will contain a function with an argument that takes the color you want written as a string. The function then returns the block state for the wool color as an integer. The function will contain the bulk of the code for the program. However, you'll add a couple of code lines to take input from a user and place the block in the game, and you'll use your fancy new function to set the color.

First, you'll need to find out the block states for the different colors of wool. You can find them in the "Block ID Cheat Sheet" on page 285. Here's some code to get you started (pink is block state 6):

woolColors.py
```
def getWoolState(color):
    """ Takes a color as a string and returns the wool block state for
    that color """
❶   if color == "pink":
        blockState = 6
```

```
      elif # Add elif statements for the other colors
      # Return the blockState here

❷ colorString = input("Enter a block color: ")
   state = getWoolState(colorString)

❸ pos = mc.player.getTilePos()
   mc.setBlock(pos.x, pos,y, pos.z, 35, state)
```

At the moment, the program has just the beginnings of the getWoolState()
function. It only has an if statement for the color pink ❶. Also included
is code at the end of the program to take user input for the block color ❷
and code to place the wool block at the player's position ❸.

Add to the getWoolState() function using elif statements for other wool
colors and their corresponding block states. The program should take an
argument for the color of the block and return the integer value of the
block state. For example, providing the argument "pink" will return the
value 6. You'll also need to add a return statement to the program. Use the
comments to guide you.

Save the file as *woolColors.py* in the *functions* folder.

If you want to make the program more user friendly, you can post a
message to chat if the argument is not a valid color. Figure 8-4 shows the
input in the Python shell and the wool block being placed in the game.

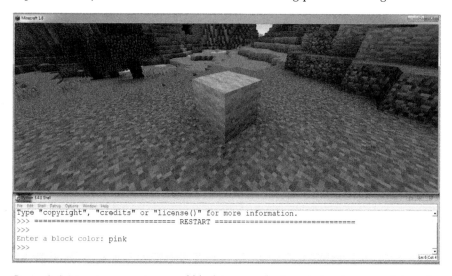

Figure 8-4: Now I can create a wool block in any color by entering the name of the color
I want.

WHILE LOOPS

Just like if statements, loops can be written inside functions. The syntax for
a loop inside a function is the same as that for a regular loop. You just need
to remember that the loop should be indented by an extra four spaces on
each line to indicate that it belongs to the function.

In the following example, the `while` loop within the function will print the `toPrint` argument. The number of times the loop repeats is determined by the `repeats` argument.

```
def printMultiple(toPrint, repeats):
    """ Prints a string a number of times determined by the repeats variable """
    count = 0
    while count < repeats:
        print(toPrint)
        count += 1
```

You can also use `return` statements and `while` loops in the same function. In most cases, you'll want the `return` statement to be outside the loop. (If you use the `return` statement inside a loop, it will break the loop and end the function.) Let's look at an example:

```
def doubleUntilHundred(numberToDbl):
    """ Doubles a number until it is greater than 100. Returns the number of
    times the number was doubled """
    count = 0
    while numToDbl < 100:
        numberToDbl = numberToDbl * 2
        count += 1
❶   return count

print(doubleUntilHundred(2))
```

This program doubles a number until it is greater than 100. It then returns the number of times the loop repeated ❶.

You can also put function calls within loops, as you did in previous chapters.

MISSION #45: BLOCKS, EVERYWHERE

By using loops inside functions, you can use an argument to determine the number of times a loop repeats. By using the `setBlock()` function, you can also determine the type of block to be placed within the loop.

WARNING *The program in this mission could be destructive, so you might want to try it in a new world to preserve your precious creations.*

In this mission, you'll create a function that places blocks randomly around the map. The number of blocks it places and the block type it places are determined by function arguments.

Listing 8-4 generates a melon at a random location on the map.

```
from mcpi.minecraft import Minecraft
mc = Minecraft.create()
import random

def randomBlockLocations(blockType, repeats):
❶    count = 0
❷    # Add the loop here
     x = random.randint(-127, 127)
     z = random.randint(-127, 127)
❸    y = mc.getHeight(x, z)
     mc.setBlock(x, y, z, blockType)
     count += 1
```

Listing 8-4: When called, this function will place a block randomly in the game.

Copy Listing 8-4 into a new file in IDLE and save it as *blocksEverywhere.py* in the *functions* folder. At ❷, add a while loop inside the function so the code repeats. The count variable ❶ makes it easier for you to tell how many times the loop has repeated. Compare the repeats argument to the count variable in the loop's condition to set how many times the loop should repeat. Indent all the lines inside the function after ❷ so they are also inside the loop. The getHeight() function ensures that the block is placed above the ground ❸.

Finally, add three function calls to create blocks. The first function should create 10 blocks, the second one should create 37 blocks, and the third should create 102 blocks. Choose any block types that you want.

Save the program and run it. The program should create blocks randomly around the map. Figure 8-5 shows an example.

Figure 8-5: You can see some of the blocks that the program has placed randomly. I created a new world to demonstrate this program so it didn't damage any of my buildings.

GLOBAL AND LOCAL VARIABLES

When you're defining functions, you have a new challenge to deal with, namely the scope of a variable. The *scope* of a variable describes how your program can access its data. The best way to learn about scope is to see it in action, so let's look at some code. Let's say you're using the following code, which increases the number of eggs you have for a party:

```
❶ eggs = 12

  def increaseEggs():
❷     eggs += 1
      print(eggs)

increaseEggs()
```

Two variables are named eggs, one outside the function ❶ and another inside the function ❷. Nothing looks terribly wrong, but Python will throw an error. Here's part of the error message:

```
UnboundLocalError: local variable 'eggs' referenced before assignment
```

The problem is that the eggs variable is defined outside the function, but when you try to add to it inside the function, Python can't see the variable. To Python, the variable inside the function is totally different from the one outside the function, even though they have the same name. Python does this on purpose to stop variables inside different functions from accidentally sharing the same names and causing unexpected bugs.

In Python code, you have two ways to approach the variables in a file: you can either make a variable *global*, which means it affects an entire program or file, or make a variable *local*, which means it can be seen only by the code in a particular function or loop. In other words, you can use the same variable inside and outside a function, or you can make two different variables that affect different parts of the code.

A *global* variable will be treated as the same variable inside and outside a function. Any changes to the variable inside the function will affect the variable that was defined outside the function and vice versa. To make a global variable, use the global keyword ❶:

```
  eggs = 12

  def increaseEggs():
❶     global eggs
      eggs += 1
      print(eggs)

increaseEggs()
```

In this example, the value of eggs will be 13 when it is printed.

You can treat the variable as a *local* variable instead to produce a different effect. In this case, the variables inside and outside the function will be treated as different variables. Changes to the variable inside the function will not affect the variable outside the function and vice versa. So you could change the code to make the variable a local variable ❶, like this:

```
eggs = 12

def increaseEggs():
❶     eggs = 0
      eggs += 1
❷     print(eggs)

increaseEggs()
❸ print(eggs)
```

When the value of eggs in the function is printed ❷, it will be 1 because the value of the eggs variable outside the function does not affect the local variable inside the function. The value of eggs inside the increaseEggs() function is 1, and the global eggs variable still has the value of 12 ❸.

MISSION #46: A MOVING BLOCK

A while ago, I thought it would be cool to make a block move around the Minecraft world by itself. Every second it would move forward. If it hit a wall, a tree, or something tall, it would turn and make its way in a different direction. If it fell in a hole, however, it would get stuck and wouldn't be able to escape.

Listing 8-5 is the start of a program to make a magical block that moves on its own.

movingBlock
.py

```
from mcpi.minecraft import Minecraft
mc = Minecraft.create()

import time


def calculateMove():
    """ Changes the x and z variables for a block. If the block
    in front of the block is less than 2 blocks higher, it will move
    forward; otherwise it will try to move left, then backward,
    then finally right. """
❶     # Create global variables here

    currentHeight = mc.getHeight(x, z) - 1

    forwardHeight = mc.getHeight(x + 1, z)
    rightHeight = mc.getHeight(x, z + 1)
    backwardHeight = mc.getHeight(x - 1, z)
    leftHeight = mc.getHeight(x, z - 1)
```

```
        if forwardHeight - currentHeight < 3:
            x += 1
        elif rightHeight - currentHeight < 3:
            z += 1
        elif leftHeight - currentHeight < 3:
            z -= 1
        elif backwardHeight - currentHeight < 3:
            x -= 1

        y = mc.getHeight(x, z)


pos = mc.player.getTilePos()
x = pos.x
z = pos.z
y = mc.getHeight(x, z)

while True:
    # Calculate block movement
    calculateMove()

    # Place block
    mc.setBlock(x, y, z, 103)

    # Wait
    time.sleep(1)

    # Remove the block
    mc.setBlock(x, y, z, 0)
```

Listing 8-5: Unfortunately, this code won't work until global variables are added.

But this code won't run yet because the variables in the calculateMove() function aren't global.

Your mission is to finish the code in Listing 8-5. Copy it into IDLE and save it as *movingBlock.py* in the *functions* folder. Add code to the start of the function to make the x, y, and z variables global. The global definitions should be placed at ❶.

After you've declared some global variables, run the program. Your block should move around. Figure 8-6 shows the block move up to a wall and then start to move around it.

BONUS OBJECTIVE: A MORE INTELLIGENT MELON BLOCK

When you run the *movingBlock.py* program, you might notice that the block moves forward along the x-axis the most, sometimes causing it to get stuck in a loop between two blocks. The reason is that the code doesn't take into account the directions that the block has already moved in and will always try to move along the x-axis first. Can you work out how to store the last direction that the block moved in and change the if statement to move in that direction first?

Figure 8-6: It was fun watching the melon move forward and then try to move around the wall.

WHAT YOU LEARNED

Hooray! In this chapter, you learned how to create and call functions. With return statements you can make functions return values, and you can write loops and if statements inside functions. In Chapter 9, you'll learn about lists, which allow you to store several pieces of data in a single variable.

9

HITTING THINGS WITH LISTS AND DICTIONARIES

We use lists, such as shopping lists or lists of instructions, to remember a group of items or to work through steps in a certain order. Lists in Python are very similar: they're used to store a collection of data within a sequence. A *list* can store several types of data, including strings, numbers, Booleans, and even other lists.

Normally, variables can hold only one value. Lists are useful because they allow you to store several values in a single variable, such as the numbers from 1 to 100 or your friends' first names. In other programming languages, lists are sometimes called *arrays*.

You can use lists of block IDs, coordinates, or a variety of other things to gain lots of power over your Minecraft world. Because lists can store several kinds of values in a single variable, they give you flexibility that a regular variable can't offer.

In this chapter, you'll learn how to use lists with the Minecraft Python API to create a mini-game for recording height, make a progress bar, and write a program that randomly slides the player around the game.

USING LISTS

Making a list with Python is straightforward. To define a list, use square brackets around any number of values—or no values at all, which is called an *empty* list. Each item in a list needs to be separated by a comma.

For example, a list of ingredients for noodle soup might look like this:

```
>>> noodleSoup = ["water", "soy sauce", "spring onions", "noodles", "beef"]
```

The noodleSoup list contains several items and all of them are strings. You can create an empty list like this:

```
>>> emptyList = []
```

Use an empty list when you want to add values later in your program.

You can store any data type in your list and even mix different data types. For example, you could have a list that contains integers and strings:

```
>>> wackyList = ["cardigan", 33, "goofballs"]
```

Sometimes your lists will be very long, making them difficult for humans to read. But you can format long lists across several lines in Python so programmers can read them easily. Using several lines for items has no effect on how the Python code runs. For example, the following format for soup ingredients works the same as the earlier noodleSoup list:

```
>>> noodleSoup = ["water",
        "soy sauce",
        "spring onions"
        "noodles",
        "beef"]
```

Next, we'll look at how you can access and change items in a list.

ACCESSING A LIST ITEM

To access a value in a list, reference the item's position in the list, which is known as its *index*. Using the noodle soup example, you can access the first item in the list like this:

```
>>> print(noodleSoup[0])
water
```

It's important to note that the first index in a list is 0. The second item is index 1, the third is index 2, and so on. The reason for this is that computers count from zero when using lists.

Counting from zero might seem silly, but there's a good reason for it. Early computers were very slow and had a very little memory. It was faster and more efficient to start counting indexes from zero. Even though computers are much faster these days, they still count from zero.

It's also important to note that if you try to access a list index that is greater than the number of items in the list, you'll get an error message. The following line tries to print the item in index position 5:

```
>>> print(noodleSoup[5])
```

Here's part of the error message:

```
IndexError: list index out of range
```

The IndexError tells me that there is no data in the index I want to access. Index position 5 in the list has no data because it's outside the length of the list. Python can't return a value that doesn't exist!

CHANGING A LIST ITEM

Just like you can change the value of variables, you can change individual items in lists as well. This is because lists are *mutable*, which means they can be changed. To change an item in a list, you use the item's index position and set its value the same way you would set the value of a variable (by using an equal sign).

Let's change the beef item in the noodle soup to chicken. Beef is the fifth item in the list, so it has an index of 4 (remember, you count from zero in lists). We can easily change item 4 to chicken, like so:

```
>>> noodleSoup[4] = "chicken"
```

Now let's do something cool with lists in Minecraft.

MISSION #47: HIGH AND LOW

When I'm exploring the Minecraft world, it's interesting to look back over my journey. From the highest mountains to the lowest caves, exploration is one of my favorite activities in the game. Sometimes when I'm playing with friends, we race each other to see who can get to the highest or lowest point in the game the fastest. So no one cheats, I wrote a program that stores the lowest and highest y-coordinates the player reaches within 60 seconds.

When I run the program, it tells me the highest and lowest places in the game that I traveled to during one minute. Listing 9-1 contains the code I've started for you. Copy it into a new file and save it as *highAndLow.py* in a new folder called *lists*.

```
from mcpi.minecraft import Minecraft
mc = Minecraft.create()

import time

❶ heights = [100, 0]
count = 0

while count < 60:
    pos = mc.player.getTilePos()

    if pos.y < heights[0]:
❷       # Set the lowest height to the y variable
    elif pos.y > heights[1]:
❸       # Set the highest height to the y variable

    count += 1
    time.sleep(1)

❹ mc.postToChat("Lowest: ")   # Output lowest height
❺ mc.postToChat("Highest: ")  # Output highest height
```

Listing 9-1: The start of the code to get the lowest and highest positions the player visits

The program will store the lowest and highest y-coordinates you've traveled to in a list called heights ❶. The first item in the list (index position 0) stores the lowest coordinate and the second (index position 1) stores the highest. We need to start with a high "lowest" value and a low "highest" value so that the first time we run the program, the player's position will be the new lowest or highest value and will be displayed in the chat. Here I've used a default lowest value of 100 and a default highest value of 0.

The while loop runs once per second for 60 seconds to constantly update the values in heights. The if statement checks whether the player's current height is lower than the lowest value stored in the list ❷. Then the elif statement checks whether the current height is greater than the highest position stored in the list ❸.

To complete the code, you need to set the value of the lowest height, height[0], to the value of pos.y at ❷. Remember that you set the values in lists like you would a variable, so the line of code should look like this: height[0] = pos.y. You also need to set the highest height, height[1], to the value of pos.y ❸.

Finally, you need to output the value of the lowest ❹ and highest ❺ heights in the last two lines of the program. To do this, you'll need to access the index positions for the lowest and highest heights from the heights list (again, index 0 is the lowest height and index 1 is the highest height).

Run the program and start running around the game. See how high and how low you can get. After 60 seconds, the loop will stop, and the program will display your highest and lowest heights. Run the program several times and see if you can beat your record!

Figure 9-1 shows one of my attempts.

Figure 9-1: The lowest y-coordinate I visited was 15 and the highest was 102.

BONUS OBJECTIVE: AN UNEXPECTED BUG

In *highAndLow.py*, the default values for the lowest and highest positions are set to 100 and 0. This isn't a problem as long as you go lower than 100 and higher than 0. However, if you don't go lower than 100 and higher than 0, the value won't change, which can make the program inaccurate. Can you work out how to fix this?

MANIPULATING LISTS

Lists have a set of built-in functions that let you manipulate them. These functions include common operations like adding an item to a list, inserting an item, or deleting an item.

ADDING AN ITEM

You can add an item to the end of a list using the append() function: just include the value of the item you want to append as an argument.

The noodle soup would be better if we added some vegetables. To do this, use the append() function:

```
>>> noodleSoup.append("vegetables")
```

Now the noodleSoup list contains a "vegetables" string as the last item in the list.

Appending items is very useful when you start with an empty list. By using the append() function, you can add the first item to an empty list:

```
>>> food = []
>>> food.append("cake")
```

INSERTING AN ITEM

It's also possible to insert an item into the middle of a list. The insert() function places an item between two existing items and changes the index positions for all the items after the newly inserted item.

This function takes two arguments, the index position where you want to insert the item and the value that you want to insert.

For example, here's our current noodleSoup list:

```
>>> noodleSoup = ["water", "soy sauce", "spring onions", "noodles", "beef",
"vegetables"]
```

Let's add "pepper" to the list in the third index position:

```
>>> noodleSoup.insert(3, "pepper")
```

The updated list holds the following values after the insert:

```
["water", "soy sauce", "spring onions", "pepper", "noodles", "beef", "vegetables"]
```

If you try to insert an item at an index position that is greater than the length of the list, the item will be added after the last item. For example, if your list has seven items, but you try to insert at item position 10, the item will just be added to the end of the list.

```
>>> noodleSoup.insert(10, "salt")
```

After running this code, the last item in the list will be "salt":

```
["water", "soy sauce", "spring onions", "pepper", "noodles", "beef",
"vegetables", "salt"]
```

Notice that salt isn't in index position 10; instead it is in index position 7.

DELETING AN ITEM

Sometimes you'll want to get rid of an item in a list. You use the del keyword for this. The keyword goes before the name of the list, with the index position of the item you want to delete in the square brackets.

For example, to delete the "beef" item, which is now in index position 5 in the noodleSoup list, do this:

```
>>> del noodleSoup[5]
```

You can also use the del keyword in combination with the index() function if you want to find the index position of a value and then delete it:

```
>>> beefPosition = noodleSoup.index("beef")
>>> del noodleSoup[beefPosition]
```

After deleting an item, the index positions in a list will change. This is what the list will look like after we delete "beef" at index position 5:

```
["water", "soy sauce", "spring onions", "pepper", "noodles", "vegetables", "salt"]
```

The "vegetables" index position changes from 6 to 5, and the "salt" index position changes from 7 to 6. Note that only indexes after the deleted item will be affected; any indexes before the deleted item will be unchanged. Keep this in mind when deleting items from your lists.

MISSION #48: PROGRESS BAR

Let's use some of the list functions to create a progress bar in Minecraft. It will look like the one you see onscreen when you're downloading a file from the Internet or when you're keeping track of your next level up in a role-playing game.

The program will use the progress bar to count to 10 seconds. When the program starts, the progress bar will be made of glass blocks. For every second that passes, the progress bar will replace a glass block with a lapis lazuli block. Figure 9-2 shows the first five steps in the progress bar.

Figure 9-2: The progress bar shows the progress at 50 percent (5 out of 10 blocks are lapis lazuli).

Open IDLE and create a new file. Save it as *progressBar.py* in the *lists* folder. An incomplete version of the program is in Listing 9-2. Copy it into your text editor.

```
from mcpi.minecraft import Minecraft
mc = Minecraft.create()

import time

pos = mc.player.getTilePos()
x = pos.x + 1
y = pos.y
z = pos.z

# Add 10 glass blocks (ID 20) to this empty list
❶ blocks = [ ]
barBlock = 22  # Lapis lazuli

count = 0
while count <= len(blocks):

    mc.setBlock(x, y, z, blocks[0])
    mc.setBlock(x, y + 1, z, blocks[1])
    mc.setBlock(x, y + 2, z, blocks[2])
❷   # Add setBlock() for the remaining blocks in the list

    count += 1

❸   # Delete the last block in the list

❹   # Insert a lapis lazuli block at the first position in the list

    time.sleep(2)
```

Listing 9-2: Incomplete code to make a progress bar

To complete the program in Listing 9-2, you'll need to do the following:

1. Add 10 glass blocks (ID 20) to the empty blocks list at ❶.
2. Use the setBlock() function to set all 10 blocks ❷ from the list in the game world. The first three blocks have been set for you.
3. Write a statement that deletes the last block in the list (index position 9) ❸. Remember that you use the del keyword to delete an item from a list.
4. Insert a new lapis lazuli block at the start of the list ❹. Use the insert() function with the barBlock variable to insert a new lapis lazuli block in index position 0.

Comments are included in the code to help you find where you need to do these tasks.

TREATING STRINGS LIKE LISTS

Strings can be treated like lists, because a string is also a *sequence* of data. You can access individual characters in a string using their index; however, you cannot change the characters in each index position using the append or insert functions because strings are *immutable*. That means that they cannot be changed.

The following code will print the second letter in the string "Grape":

```
>>> flavor = "Grape"
>>> print(flavor[1])
r
```

This shows that you can access parts of a string like you would items in a list. For example, you could access the first letters of someone's first and last names to print their initials:

```
>>> firstName = "Lyra"
>>> lastName = "Jones"
>>> initials = firstName[0] + " " + lastName[0]
>>> print(initials)
L J
```

The new string "L J" that you get by accessing parts of a string using index positions is called a *substring*. Note that the index for a string also counts from zero!

TUPLES

Tuples are a type of list that is immutable. But like other lists, they're a sequence of items of any variable type. Tuples use parentheses instead of square brackets, and they use commas to separate items.

For example, say a nation's only Olympic athlete, from an underfunded training program, records a number of distances for their long jumps in meters:

```
>>> distance = (5.17, 5.20, 4.56, 53.64, 9.58, 6.41, 2.20)
```

If the athlete jumped only once, you could also create a tuple with a single value. To write a tuple with a single value, you still have to include a comma:

```
>>> distance = (5.17,)
```

When you're defining a tuple, the parentheses are optional, so you can just define a tuple by placing commas between values, like this:

```
>>> distance = 5.17, 5.20, 4.56, 53.64, 9.58, 6.41, 2.20
```

To access values of tuples, use the square bracket notation that you use with regular lists. Let's assign the value in index 1 of the distance tuple to the variable jump:

```
>>> jump = distance[1]
>>> print(jump)
5.20
```

The main difference between lists and tuples is that tuples are immutable: you can't change their contents. You can't append items to the end of the tuple, insert items, delete items, or update any values. You use tuples instead of lists when your program doesn't need to change the values of the items in the tuple.

SETTING VARIABLES WITH TUPLES

A useful feature of tuples is that you can use them to set more than one variable at the same time. This saves space and can keep related variables clustered together.

Normally, you would refer to a tuple like you would a list, by using a single variable name:

```
measurements = 6, 30
```

However, let's say we want to store the values in two variables instead of one. The syntax to do so isn't complex. You separate the variable names with commas, then use an equal sign, and then write the tuples on the other side of the equal sign. Each tuple value will be assigned to the variable in the corresponding position. Let's take a look.

In this example, two variables, width and height, are set to the values 6 and 30, respectively:

```
width, height = 6, 30
```

Now we have two variables. One is called width and has a value of 6, and the other is called height and has a value of 30. And we did it by using just a single line of code!

Setting variables with tuples is a quick and easy way to save space in your programs. It's also useful for setting related variables together in one place in your program. For example, throughout the book you've used code like this for setting the values of the x, y, and z variables:

```
x = 10
y = 11
z = 12
```

Instead, you can use a tuple to set all of these values in one line:

```
x, y, z = 10, 11, 12
```

Next, you'll put your new code-writing abilities to use! Your mission is to create a program that moves the player randomly around the game world in small steps, making it look like you're skating on ice. I've started the program for you in Listing 9-3; some bits are missing and you need to complete them.

sliding.py

```
from mcpi.minecraft import Minecraft
mc = Minecraft.create()

import random
import time

❶ # Get the player's position

❷ # Set the x, y, and z variables on the same line using a tuple

while True:
❸     x += random.uniform(-0.2, 0.2)
       # Change the z variable by a random float
❹     z +=
       y = mc.getHeight(x, z)

       mc.player.setPos(x, y, z)
       time.sleep(0.1)
```

Listing 9-3: The start of the code to make the player slide around the map

Copy Listing 9-3 into a new file and save it as *sliding.py* in your *lists* folder. To finish the program, you need to get the player's starting position ❶ and set the values of the x, y, and z variables ❷. Use a tuple to set these values. This program also uses the uniform() function ❸, which is like the randint() function (see "Playing with Random Numbers" on page 62) but returns a random float value instead of an integer value. Use the uniform() function to change the value of the z variable in the loop ❹. This has already been done for the x variable ❸.

Figure 9-3 shows my player sliding slowly around my game.

Figure 9-3: Slowly sliding backwards around my garden

BONUS OBJECTIVE: SLIDING BLOCKS

The *sliding.py* program makes the player slide randomly around the game. Can you work out how to change the program so it makes a block slide around?

RETURNING A TUPLE

Some of Python's built-in functions return a tuple. When you define your own functions, they can return the result as a tuple as well. To do that, you put a tuple after the return keyword. For example, let's create a function to convert a date into a tuple. We give the date as a string argument, and the function will return the year, the month, and the day in a tuple. Here's the code:

```python
def getDateTuple(dateString):
    year = int(dateString[0:4])
    month = int(dateString[5:7])
    day = int(dateString[8:10])
    return year, month, day
```

When we call the function and give it a date as a string, it returns a tuple containing the year, month, and day in that order:

```python
>>> getDateTuple("1997-09-27")
(1997, 9, 27)
```

When we call the function, we can store the returned tuple however we want. This code stores each value in a separate variable:

```python
year, month, day = getDateTuple("1997-09-27")
```

Now we can quickly convert date strings to individual variables. In my work as a software developer, I use code that's very similar to this all the time.

OTHER USEFUL FEATURES OF LISTS

You can do many other tasks with lists. This section explains how to find the length of a list, how to randomly choose an item from a list, and how to use an if statement to check whether a value is in a list.

LIST LENGTH

The len() function is a quick way to find the length of any list in Python. The function returns the number of items in a list when a list is used as an argument. Let's see it in action:

```python
>>> noodleSoup = ["water", "soy sauce", "spring onions", "noodles", "beef",
"vegetables"]
>>> print(len(noodleSoup))
6
```

Although Python starts counting indexes at zero, it counts how many items are in a list in regular counting numbers. The highest index in this list is 5, but Python knows there are 6 total items!

MISSION #50: BLOCK HITS

The Minecraft Python API has a handy function that returns a list of locations you've hit with your sword. You can use the items in the list to get the coordinates of blocks you've hit. You'll see how useful this is in programs later in this chapter and later in the book.

You can also make a short and fun game that counts the number of blocks you can hit in a minute. In this mission, you'll do just that. It's quite a fun game: play against a friend and try to beat each other's scores! You can also expand it, for example, by keeping a high score.

Figure 9-4 shows the program in action.

Figure 9-4: In 60 seconds I hit 197 blocks.

Not much code is required to make this game. Here's a summary of the code structure:

1. Connect to the Minecraft game.
2. Wait 60 seconds.
3. Get the list of block hits.
4. Display the length of the block hits list to chat.

The following code shows the only part you haven't seen so far, which is the code that gets the list of block hits from the game:

```
blockHits = mc.events.pollBlockHits()
```

This code uses the pollBlockHits() function to return a list of block hits and stores that list in a variable named blockHits. The blockHits variable will act like any other kind of list, so you can access data from index positions and get the length of the list.

When you play this game, you'll have to right-click blocks to keep count of them. The reason is that the pollBlockHits() function records all the blocks you *right-click* with a sword. On the PC version of Minecraft, right-clicking with your sword looks more like you're defending yourself than hitting something, but it still records which blocks you've clicked. Figure 9-5 shows what this looks like. Make sure you only right-click with your sword: left clicks with your sword won't be recorded, and neither will right-clicking with something else in your hand! But you can use any type of sword, including iron, gold, and diamond.

Figure 9-5: When I right-click, the player holds the sword like this.

When you print the output of the list, it should look similar to this, although the values will change each time depending on where you hit:

```
[BlockEvent(BlockEvent.HIT, 76, -2, 144, 1, 452),
BlockEvent(BlockEvent.HIT, 79, -2, 145, 1, 452),
BlockEvent(BlockEvent.HIT, 80, -3, 147, 1, 452),
BlockEvent(BlockEvent.HIT, 76, -3, 149, 1, 452)]
```

This list output stores the details of four block hits. Each item contains the hit's coordinates. You'll learn how to access these coordinates in Mission #55 (page 196).

To help you get started with the program, I've written the basic structure in Listing 9-4.

swordHits.py

```
# Connect to the Minecraft game
from mcpi.minecraft import Minecraft
mc = Minecraft.create()

import time

# Wait 60 seconds
time.sleep(60)

# Get the list of block hits
❶ blockHits =

# Display the length of the block hits list to chat
❷ blockHitsLength =
mc.postToChat("Your score is " + str(blockHitsLength))
```

Listing 9-4: Beginnings of the sword hits game

To complete this program, open IDLE, create a new file, and copy Listing 9-4 into it. Save this file as *swordHits.py* in the *lists* folder. Set the blockHits variable using the pollBlockHits() function ❶ and set the blockHitsLength variable by getting the length of the blockHits variable ❷.

RANDOMLY CHOOSING AN ITEM

By now you might have realized that I really like using randomly generated things in my programs. Randomness makes a program behave somewhat unpredictably every time you run it.

When you're using lists, you'll want to access random items from the list from time to time. For example, you might want to choose a block at random from a list of blocks.

The choice() function in the random module is the go-to function for choosing a list item at random. The function takes one argument, the list that you want to use, and returns a random item from within the list.

In Listing 9-5, the colors list contains the names of several colors. It chooses one at random using the choice() function and then prints it:

```
import random
colors = ["red", "green", "blue", "yellow", "orange", "purple"]
print(random.choice(colors))
```

Listing 9-5: Printing a random color from a list of colors

When you run the code, the program will output an item from the list at random.

MISSION #51: RANDOM BLOCK

In Minecraft, selecting a random block ID from a range of numbers can cause problems in the program because some block IDs don't have corresponding blocks. One solution is to use a list of valid blocks to select from at random. Lists allow you to create a limited number of items and then select one at random using the choice() function.

Your mission is to create a list of block IDs, select a random block from that list, and then set the block to the player's position. You can use Listing 9-5 as a starting point.

First, create a list of block IDs. Second, use the random.choice() function to select a block from the list. Third, use the setBlock() function to place the random block in the Minecraft game.

Save the program as *randomBlock.py* in the *lists* folder.

Include as many blocks as you want in your list. For my list I chose five blocks, including melon, diamond, and gold. You can see the result of running the program in Figure 9-6.

Figure 9-6: The program randomly selected a gold block.

COPYING A LIST

Copying lists is quite tricky in most programming languages. List variables do not actually contain values; instead, they contain a reference to an address in your computer's memory that has further references to the values contained in the list. Although your computer takes care of this capability behind the scenes, it's worthwhile to understand how it works because it will make you a smarter programmer! You can view the memory address of a list using the id() function:

```
>>> cake = ["Eggs",
            "Butter",
            "Sugar",
```

```
                "Milk",
                "Flour"]
>>> print(id(cake))
```

For example, the output of this code on my computer was 3067456428.
The value 3067456428 is the memory location where cake is stored. When
you run this code on your computer, you'll probably get a different number
because it's stored in a different place in your computer's memory.

You don't need to understand this behavior fully, but you do need to
know that it has consequences when you want to copy a list into another
variable. Instead of the values in the list being copied as you would expect,
the memory location of the list is copied into the new variable. This means
that when you change a value in either list, it will affect the other.

For example, the following program creates a list called cake and then
sets the value of chocolateCake to be the same as cake. An item, "Chocolate", is
then added to the chocolateCake list:

```
>>> cake = ["Eggs",
            "Butter",
            "Sugar",
            "Milk",
            "Flour"]

>>> # Store the list in a second variable
>>> chocolateCake = cake
>>> chocolateCake.append("Chocolate")
```

Unfortunately, "Chocolate" is also added to the cake list, even though you
didn't want it to be. You can see this mistake when the lists are printed:

```
>>> print(cake)
['Eggs', 'Butter', 'Sugar', 'Milk', 'Flour', 'Chocolate']
>>> print(chocolateCake)
['Eggs', 'Butter', 'Sugar', 'Milk', 'Flour', 'Chocolate']
```

This problem happens because the variables store the memory location
of the list, not the items in the list.

A simple way to overcome this problem is to use a *list slice*. When you
slice food with a knife, you are cutting it into different parts. A list slice in
Python is similar. When you slice a list, you take a piece of the list. You can
use a list slice to take only certain items in a list, but in this case, you'll be
using a list slice to copy every item in a list. To copy the cake list into the
chocolateCake variable, use this code:

```
>>> chocolateCake = cake[:]
```

The chocolateCake variable will now contain the values of the cake list but
with a different memory address.

The code for the cake ingredients can be corrected using the list slice:

```
>>> cake = ["Eggs",
            "Butter",
            "Sugar",
            "Milk",
            "Flour"]

>>> # Store the list in a second variable
❶ >>> chocolateCake = cake[:]
  >>> chocolateCake.append("Chocolate")
```

You can see that the items in cake have been copied to chocolateCake using [:] at ❶.

Here's the output:

```
>>> print(cake)
['Eggs', 'Butter', 'Sugar', 'Milk', 'Flour']
>>> print(chocolateCake)
['Eggs', 'Butter', 'Sugar', 'Milk', 'Flour', 'Chocolate']
```

Notice that the values in both lists are now different—only chocolateCake contains the "Chocolate" value.

ITEMS AND IF STATEMENTS

To find out whether a value is in a list, you can use the in operator. The in operator goes between a value and the list you want to check. If the value is in the list, the expression will evaluate to True; if the value is not in the list, the expression will evaluate to False.

The following example checks whether the value "Eggs" is in the cake list:

```
>>> cake = ["Eggs", "Butter", "Sugar", "Milk", "Flour"]
>>> print("Eggs" in cake)
```

The value True will be printed, because "Eggs" is in the list.

You can of course use the in operator as part of an if statement condition. The following code extends and adapts this example to use an if statement instead of printing the Boolean value. It checks whether "Ham" is in the cake list and prints different messages depending on whether it is or isn't in the list:

```
>>> cake = ["Eggs", "Butter", "Sugar", "Milk", "Flour"]
>>> if "Ham" in cake:
>>>     print("That cake sounds disgusting.")
>>> else:
>>>     print("Good. Ham in a cake is a terrible mistake.")
```

You can combine the not operator with the in operator to produce the opposite effect. Instead of returning True when an item is in a list, the code will return False and vice versa. Here's how that looks (note that the bodies of the if and else statements have also been swapped):

```
>>> cake = ["Eggs", "Butter", "Sugar", "Milk", "Flour"]
>>> if "Ham" not in cake:
>>>     print("Good. Ham in a cake is a terrible mistake.")
>>> else:
>>>     print("That cake sounds disgusting")
```

You can use either technique in your programs. Just choose the one that you think makes the most sense!

MISSION #52: NIGHT VISION SWORD

Do you forget to bring enough torches with you when you're exploring caves in Minecraft? I do that all the time. Sometimes I forget to bring any torches, and I'm too far into the cave to go back. So I fumble around in the dark, not really sure if I'm finding anything useful. But with your Python knowledge, you can make a program to help you find diamonds with your sword.

Let's write a basic program that uses the pollBlockHits() function to check whether any of the blocks you've hit are diamond ore. This is useful for exploring caves with no light or playing a game of "find the diamond ore" in the dark. The code is in Listing 9-6. Copy it into a new file and save it as *nightVisionSword.py* in the *lists* folder.

nightVision Sword.py

```
from mcpi.minecraft import Minecraft
mc = Minecraft.create()

import time

blocks = []

while True:
    hits = mc.events.pollBlockHits()
    if len(hits) > 0:
        hit = hits[0]
❶       hitX, hitY, hitZ = hit.pos.x, hit.pos.y, hit.pos.z
        block = mc.getBlock(hitX, hitY, hitZ)
        blocks.append(block)

❷       # Add the if statement here

    time.sleep(0.2)
```

Listing 9-6: This program will help you find diamond ore in the dark.

Notice how hit.pos.x, hit.pos.y, and hit.pos.z are used ❶. Each hit stores the coordinates of the block that was clicked using a tuple. You can access these coordinates using dot notation. In this example, the variable name hit is used to name the list that contains each block hit, so I access the coordinates using hit.pos.x, hit.pos.y, and hit.pos.z.

The code is nearly complete. The only remaining task is to check whether you've found some diamond. Add an if statement ❷ to check whether diamond ore (block ID 56) is in the blocks list and post a message to chat saying "You found some diamond ore!" if it is. Add a break statement inside the if statement as well so the loop stops repeating when you find the ore.

Figure 9-7 shows the program in action.

Figure 9-7: It's dark, but I found some diamond ore. Yay!

If you're not as forgetful as I am and remember to bring torches with you into caves, you can still use this code—as a game. Make an underground room with no light and put a single diamond ore somewhere on the wall. Run the program and see how long it takes you to find the diamond ore in the dark. Remember to right-click with a sword! That's the only way the pollBlockHits() function can record which blocks you're hitting.

BONUS OBJECTIVE: DIAMOND CHALLENGE

It would be cool to change the *nightVisionSword.py* program into a full mini-game. Can you automatically generate a room with a single diamond block placed at random, put the player in that room, and then time how long it takes them to find the block in the dark?

DICTIONARIES

Dictionaries are a type of list that uses a different approach. Instead of using an index to identify items, dictionaries identify items using a set of keys defined by the programmer.

For example, this raceTimes dictionary stores the names of people who ran in a race and their race times:

```
raceTimes = {'Katy': 26,
             'Alex': 30,
             'Richard': 19}
```

The key uniquely identifies each value in the dictionary. In this example, the key is the name of the person. The 'Katy' key has an associated value of 26.

Like lists, dictionaries are mutable; their content can be changed.

DEFINING A DICTIONARY

To define a dictionary, use a pair of curly brackets around a set of key-value pairs. For example, you can use a dictionary to describe a person. You can use keys like 'name' and 'favoriteAnimal' to store information about the person, like so:

```
person = {'name': 'David',
          'age': 42,
          'favoriteAnimal': 'Snake',
          'favoritePlace': 'Inside a cardboard box'}
```

In this example, every key is a string. Each key is paired with a value using a colon. For example, 'age' is a key and 42 is its corresponding value. Items in the dictionary are then separated by commas.

You may have noticed that using dictionaries makes it easy for a programmer to understand what each item in the list represents; for example, it's easy to understand that the 'name' key stores a name, not a number or some other random information.

You can also use integers and floats as dictionary keys. Using floats or integers in dictionaries is very useful when the keys you want to match with values don't follow a strict sequence.

The following example creates a dictionary of train times. The train time (which is a float) is stored as the key, and the destination of the train is stored as the value:

```
trainTimes = {1.00: 'Castle Town',
              2.30: 'Sheep Farm',
              3.15: 'Lake City',
```

```
      3.45: 'Castle Town',
      3.55: 'Storage Land'
      }
```

Because dictionaries can store two pieces of data that go together as a pair, they're ideal for a situation like this. If I used a list of train destinations instead of a dictionary, I wouldn't be able to match up the times to the destinations. I would only be able to use the list's index positions, which would be 0, 1, 2, 3, 4, and so on, instead of the times.

ACCESSING ITEMS IN DICTIONARIES

To access the value of an item in a dictionary, you use square brackets and a key instead of an index. The key is usually a string or an integer. When you're creating a dictionary that uses strings as keys, make sure you put them in quotation marks.

For example, to access the value of the 'name' key in the person dictionary created earlier, you would use this syntax:

```
person = {'name': 'David',
       'age': 42,
       'favoriteAnimal': 'Snake',
       'favoritePlace': 'Inside a cardboard box'}

agentName = person['name']
```

The agentName variable will contain the value 'David' because it accesses the value of the 'name' key. In the same way, if you wanted to access the age of the agent, you would use the 'age' key:

```
agentAge = person['age']
```

This would store the value 42 in the agentAge variable.

In the trainTimes example, you can access the values in the dictionary (the destinations) using their key values (the train times), which are floats:

```
trainTimes = {1.00: 'Castle Town',
            2.30: 'Sheep Farm',
            3.15: 'Lake City',
            3.45: 'Castle Town',
            3.55: 'Storage Land'
            }

myTrain = trainTimes[3.15]
```

Accessing the 3.15 key in the trainTimes dictionary sets the myTrain variable to 'Lake City'.

When you're using dictionaries, you can store any data type as the value, even lists and tuples. For example, you could store a tuple containing values for x, y, and z. Here's an example of code that does just that:

```
places = {'Living room': (76, 1, -61), 'Bedroom': (61, 9, -61)}
```

The places dictionary stores two items. The dictionary key is the name of a location in my Minecraft game (such as my living room or bedroom), and the value is a tuple of the coordinates. If I wanted to access the coordinates of my living room, I would use the following code:

```
location = places['Living room']
x, y, z = location[0], location[1], location[2]
```

Your mission is to create a program that uses a dictionary to store the locations of different places in your Minecraft game so you can teleport to them by name. Include as many locations in the dictionary as you want. To teleport to those locations, you need to access the tuple of coordinates stored in the dictionary and then set x, y, and z to the values stored in the tuple. Comments in the code show where to do this.

Copy Listing 9-7 into the IDLE text editor and save it in the *lists* folder as *sightseeingGuide.py*.

sightseeing Guide.py

```
from mcpi.minecraft import Minecraft
mc = Minecraft.create()

# Add locations to the dictionary
places = {}

choice = ""
while choice != "exit":
❶     choice = input("Enter a location ('exit' to close): ")
❷     if choice in places:
          # Store the dictionary item's value using its key (choice)
          location =
          # Store the values stored in the tuple in the x, y, and z variables
          x, y, z =
          mc.player.setTilePos(x, y, z)
```

Listing 9-7: Some neat code to teleport to different locations

I've included a statement that asks you to enter the name of the location you want to go to. This input is stored in the choice variable ❶. The program then uses an if statement to check whether the value of choice is in the dictionary ❷. The last line uses the x, y, and z variables to teleport the player to the position stored in the dictionary.

When the program runs, enter the name of the location that you want to go to. Figure 9-8 shows my version of the program teleporting me to different places in my game.

Figure 9-8: I teleported to my living room (top) and my bedroom (bottom).

CHANGING OR ADDING AN ITEM IN A DICTIONARY

It doesn't take much work to change the value of an item in a dictionary. You use square brackets with a key to access the item and set it as you would a normal variable (with an equal sign). You can also add a new item using this approach.

Let's change the value of the age item in the person dictionary from 42 to 43:

```
person['age'] = 43
```

Let's also add a new item called location with the value 'USS Discovery':

```
person['location'] = 'USS Discovery'
```

After running this code, the dictionary will have a new key called location that has the value of 'USS Discovery'.

DELETING ITEMS IN DICTIONARIES

Sometimes you'll want to delete an item in a dictionary. As with a list, you use the del keyword to do this. For example, to delete the favoriteAnimal item in the person dictionary, you would do this:

```
del person['favoriteAnimal']
```

As you can see, it works just like deleting items from a list.

MISSION #54: BLOCK HITS SCORE

In Mission #50 (page 180), you wrote a program that counts the number of times the player hits a block with their sword in 60 seconds. As fun as the program is, it would be even cooler if you could record the scores of everyone who played.

To add a scoreboard to the game, you'll use a dictionary. The dictionary will store the player's name and their score, which can then be displayed alongside everyone else's scores.

To get started, open *swordHits.py* and save it as *swordHitsScore.py* in the *lists* folder. Update the code to match Listing 9-8, where I've made some changes to the program so it repeats, asks the player for their name, and then prints all the scores. (I've also included the solutions to the missing code from *swordHits.py*.) The older sections are grayed out. (Remember to indent everything inside the loop.)

swordHits Score.py

```
# Connect to the Minecraft game
from mcpi.minecraft import Minecraft
mc = Minecraft.create()

import time

name = ""
scoreboard = {}

while True:
    # Get the player's name
    name = input("What is your name? ")
```

```
# Break loop if name is exit
if name == "exit":
    break
mc.postToChat("Go!")

# Wait 60 seconds
time.sleep(60)

# Get the list of block hits
blockHits = mc.events.pollBlockHits()

# Display the length of the block hits list to chat
blockHitsLength = len(blockHits)
mc.postToChat("Your score is " + str(blockHitsLength))
```
❶
```
# Add the player to the scoreboard

# Display the scoreboard
print(scoreboard)
```

Listing 9-8: When the code is complete, it will add a scoreboard to the block hits game.

To finish the program, you need to store the name and score of every player who plays the game. Do this by adding a new dictionary item using the pieces of data in the code at ❶. The dictionary is called scoreboard, and the name of the player is stored in the name variable.

Figure 9-9 shows the output of my scoreboard.

Figure 9-9: My friends and I played a game, and Jim is the winner with 274 block hits.

NOTE *You might have noticed that when the scoreboard dictionary is printed, it isn't easy to read. You'll learn how to fix this in Mission #59 (page 205).*

WHAT YOU LEARNED

Excellent job! In this chapter you learned about lists, tuples, and dictionaries. You saw that they can store several data values in a single variable. They are a very useful way to structure and store data in your programs.

In the missions, you created several fun programs that use lists, dictionaries, and tuples. With lists, you created a progress bar using lapis lazuli and glass. Using tuples, you learned a quicker way to set the x, y, and z variables. And dictionaries allowed you to store the coordinates of things you've built and then teleport to them by entering their names.

In Chapter 10, you'll further develop your knowledge of lists by learning about for loops. You'll create some very cool programs, including one that you can use to duplicate items you've built.

10

MINECRAFT MAGIC WITH
FOR LOOPS

Now it's time to learn about for loops.
for loops are super useful because they
iterate over lists of items, like the lists you
saw in Chapter 9. This means that they are perfect when you want to use loops with lists in your
programs.

While following along with the missions in this chapter, you'll use for
loops to generate stairs, pillars, pyramids, and weather-beaten walls. With
nested for loops and lists, you'll be able to create pixel art and generate
new structures in seconds. for loops are very powerful tools for building in
Minecraft!

A SIMPLE FOR LOOP

A for loop repeats a block of code for each item in a list until the list ends,
rather than using a condition like a while loop or an if statement.

The list you use in a for statement can contain any number of items of any data type. The for loop will iterate through each one in order, that is, by its index. For example, to print every item in the noodle soup list, we would use the following code:

```
noodleSoup = ["water", "soy sauce", "spring onions", "pepper", "noodles",
"beef", "vegetables"]

for ingredient in noodleSoup:
    print(ingredient)
```

We use the for operator to tell Python we're using a loop.

After the for operator is a variable, ingredient, that represents the item that the loop is currently using. The value changes every time the loop iterates until it has looped through each item in the list. The first time the loop executes, the value will be the item in index position 0 (in this case "water"), the second time the value will be the item in index 1 ("soy sauce"), the third time the value will be the item in index 2 ("spring onions"), and so on.

The in operator and the list name at the end of the statement tell Python which list you're using. The name of the list in this example is noodleSoup.

The loop executes once for each item in the list and then ends when it reaches the end of the list. Here's the output for this program:

```
water
soy sauce
spring onions
pepper
noodles
beef
vegetables
```

Every item in the list is printed! Now let's have some fun with for loops in Minecraft.

MISSION #55: MAGIC WAND

Every tool in Minecraft has its own purpose. The shovel digs dirt, the pickaxe breaks stone blocks, the axe cuts wood, and the sword hits baddies. Usually, you can't change how the tools behave; you just have to accept that the sword only hits enemies. But with Python, you can change how the tools work. In this program, we'll turn the sword into a magic wand.

In Chapter 9, you learned about the pollBlockHits() function. This function returns a list of block coordinates that the sword has hit. Using a for loop, you can access each set of coordinates in this list. We're going to turn all the blocks we hit in the last 60 seconds into melons. You can see how this works in Figure 10-1.

Figure 10-1: Abracadabra! All the blocks I hit are now melons.

Listing 10-1 contains the start of the program. Save it as *magicWand.py* in a new folder called *forLoops*.

magicWand
.py

```
from mcpi.minecraft import Minecraft
mc = Minecraft.create()

import time

time.sleep(60)

❶ hits = mc.events.pollBlockHits()
   block = 103

❷ for
❸ x, y, z = hit.pos.x, hit.pos.y, hit.pos.z
❹ # Set melon blocks at the coordinates
```

Listing 10-1: The start of the magic wand program

To get the list of block hits, we call the `pollBlockHits()` function and store the result in the hits variable ❶.

Included is a line of code that will get the position of any block you hit and store its coordinates in the x, y, and z variables ❸. It uses a tuple (introduced in "Tuples" on page 175) to assign the three variables in a single line.

At the moment, this line of code won't work because the hit variable doesn't exist. Create a for loop at ❷ and call the variable of the for loop hit. The for loop should iterate over the hits list. The code for the first part of the for loop should look like this:

```
for hit in hits:
```

Make sure you indent the line of code that gets the x, y, and z values inside the for loop at ❸. On the last line of the for loop, add the setBlock() function to set a melon block at the x-, y-, and z-coordinates ❹.

When the user runs the completed program, they'll have 60 seconds to run around and right-click as many blocks as they can with their sword. After 60 seconds, all the blocks that were hit with the sword will turn to melons.

BONUS OBJECTIVE: YOU'RE A WIZARD

Change the *magicWand.py* program so it teleports the player: the first hit sets the location, and the second hit takes them there.

THE RANGE() FUNCTION

The range() function creates a list of integers. It's a good way to create a list of numbers for your for loops very quickly. Let's take a look and pass two arguments, 0 and 5, to the range() function:

```
aRange = range(0, 5)
```

This is a faster way to create a list than writing each item in the list individually, which would look like this:

```
aRange = [0, 1, 2, 3, 4]
```

Notice that the range() function's second argument is 5, but the last item in the list is 4. This is because the function only creates values that are less than but not equal to the second argument.

To create a loop that uses the range() function to print the numbers 1 to 15, you would use the following code:

```
for item in range(1, 16):
    print(item)
```

You could print double the value of every item in a list like so:

```
for item in range(1, 16):
    print(item * 2)
```

You can do the same thing with a while loop, which you learned about in Chapter 7. The following code uses a while loop instead of a for loop to print the numbers 1 to 15:

```
count = 1
while count < 16:
    print(count)
    count += 1
```

Notice that the for loop is simpler and easier to read. In large and complex programs, a for loop is often a better choice than a while loop with count.

MISSION #56: MAGIC STAIRS

One of the best features of using Minecraft with Python is that you can build things quickly with just a few lines of code. Instead of spending lots of time building walls, you can just run some code and it's done. You can also reuse the code as many times as you want, saving time and effort.

Building stairs is one task that often takes a long time to do. Fortunately, with just a few lines of Python code, you can quickly create a staircase in Minecraft. In this mission, you'll use a for loop to make a staircase appear in the game world.

Listing 10-2 creates a staircase in Minecraft using a while loop. Save it as *stairs.py* in the *forLoops* folder.

stairs.py
```
from mcpi.minecraft import Minecraft
mc = Minecraft.create()

pos = mc.player.getTilePos()
x, y, z = pos.x, pos.y, pos.z

stairBlock = 53

step = 0
while step < 10:
    mc.setblock(x + step, y + step, z, stairBlock)
    step += 1
```

Listing 10-2: A program that creates a staircase using a while loop

Although you can use a while loop for this program, as shown here, a for loop is actually more suitable. Unlike the while loop, a for loop doesn't require a count or step variable. Instead, you can use the range() function to determine how many times the loop repeats.

To complete the program, change the code so it uses a for loop instead of a while loop.

You can see the result of the program in Figure 10-2.

BONUS OBJECTIVE: GOING DOWN?

At the moment, the *stairs.py* program only builds stairs in one direction. Try to work out how to build stairs in other directions. Hint: You'll use the optional block states argument in the setBlock() function and add to or take away from the x or z variables.

Figure 10-2: Where will your magic staircase lead?

PLAYING AROUND WITH RANGE()

You've learned a bit about the range() function and what happens when you pass two arguments to the function. What if you pass just one argument? Enter this code in the IDLE shell to see what happens:

```
>>> aRange = range(5)
>>> list(aRange)
[0, 1, 2, 3, 4]
```

When you give the range() function only one argument, it will start at 0 and store each value up to one less than the value you pass in as an argument. In other words, it's as if you passed 0 for the first argument and 5 for the second argument. In this example, the list() function shows the list values created by the range() function (otherwise, you wouldn't see them!). As you can see, the value of list(aRange) is a list of five numbers that start at 0: [0, 1, 2, 3, 4]. This is a fast way to create a range if you want to start with 0 as the first value.

As you've seen, when you pass two arguments to range(), the list starts at the first argument provided and ends before the second argument:

```
>>> aRange = range(2, 5)
>>> list(aRange)
[2, 3, 4]
```

This example creates a range equivalent to the list [2, 3, 4].

When you give range() three arguments, the third argument defines the *step* between items. Normally, each value in the list created by the range() function is one larger than the previous value. By changing the step, you change the difference between values. For example, a step of 2 would make the next value in a list 2 more than the previous item. A step of 3 would make it 3 more than the previous item, and so on.

For example, this list adds 2 to the previous value to get the next value:

```
>>> aRange = range(3, 10, 2)
>>> list(aRange)
[3, 5, 7, 9]
```

Notice that each item is 2 more than the previous item (5 is 3 + 2, 7 is 5 + 2, and 9 is 7 + 2).

You can even give range() a negative step value, like this:

```
>>> newRange = range(100, 0, -2)
>>> list(newRange)
[100, 98, 96, 94, 92, 90, 88, 86, 84, 82, 80, 78, 76, 74, 72, 70, 68, 66, 64,
62, 60, 58, 56, 54, 52, 50, 48, 46, 44, 42, 40, 38, 36, 34, 32, 30, 28, 26,
24, 22, 20, 18, 16, 14, 12, 10, 8, 6, 4, 2]
```

Notice that the values in the list decrease by 2 because of the negative step value.

OTHER LIST FUNCTIONS

Because we're working with lists, let's explore a few other functions designed to interact with lists.

The reversed() function takes one argument, the list you want to use, and returns the list reversed. The last item will be the first item, the second-to-last item will be the second item, and so on. Let's reverse an earlier list:

```
>>> backwardsList = reversed(aRange)
>>> list(backwardsList)
[9, 7, 5, 3]
```

Items in the list have been reversed, just as we wanted. This kind of list manipulation comes in handy when you're writing for loops.

The following example generates a list of numbers from 1 to 100 using the range() function. It then reverses the list and prints it using a for loop, effectively creating a countdown from 100 to 1:

```
countDown = range(1, 101)
countDown = reversed(countDown)
for item in countDown:
    print(item)
```

Run it to see the output!

```
100
99
98
97
96
```

```
--snip--
3
2
1
```

You can also reverse the list when you declare the for loop without needing a variable to store the list:

```
for item in reversed(range(0, 101)):
    print(item)
```

This program requires fewer lines of code while having the same effect. Use this trick to save time so you can focus on building!

MISSION #57: PILLARS

Wouldn't it be cool to build a palace in Minecraft? Because palaces should be grand, ours should have rows of tall, imposing pillars. Obviously, we don't want to build them by hand, so using a loop to build them is the best solution.

We'll create a function that builds a pillar and then call the function when we want to build one. Listing 10-3 contains the function to build a pillar. Copy it into a new file called *pillars.py* and save it in the *forLoops* folder.

pillars.py
```
from mcpi.minecraft import Minecraft
mc = Minecraft.create()

def setPillar(x, y, z, height):
    """ Creates a pillar. Args set position and height of pillar """
    stairBlock = 156
    block = 155

    # Pillar top
    mc.setBlocks(x - 1, y + height, z - 1, x + 1, y + height, z + 1, block, 1)
    mc.setBlock(x - 1, y + height - 1, z, stairBlock, 12)
    mc.setBlock(x + 1, y + height - 1, z, stairBlock, 13)
    mc.setBlock(x, y + height - 1, z + 1, stairBlock, 15)
    mc.setBlock(x, y + height - 1, z - 1, stairBlock, 14)

    # Pillar base
    mc.setBlocks(x - 1, y, z - 1, x + 1, y, z + 1, block, 1)
    mc.setBlock(x - 1, y + 1, z, stairBlock, 0)
    mc.setBlock(x + 1, y + 1, z, stairBlock, 1)
    mc.setBlock(x, y + 1, z + 1, stairBlock, 3)
    mc.setBlock(x, y + 1, z - 1, stairBlock, 2)

    # Pillar column
    mc.setBlocks(x, y, z, x, y + height, z, block, 2)

pos = mc.player.getTilePos()
x, y, z = pos.x + 2, pos.y, pos.z
```

```
❶ # Add the for loop here
❷ # Call the function here
```

Listing 10-3: A function that creates a pillar

The setPillar() function creates a pillar. It takes four arguments: the x-, y-, and z-coordinates and the pillar height.

To finish the program, add a for loop ❶ that calls the setPillar() function ❷. We want to create a row of 20 pillars that are each 5 blocks apart. To do that, use a range() function with three arguments to determine how many pillars will be created and how far apart they will be. By adding the values stored in the for loop's variable to the x or z variable in the setPillar() function call, you can make each pillar an equal distance apart.

Figure 10-3 shows some of the pillars.

Figure 10-3: A brilliant row of pillars

MISSION #58: PYRAMID

Continuing the theme of building awesome stuff with for loops, let's build a pyramid. A pyramid is made up of many levels. The bottom level is the widest, and the top level—the peak—is the narrowest. Each level is a square of blocks. We'll make a pyramid that's two blocks narrower on each level. For example, if the base level is seven blocks wide, the next level would be five blocks wide, then three blocks, and finally the top level would be one block wide.

Listing 10-4 creates a pyramid. Copy it into a new file called *pyramid.py* and save it in the *forLoops* folder.

pyramid.py
```
from mcpi.minecraft import Minecraft
mc = Minecraft.create()
```

```
  block = 24  # sandstone
❶ height = 10
❷ levels = range(height)

  pos = mc.player.getTilePos()
❸ x, y, z = pos.x + height, pos.y, pos.z

❹ for level in levels:
❺     mc.setBlocks(x - level, y, z - level, x + level, y, z + level, block)
      y += 1
```

Listing 10-4: An upside-down pyramid program

Although Listing 10-4 creates a pyramid, it contains a minor bug you need to fix! We store the pyramid's height in the height variable ❶. You can change the value of the height variable to anything you want. The levels variable uses the range() function to create a list that contains one item for each level of the pyramid ❷. The height variable is added to the player's x-coordinate when we set the x, y, and z variables ❸. If we didn't do this, the player would be trapped at the center of the pyramid when it's built.

The for loop iterates for each level in the levels list ❹. The line of code that creates each level of the pyramid uses the level variable to work out the width of each square of blocks that it creates ❺. The width and length of each pyramid level will always be twice the size of the level variable.

Remember that bug I mentioned earlier? Run the program to see what the problem is. The pyramid is upside down!

To fix this issue and make the pyramid right side up, you'll need to use the reversed() function on the levels variable to make a list that gets smaller over time. Or you could be sneaky and call the range() function with a negative value.

Figure 10-4 shows the finished pyramid.

Figure 10-4: A magnificent pyramid

LOOPING OVER A DICTIONARY

You can also use a for loop to loop over a dictionary. When you're using a dictionary with a for loop, the syntax is the same as a for loop with a list; however, the loop will only iterate through the dictionary's keys.

For example, the following code prints the for loop's variable each time the loop iterates. In this case, it prints the key of each item in the dictionary:

```
inventory = {'gems': 5, 'potions': 2, 'boxes': 1}

for key in inventory:
    print(key)
```

This code prints the following:

```
gems
potions
boxes
```

To print the value associated with each item in the dictionary, you need to use the dictionary[key] syntax. Here's how to change the code so it prints the value of each item as well as the key:

```
inventory = {'gems': 5, 'potions': 2, 'boxes': 1}

for key in inventory:
    print(key + " " + str(inventory[key]))
```

This example now prints the following:

```
gems 5
potions 2
boxes 1
```

Notice that this output is much easier to read than the dictionary itself. By using a loop to output the values of a dictionary, you have much more control over how the information is displayed.

MISSION #59: SCOREBOARD

Recall the *swordHitsScore.py* game from Mission #54 (page 192). The game recorded the number of blocks a player hit in a minute. The score was stored in a dictionary along with the name of the player. Although the program worked just fine, the scoreboard at the end of the program didn't output the scores and names in a very readable format. It just printed a dictionary without any formatting.

To improve the program, in this mission you'll modify *swordHitsScore.py* so it outputs the scoreboard dictionary in an easy-to-read format. To do this, you'll use a for loop.

Open your *swordHitsScore.py* program (it should be in the *lists* folder) and save it as *scoreBoard.py* in the *forLoops* folder. In the program, find and delete this line:

```
print(scoreboard)
```

Replace this line with a for loop that prints the name of each player and their score. These values are stored in the scoreboard dictionary: each player's name is a key in the dictionary, and their score is the value of the key.

Figure 10-5 shows the updated output.

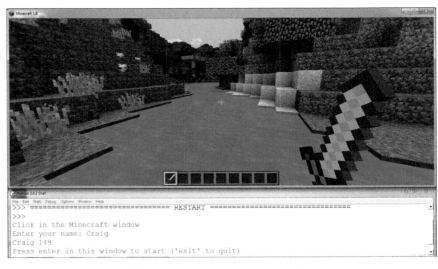

Figure 10-5: The output of the program is now easier to read.

FOR-ELSE LOOPS

You can also use the else statement with a for loop. When you use else with a for loop, it executes after the for loop reaches the end of the list. If the for loop doesn't reach the end of its list, the else statement will not execute.

For example, here's a bit of code that prints the ingredients of a sandwich and then uses an else statement:

```
sandwich = ["Bread", "Butter", "Tuna", "Lettuce", "Mayonnaise", "Bread"]

for ingredient in sandwich:
    print(ingredient)
else:
    print("This is the end of the sandwich.")
```

When you run this code, it prints the following:

```
Bread
Butter
```

```
Tuna
Lettuce
Mayonnaise
Bread
This is the end of the sandwich.
```

You might think this code is just the same as writing the following:

```
for ingredient in sandwich:
    print(ingredient)
print("This is the end of the sandwich.")
```

Well, yes it is. Both pieces of code will do the same thing. So what is the point of using else with a for loop? Well, when used with a break statement, the else statement will behave differently. Let's look at that next.

BREAKING A FOR-ELSE LOOP

Using a break statement to exit a for loop is one way to prevent the else statement from executing.

The following example incorporates a break statement within an if statement. The loop will break if the current item is "Mayonnaise":

```
sandwich = ["Bread", "Butter", "Tuna", "Lettuce", "Mayonnaise", "Bread"]

for ingredient in sandwich:
    if ingredient == "Mayonnaise":
        print("I don't like mayonnaise on my sandwich.")
        break
    else:
        print(ingredient)
else:
    print("This is the end of the sandwich.")
```

Can you predict what the output will be? Think about it before running this code, and then run the code and see what happens.

MISSION #60: THE DIAMOND PROSPECTOR

Sometimes when I'm playing Minecraft with friends, they won't let me use Python programs to generate diamond blocks. But I still need diamonds for armor, tools, and building diamond castles. Digging straight down for diamond is easy enough, but you don't always find it.

To save some time, I wrote a program that checks whether any diamond ore is directly below me. The program gets my current position and then uses a for loop to check the blocks below me one at a time to see whether they're diamond ore. If diamond ore is found, the program tells me how deep the ore is; if no diamond ore is found, the program posts a message to say no diamond ore is below me.

Create a new program and save it as *diamondSurvey.py* in the *forLoops* folder.

Use a for loop to change the value of the y variable by –1 each time the loop iterates. In total, the loop should repeat 50 times to check 50 blocks deep. For each iteration, use an if statement to check whether the block at that position is diamond ore (block ID 56). If it is a diamond ore block, post a message to the chat to say how far the block is below the player and break the loop. If no diamond ore blocks are found, use an else statement in your for loop to post a message that says no diamond ore blocks are directly below the player.

Figure 10-6 shows the working program.

Figure 10-6: It looks like a diamond ore block is four blocks below me. Time to start digging!

BONUS OBJECTIVE: GOLD IN THEM THAR HILLS

Change the *diamondSurvey.py* program so it looks for other ore blocks as well, such as iron ore or gold ore.

NESTED FOR LOOPS AND MULTIDIMENSIONAL LISTS

Within your programs, you can use multiple lists together for a variety of reasons. It's possible to include lists within lists, which are called *multidimensional lists*. In this section, we'll use two-dimensional (2D) and three-dimensional (3D) lists to build structures in Minecraft.

THINKING IN TWO DIMENSIONS

You've learned how to write lists, specifically *one-dimensional* lists. They're called one-dimensional lists because each position in the list contains only one item.

For example, look at the following list, called oneDimensionalRainbowList. The formatting of this list is a bit different just to emphasize that each position contains a single item; otherwise, it's the same as other lists you've worked with:

```
oneDimensionalRainbowList = [0,
                             1,
                             2,
                             3,
                             4,
                             5]
```

There are six items in this list: the numbers 0 to 5. Each item in the list has only one value, making the list a one-dimensional list.

Listing 10-5 displays this list in Minecraft as wool blocks. The program file, *rainbowStack1.py*, is available in the book's resources. Download the code files from *https://www.nostarch.com/pythonwithminecraft/* or type it yourself and play along!

rainbow Stack1.py

```
from mcpi.minecraft import Minecraft
mc = Minecraft.create()

❶ oneDimensionalRainbowList = [0, 1, 2, 3, 4, 5]

pos = mc.player.getTilePos()
x = pos.x
y = pos.y
z = pos.z

❷ for color in oneDimensionalRainbowList:
      mc.setBlock(x, y, z, 35, color)
      y += 1
```

Listing 10-5: Building a rainbow stack of blocks

The program creates a list of block colors ❶ and then uses a for loop to create a stack of wool blocks with colors based on the colors in the list ❷.

When you run the program, you'll get a single stack of wool blocks, as you can see in Figure 10-7. Notice that the stack is six blocks high and one block wide. You've used the x, y, and z variables throughout this book. Each of these variables can also be referred to as a *dimension*. This program creates a stack of six blocks on the y-dimension. By changing the x variable on the last line of the code instead of the y variable, you can build a stack of blocks on the x-dimension, which you can see in Figure 10-8.

Figure 10-7: The rainbow stack of blocks created by rainbowStack1.py

Figure 10-8: Swapping the y variable for the x variable on the last line of the program builds the blocks in a horizontal row.

Because the list is one-dimensional, you can change the value of only one variable on a single dimension at a time. In other words, you can change the value of the y variable, x variable, or z variable but can't change all of them at once.

So, it's time to start thinking about two dimensions! One-dimensional lists allow you to have a single list with only one value in each position, but two-dimensional lists allow you to have many values in each position of a list. You do this by putting a list at each position of the original list, as follows.

```
❶ twoDimensionalRainbowList = [[0, 0, 0],
❷                             [1, 1, 1],
❸                             [2, 2, 2],
                              [3, 3, 3],
                              [4, 4, 4],
❹                             [5, 5, 5]]
```

Look closely and you'll see an opening square bracket on the first line followed by a list full of zeroes and then a comma ❶. That is a list inside a list! We can call the main list the *outer list* and say that it contains *nested lists*.

In index position 1 is a list that contains three 1s ❷. In index position 2 is another list, this one containing three 2s ❸. This repeats on every line. On the last line is a list of three 5s, followed by a square bracket, which closes the outer list ❹. This code shows a list with six items in it, each of which is also a list. This is a two-dimensional list!

You'll better understand two-dimensional lists when you use them in Minecraft. Let's look at an example. By modifying *rainbowStack1.py*, we can make it work with the two-dimensional list. This new program is named *rainbowRows.py*:

rainbowRows .py
```
from mcpi.minecraft import Minecraft
mc = Minecraft.create()

twoDimensionalRainbowList = [[0, 0, 0],
                            [1, 1, 1],
                            [2, 2, 2],
                            [3, 3, 3],
                            [4, 4, 4],
                            [5, 5, 5]]

pos = mc.player.getTilePos()
x = pos.x
y = pos.y
z = pos.z
```
❶
```
startingX = x
```
❷
❸
❹
❺
❻
❼
```
for row in twoDimensionalRainbowList:
    for color in row:
        mc.setBlock(x, y, z, 35, color)
        x += 1
    y += 1
    x = startingX
```

Before I explain the code, look at Figure 10-9 to see the output of *rainbowRows.py*, which is a set of blocks six blocks high on the y-dimension and three blocks wide on the x-dimension.

Figure 10-9: Using a two-dimensional list to make a rainbow wall

Because we're working with two dimensions, we need two for loops to output the values in the twoDimensionalRainbowList list. The first loop iterates through each item in the outer list ❷. The second loop ❸, called a *nested* loop because it is inside another loop, then goes through each item in each nested list.

For example, the first time the outer loop runs, it gets the item stored in index position 0 of the twoDimensionalRainbowList list and stores it in a variable called row ❷. The value of row is [0, 0, 0] because it's the first item in the list.

The second loop then works through each item in the row list and stores it in the color variable ❸. In this case, each item will be 0. The program then sets the blocks using the color variable to determine the color of each wool block ❹. The nested loop finishes after it has placed all three blocks for that row, and then the outer loop runs again. Next, the outer loop moves to index position 1 and stores the value in the row variable, which is now [1, 1, 1]. It then runs through the nested loop to set the blocks again and iterates again until it reaches the end of the twoDimensionalRainbowList list.

When you're working in two dimensions, you can change two coordinate variables at the same time. In this example, we increment the y variable on the second-to-last line of the outer for loop ❻ so each row of blocks will be placed above the previous row. We also increment the x variable inside the nested for loop ❺ to make sure the blocks are placed in a row. Then we need to reset the x variable to its original value (which is stored in the startingX variable ❶) every time the outer for loop iterates ❼. Resetting the x variable causes the first block of each row to be placed directly on top of the first block in the previous row, and so on, so the rows line up correctly with one another.

ACCESSING VALUES IN 2D LISTS

When getting or setting a value in a one-dimensional list, you use square brackets and the index position. For example, this code creates a list called scores that records a player's scores, and then it changes the item in index position 2 from 6 to 7:

```
scores = [1, 5, 6, 1]
scores[2] = 7
```

Using or changing values in a two-dimensional list isn't much different. You still use square brackets and the index position, but because you're accessing two lists at the same time, you use two sets of indexes and square brackets. Let's have a look!

Here's the list you saw earlier:

```
twoDimensionalRainbowList = [[0, 0, 0],
                             [1, 1, 1},
                             [2, 2, 2],
                             [3, 3, 3],
                             [4, 4, 4],
                             [5, 5, 5]]
```

If we wanted to change the second item (index position 1) in the first list (index position 0) to the value of 7, we would use this code:

```
twoDimensionalRainbowList[0][1] = 7
```

Because we're using two lists and one list is nested inside the other, we need to use two sets of square brackets. The first one picks the index position 0 of the twoDimensionalRainbowList list, which is its first nested list. In the second bracket we put the index position we want to access in the nested list, 1. We then set the value of this position to 7 using the equal sign.

I added this code to the *rainbowRows.py* program (page 211) and reran it. Figure 10-10 shows the result. Notice that the second block on the first row has changed because we changed the value in the nested list to 7.

If you wanted to get the value of an item in a two-dimensional list, you would also use two sets of square brackets. For example, if you wanted to print the value in the first position (index 0) of the last row (index 5), you would use this code:

```
print(twoDimensionalRainbowList[5][0])
```

This code outputs the value 5.

Figure 10-10: Changing one of the values in a nested list to get a different result

MISSION #61: PIXEL ART

Pixels are single-colored squares that make up images on your computer. By combining lots of pixels in a grid, your computer can display text, images, videos, and everything else shown on your monitor. All photos and drawings on your computer are displayed using pixels.

Pixel art is quite popular in Minecraft. Using different colored blocks in the Minecraft game, players build pictures in Minecraft. Pictures of characters from 2D video games are some of the most popular. You can create pixel art by hand, or of course, you can use a Python program to generate the pixel art.

In this program, you'll use a 2D list and nested loops to create pixel art in Minecraft. Listing 10-6 contains the beginning of the program. Copy it into a new file called *pixelArt.py* and save it in the *forLoops* folder.

pixelArt.py

```
from mcpi.minecraft import Minecraft
mc = Minecraft.create()

pos = mc.player.getTilePos()
x, y, z = pos.x, pos.y, pos.z

❶ blocks = [[35, 35, 35, 35, 35, 35, 35, 35],
           [35, 35, 35, 35, 35, 35, 35, 35],
           [35, 35, 35, 35, 35, 35, 35, 35],
           [35, 35, 35, 35, 35, 35, 35, 35]]
```

```
❷ for row in reversed(blocks):
      for block in row:
          mc.setBlock(x, y, z, block)
          x += 1
      y += 1
      x = pos.x
```

Listing 10-6: A two-dimensional list that draws a smiley face

The program creates a two-dimensional list called blocks that contains block IDs ❶ and then uses two loops to set the blocks in the Minecraft world ❷. To make sure the first row of the list is at the top when it is placed in Minecraft and the bottom row of the list is placed at the bottom, the reversed() function is included with the first for loop ❷. If it wasn't, the image would be upside down compared to the order of the blocks list.

At the moment, the blocks are all white wool blocks and don't display a picture. To finish the program, you need to rewrite the two-dimensional blocks list so it draws a smiley face, as shown in Figure 10-11.

Figure 10-11: A smiley face drawn with blocks

Change the values inside the lists so the output matches Figure 10-11. You'll need to change some of the values in the lists from wool blocks (block ID 35) to lapis lazuli blocks (block ID 22). For example, change the first line to this:

```
blocks = [[35, 35, 22, 22, 22, 22, 35, 35],
```

You'll also need to add more rows to the blocks list so the height of the image matches the one in the picture.

GENERATING 2D LISTS WITH LOOPS

Programs that use random numbers are fun because they behave differently every time you run them. In the past, I've created lots of programs that use random numbers in two-dimensional lists to create pictures. Each random number might display a color, or in the case of Minecraft, a different block.

Here's the beginning of a program that generates random numbers and stores them in a two-dimensional set of lists:

```
import random
❶ randomNumbers = []
  for outer in range(10):
❷     randomNumbers.append([])
      for inner in range(10):
❸         number = random.randint(1, 4)
          randomNumbers[outer].append(number)
  print(randomNumbers)
```

The program starts with an empty list called randomNumbers ❶. Every time the outer for loop repeats, it adds a new empty list into the randomNumbers list ❷. In the inner loop, the program then generates a random number between 1 and 5 and stores this in the inner list ❸. The inner loop repeats 10 times to generate 10 items in each inner list.

After we add line breaks for readability, the output of the program looks like this (notice the 10 items in the 10 inner lists):

```
[[3, 1, 4, 1, 4, 1, 2, 3, 2, 2],
 [1, 3, 4, 2, 4, 3, 4, 1, 3, 2],
 [4, 2, 4, 1, 4, 3, 2, 3, 4, 4],
 [1, 4, 3, 4, 3, 4, 3, 3, 4, 4],
 [3, 1, 4, 2, 3, 3, 3, 1, 4, 2],
 [4, 1, 4, 2, 3, 2, 4, 3, 3, 1],
 [2, 4, 2, 1, 2, 1, 4, 2, 4, 3],
 [3, 1, 3, 4, 1, 4, 2, 2, 4, 1],
 [4, 3, 1, 2, 4, 2, 2, 3, 1, 2],
 [3, 1, 3, 3, 1, 3, 1, 4, 1, 2]]
```

By incorporating random numbers into your 2D Minecraft creations, you can create some very cool effects that would be difficult to make by hand!

When I build walls in Minecraft, I don't use a single block type. By swapping some cobblestone blocks for mossy cobblestone blocks, I can turn a plain wall into a wall that looks damaged, weather-beaten, organic, and cool. As fun as it is to build a wall by hand, I can never get the blocks I've added randomly to look random enough. You've probably guessed that the solution to making broken walls look more random is to use a Python program.

To generate a weather-worn wall with Python, you need to break down the program into two main steps:

1. Create a two-dimensional list and store block values in the list.
2. Output the two-dimensional list into the Minecraft world.

To get you started, Listing 10-7 includes the code to choose a random block value, set up the list, and get the player's position. Copy the listing into a new file called *brokenWall.py* and save it in the *forLoops* folder.

brokenWall.py

```
from mcpi.minecraft import Minecraft
mc = Minecraft.create()

import random


❶ def brokenBlock():
      brokenBlocks = [48, 67, 4, 4, 4, 4]
      block = random.choice(brokenBlocks)
      return block

pos = mc.player.getTilePos()
x, y, z = pos.x, pos.y, pos.z

brokenWall = []
height, width = 5, 10

# Create the list of broken blocks

# Set the blocks
```

Listing 10-7: The start of the program to create a broken wall

The brokenBlock() function returns a random block value that's used to build the wall ❶. The width and height variables set the width and the height of the wall.

To finish the program, you need to generate a two-dimensional list of block values, then use those values to build the design in Minecraft.

Start with the blank list brokenWall. Using a for loop nested inside another for loop, generate random block values with the brokenBlock() function. Store the block values in lists, and store those lists in the brokenWall list. Then use another set of nested loops to place the blocks in Minecraft.

When your program is complete, move to where you want to build your weather-worn wall in your Minecraft world and run the code. You can use the program to decorate a castle or create spooky-looking ruins in the forest. Experiment with different locations to see what you like best! Figure 10-12 shows what a wall will look like when you run the program.

Figure 10-12: A wall with randomly generated broken blocks. It looks like it might be haunted!

BONUS OBJECTIVE: CREATE A COLORFUL WALL

In the *brokenWall.py* program, change the block values in the brokenBlock() function's brokenBlocks list to create all kinds of walls. Try changing the block values to different colors of wool and see what happens!

THINKING IN THREE DIMENSIONS

Of course, Minecraft is a game that uses three dimensions. And you've used three dimensions throughout this book. Each of the x, y, and z variables you used in most programs represents a dimension.

You've seen how to put one group of lists inside another to get a two-dimensional list and create cool pixel art and weathered walls. Putting a third group of lists inside a two-dimensional list creates a three-dimensional list, which lets you take your building skills to a whole new dimension!

Three-dimensional lists are extremely useful in Minecraft because you can use them to duplicate 3D structures, such as buildings, sculptures, and lots of other things.

The three-dimensional list in Listing 10-8 has four lists nested inside it. The kicker is that inside each index of those nested lists is another list! Basically, each item in this list is a 2D list. I've added blank comments to make the list easier to read.

```
cube = [[[57, 57, 57, 57],
         [57, 0, 0, 57],
         [57, 0, 0, 57],
         [57, 57, 57, 57]],
        #
        [[57, 0, 0, 57],
         [0, 0, 0, 0],
         [0, 0, 0, 0],
         [57, 0, 0, 57]],
        #
        [[57, 0, 0, 57],
         [0, 0, 0, 0],
         [0, 0, 0, 0],
         [57, 0, 0, 57]],
        #
        [[57, 57, 57, 57],
         [57, 0, 0, 57],
         [57, 0, 0, 57],
         [57, 57, 57, 57]]]
```

Listing 10-8: A three-dimensional list with nested lists

Code like this can be used to make a cool cube structure! Next we'll dig into a program that does just that.

OUTPUTTING 3D LISTS

Lists that have three dimensions are perfect for storing data about three-dimensional objects, such as your awesome Minecraft buildings. Storing three-dimensional objects is important, and correctly outputting them to Minecraft is just as important. Because a three-dimensional list is a list within a list that is within a list, you can use a for loop inside another for loop that is also inside another for loop to access all the data. In other words, you can use three nested for loops.

In Listing 10-9, I've copied the three-dimensional list from Listing 10-8 and created a program called *cube.py*. This program uses three nested for loops to output all the values of the three-dimensional list one at a time to build a cube structure in the Minecraft world.

cube.py
```
from mcpi.minecraft import Minecraft
mc = Minecraft.create()

pos = mc.player.getTilePos()
x = pos.x
y = pos.y
z = pos.z
cube = [[[57, 57, 57, 57], [57, 0, 0, 57], [57, 0, 0, 57], [57, 57, 57, 57]],
        [[57, 0, 0, 57], [0, 0, 0, 0], [0, 0, 0, 0], [57, 0, 0, 57]],
        [[57, 0, 0, 57], [0, 0, 0, 0], [0, 0, 0, 0], [57, 0, 0, 57]],
        [[57, 57, 57, 57], [57, 0, 0, 57], [57, 0, 0, 57], [57, 57, 57, 57]]]

startingX = x
❶ startingY = y
```

```
❷ for depth in cube:
      for height in reversed(depth):
          for block in height:
              mc.setBlock(x, y, z, block)
              x += 1
          y += 1
          x = startingX
❸     z += 1
❹     y = startingY
```

Listing 10-9: Code to create a three-dimensional cube made of diamonds

Figure 10-13 shows the result of this program.

Figure 10-13: The cube created by the cube.py program

The code in *cube.py* is very similar to the two-dimensional *rainbowRows*
.py program (page 211) that builds a rainbow wall. The main difference
is that *cube.py* uses three for loops instead of two, because it works with a
three-dimensional list. The extra for loop adds an extra dimension to the
structure, depth ❷. So now the structure has width, height, and depth.

Each time the outer loop for depth in cube runs, it creates a two-
dimensional list using the two nested loops, for height in reversed(depth)
and for block in height. The code in the two nested loops is similar to the
code in the *rainbowRows.py* program, which means these loops build a wall
in Minecraft.

Let's look at the result of the outer loop each time it repeats so we can
see it build the cube step-by-step. The first time the outer loop runs, it outputs the blocks in index position 0 of the cube list. That list looks like this:

```
[[57, 57, 57, 57],
 [57, 0, 0, 57],
 [57, 0, 0, 57],
 [57, 57, 57, 57]]
```

Figure 10-14 shows the output: our first wall of blocks.

Figure 10-14: The result of the first two-dimensional loop, cube index 0

After each two-dimensional list is built in the game, the value of the z variable in *cube.py* ❸ is increased to move one block farther along the z-axis. This gives the cube depth, so we're not just building a wall. We also need to reset the value of the y variable at ❹ to its original value ❶ so the blocks on the bottom of the cube line up with each other every time the outer loop repeats. If the y variable wasn't reset, the y-coordinate of each set of blocks would keep getting higher and higher, creating some weird-looking stairs! Figure 10-15 shows what this would look like.

Figure 10-15: We reset the y variable so this won't happen!

The second time the outer loop runs, it outputs the blocks in index position 1 of the cube list, which looks like this:

```
[[57, 0, 0, 57],
 [0, 0, 0, 0],
 [0, 0, 0, 0],
 [57, 0, 0, 57]]
```

This adds the next part of the cube, as you can see in Figure 10-16. After this part of the cube is built, the z variable increases by 1 ❸ and the y variable is reset to its original value again ❹.

Figure 10-16: The result of the second two-dimensional loop, cube index 1

The next time the loop repeats, it outputs the two-dimensional list in index position 2 of cube:

```
[[57, 0, 0, 57],
 [0, 0, 0, 0],
 [0, 0, 0, 0],
 [57, 0, 0, 57]]
```

Figure 10-17 shows the result. Again, the z value is increased by 1 and the y value is reset.

Then the loop repeats a fourth and final time, outputting index position 3 of cube:

```
[[57, 57, 57, 57],
 [57, 0, 0, 57],
 [57, 0, 0, 57],
 [57, 57, 57, 57]]
```

Figure 10-18 shows the finished cube structure.

Figure 10-17: The result of the third two-dimensional loop, cube index 2

Figure 10-18: The result of the last two-dimensional loop, in the final cube index position

Experiment with this program—use a different block type, try making a larger cube, or anything else you can imagine! In the next section, I'll show you how to access values in three-dimensional lists so you can make some of these changes.

ACCESSING VALUES IN 3D LISTS

The values inside three-dimensional lists can be changed just as in one-dimensional and two-dimensional lists, using square brackets and index positions.

Let's start with our three-dimensional diamond cube list:

```
cube = [[[57, 57, 57, 57],
         [57, 0, 0, 57],
         [57, 0, 0, 57],
         [57, 57, 57, 57]],
         #
        [[57, 0, 0, 57],
         [0, 0, 0, 0],
         [0, 0, 0, 0],
         [57, 0, 0, 57]],
         #
        [[57, 0, 0, 57],
         [0, 0, 0, 0],
         [0, 0, 0, 0],
         [57, 0, 0, 57]],
         #
        [[57, 57, 57, 57],
         [57, 0, 0, 57],
         [57, 0, 0, 57],
         [57, 57, 57, 57]]]
```

I want to change the bottom-left block on the front of my cube to gold. First I need to access the index of the cube list that contains the front of the cube, which is 0. So the first part of the expression will look like this:

```
cube[0]
```

If I printed the value of this expression, I would get the following output (which I've formatted to make it easier to read):

```
[[57, 57, 57, 57],
 [57, 0, 0, 57],
 [57, 0, 0, 57],
 [57, 57, 57, 57]]
```

This two-dimensional list represents the front of the cube. Next, I want to access the bottom row, which is index 3. So I add [3] to my expression:

```
cube[0][3]
```

If I printed the list stored at this position, I would get the following:

```
[57, 57, 57, 57]
```

Finally, I want to access the leftmost block in the row, which is index 3. So the final expression to change the bottom-left block to a gold block looks like this:

```
cube[0][3][3] = 41
```

When I run the *cube.py* program with this line added, I get a cube made of diamonds with one single golden block, as in Figure 10-19.

Figure 10-19: The modified cube with a single golden corner

MISSION #63: DUPLICATE A BUILDING

Even though building things in Minecraft using a Python program saves a lot of time, if you're like me, you might still spend a considerable amount of effort adding details, like pictures and furniture, to your buildings. Sometimes you might need to make an identical copy of a particular object, and copying an object by hand can take lots of time. Placing each block one by one is a lot of work as well, and you might place a block in the wrong spot. The obvious solution is to make a program that copies a building in Minecraft and builds a copy of it in the game for you!

The finished program will need to do two things: first it will copy an area of the game and store it in a three-dimensional list, and then it will build the copied structure using that three-dimensional list.

I've included the start of the program in Listing 10-10 to help you. Copy the listing into a new file and save it as *duplicateArea.py* in the *forLoops* folder.

duplicateArea *.py*

```
from mcpi.minecraft import Minecraft
mc = Minecraft.create()


❶ def sortPair(val1, val2):
      if val1 > val2:
          return val2, val1
      else:
          return val1, val2
```

```
❷ def copyStructure(x1, y1, z1, x2, y2, z2):
      # Sort the highest and lowest x, y, and z values
      x1, x2 = sortPair(x1, x2)
      y1, y2 = sortPair(y1, y2)
      z1, z2 = sortPair(z1, z2)

      width = x2 - x1
      height = y2 - y1
      length = z2 - z1

      structure = []

      print("Please wait...")
❸     # Copy the structure

      return structure


❹ def buildStructure(x, y, z, structure):
      xStart = x
      yStart = y

❺     # Build the structure

  # Get the position of the first corner
❻ input("Move to the first corner and press enter in this window")
  pos = mc.player.getTilePos()
  x1, y1, z1 = pos.x, pos.y, pos.z

  # Get the position of the second corner
❼ input("Move to the opposite corner and press enter in this window")
  pos = mc.player.getTilePos()
  x2, y2, z2 = pos.x, pos.y, pos.z

  # Copy the building
❽ structure = copyStructure(x1, y1, z1, x2, y2, z2)

  # Set the position for the copy
❾ input("Move to the position you want to create the structure and press ENTER ↵
         in this window")
  pos = mc.player.getTilePos()
  x, y, z = pos.x, pos.y, pos.z
  buildStructure(x, y, z, structure)
```

Listing 10-10: When the program is finished, it will duplicate buildings.

This program is divided into several parts. First, the sortPair() function ❶ sorts a pair of values into a tuple with the lowest value in the first index position and the highest value in the second index position. For example, if I gave sortPair() the arguments 9 and 3, it would return a tuple with the value of (3, 9) because 3 is less than 9. I use this function to sort pairs of x, y, and z values so the width, length, and depth variables are always positive when calculated.

Next, the copyStructure() function ❷ copies the structure from the game world, but it's incomplete ❸. The buildStructure() function ❹ builds the structure, but it is also incomplete ❺. You'll complete both in this mission.

I've added a neat trick to get the coordinates of the building you want to copy and the location in the game where you want to build the copy: Using the input() function, the program first asks you to move your character to one corner of the building and press ENTER ❻. The input() function makes the code wait until you've moved the player to where you want them to be. As soon as you press ENTER, it gets the player's position using the getTilePos() function. We do the same again at the opposite corner of the building ❼. Then the copyStructure() function uses these two sets of coordinates to copy the building ❽. (When copying larger structures, this part of the program can take a while to run.) Finally, you move to where you want the building to be built and press ENTER ❾ to pass the player's last position to the buildStructure() function.

To finish the program, it's your job to complete the copyStructure() and buildStructure() functions. Add three nested loops to the copyStructure() function to copy all the blocks between the coordinates given in the argument into a three-dimensional list at ❸. To finish the buildStructure() function, add three nested for loops that output the block values from the three-dimensional list at ❺. The function should use the given coordinates in its arguments.

Make sure the program works through x, y, and z positions inside the structure. Use the for loops to change the x, y, and z positions.

Although *duplicateArea.py* is a long program, it's very useful and worth the effort. After you finish this mission, you'll be able to build entire cities in your Minecraft world! I used *duplicateArea.py* to duplicate an interesting cliff I found when I was exploring. Figure 10-20 shows the cliff that I wanted to copy.

Figure 10-20: I liked the look of this cliff, so I made a copy of it.

When you're using the *duplicateArea.py* program to make copies, first stand outside (if your structure is a building) and near the bottom corner of the object you want to copy. Then press ENTER in IDLE. Figure 10-21 shows me standing on the first corner.

Figure 10-21: First I moved to one corner of the structure and pressed ENTER in IDLE.

Next, fly up and around to the opposite corner of the object you want to copy and press ENTER a second time. Figure 10-22 shows that I've flown into the air and moved around the cliff.

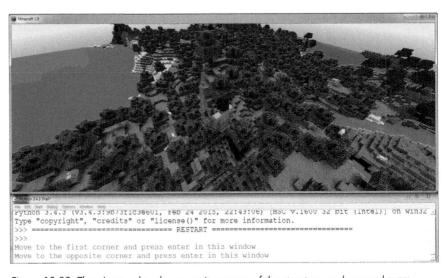

Figure 10-22: Then I moved to the opposite corner of the structure and pressed ENTER.

You'll get a message asking you to wait a moment while the structure is being copied by the program. Move to the location where you want to build the copy and wait for a message asking you where you want to build the new structure (Figure 10-23).

Figure 10-23: I waited a while for the structure to copy. Then I moved to where I wanted to build the copy and pressed ENTER to build it.

Press ENTER when you're in the right place for the new building, and a copy of it will be built right in front of you! Figure 10-24 shows my copy of the cliff.

Figure 10-24: The copy of the original cliff!

WHAT YOU LEARNED

This chapter covered a lot of ground. You learned how to use for loops with lists, and you learned how to use the range() function. You also learned more about for loops and lists, such as reversing lists, looping over dictionaries, and breaking for loops. You created two- and three-dimensional lists with nested loops, which are super useful for building an awesome Minecraft world.

From generating stairs and pyramids to duplicating structures and creating art, you now have much more control over Minecraft than ever before. The programs in this chapter are some of my favorite programs in the book, and they'll help you create your own advanced projects!

This chapter and Chapter 9 focused strongly on lists and for loops, which are closely related. In Chapter 11, you'll move on to files and modules, which are closely related to functions and which you've been using throughout this book. As part of the missions, you'll learn how to save and load structures to and from files.

11

SAVING AND LOADING BUILDINGS WITH FILES AND MODULES

Files are a major part of computing. They let you save data for long-term storage and load data for use in your programs. So far, the programs you've been working with have stored data only in variables. You've either used hard-coded data in your programs or taken data from user input. Although you can do amazing things with this data, you're limited to single sessions and your own Minecraft world. Once you learn how to store and retrieve data, you can save and load your Minecraft creations into any Minecraft world, even your friends' games!

In this chapter, you'll learn how to get input from files and how to output data to files. You'll use some built-in functions in Python and learn how to use two Python *modules*, the pickle and shelve modules, to store entire Minecraft creations.

Modules can extend what it's possible to accomplish with Python. Using modules, you can draw pictures on the screen or run websites. Modules also provide functions for common tasks so you don't have to write your own solutions.

You'll also learn about pip, which is a very useful program for installing new modules. You'll try it out by using the Flask module to make a simple website that connects to Minecraft and displays the player's position.

USING FILES

When you work with computers, you work with files all the time. Anytime you write a text document or some Python code and save it, you're working with files. Text, pictures, videos, and music are all files! Even this book was stored as a text file while I was writing it. Python's file-handling features are easy to learn and will let you create files, save files, and read information from files to do cool things in Minecraft. Let's start with the basics and learn how to read and write to a text file in Python.

OPENING A FILE

Opening a file is the first step when you're working with files. To open a file in Python, you use the open() function, which takes two arguments: the file's location and its permissions. A file's *location* is where the file is stored on your computer. You'll pass this into the open() function in the form of a string. The file's *permissions* control whether or not Python is allowed to read or modify the file.

To open (or create) a text file named *secretFile.txt* in Python, you would use the argument "secretFile.txt":

```
secretFile = open("secretFile.txt", "w")
```

The second argument, "w", is the permissions argument, which specifies what the program is allowed to do with the file. In this case, w means that the program can write data to the file *secretFile.txt*.

When a program calls the open() function with a filename, Python first checks whether a file already exists with that name. If the file exists, Python will use the contents of that file in the program. If it doesn't exist, Python will create a new file with that name.

If you don't specify a *directory* with your filename (a folder and a directory are the same thing), Python will look for the file in the directory where the program is located. If the file is stored in a different directory, you must specify that in the argument. For example, if *secretFile.txt* was in the *secrets* directory, the first argument would be "/secrets/secretFile.txt":

```
secretFile = open("/secrets/secretFile.txt", "w")
```

If you provide a directory in the argument and the directory doesn't exist, or if the file doesn't exist, you'll get an error message.

There are four options for the permissions argument:

w   This means *write only*. Write-only permissions let the program write new data to the file and overwrite content that is already in the file, but the program cannot read the contents of the file. If a file doesn't exist with the name that you provide as the first argument, the program will create a new one.

r This means *read only*. Read-only permissions let the program read the contents of the file, but the program is not allowed to modify the file's contents. This permission cannot be used to create a new file.

r+ This means *read and write*. Read-and-write permissions let the program read and change the contents of the file. The program can also write over any content that is already in the file. However, if the file doesn't exist, a new one will not be created; instead, you'll get an error.

a This stands for *append*. Append permissions let the program write new data only to the end of the file, leaving the other contents of the file intact. The program cannot read the contents of the file either. This permission can be used to create a new file.

There are different circumstances in which you'd use each kind of permission. Let's say you write some directions to an awesome diamond mine that you found, and you want to load the directions into Minecraft without accidentally changing them. In that case, you'd want to use the read-only permission to make sure nothing in the file changes. Alternatively, if you want someone to be able to add data to a file but you don't want them to see the other data stored in the file, you would use the append permission. For instance, you could use append if you want to let your friends add notes to a shared travel log without letting them peak inside and read about all your secret treasure!

Next, you'll learn how to write data to an open file, and you'll learn how to close that file to use that data later.

WRITING TO AND SAVING A FILE

The write() function writes data to a file that the program has opened. This is the bread and butter of working with files because it lets you save all kinds of data. You provide the data you want written to the file as an argument to the write() function.

For example, let's open a file and write a simple string to it:

```
secretFile = open("secretFile.txt", "w")
secretFile.write("This is a secret file. Shhh! Don't tell anyone.")
❶ secretFile.close()
```

First, you must open the file using the open() function. Next, use dot notation to call the write() function to write a string to *secretFile.txt*. Then, you need to call the close() function ❶, which saves and closes the file. It's important to remember to include the close() function; otherwise, the data will not be stored in the file.

Run the program and then open *secretFile.txt* in a text editor to see if your secret message was saved. Try changing the string to write something different to the file and run the program again. What happens? The old message should have been replaced with the new message! Try changing the message again, but instead of passing "w" pass in "a" instead. Now what happens? Pretty cool, huh?

READING A FILE

The read() function reads the entire contents of a file that a program has opened. You may want to use the data in your program, modify the data and then send it back to the file, or output the data to make it easy to look at. Whatever the reason, you'll use the read() function to read files.

To read a file, you must first open it and then remember to close it when you're finished. It's important to learn this habit when you're working with files in your programs to avoid errors!

Let's read a file and then output its contents so we can see what it says. This program, *showSecretFile.py*, outputs the contents of a file using the read() and print() functions:

showSecret
File.py

```
secretFile = open("secretFile.txt", "r")

❶ print(secretFile.read())
secretFile.close()
```

First, we open the file, and we pass in "r" as the permission argument so our program can read from the file. You could also pass in "r+", but in this case we're not writing to the file, so "r" is best. To print out the contents of *secretFile.txt*, we pass secretFile.read() to a print statement. Finally, even though we haven't written any data to the file, it's still a good idea to close it with the close() function.

Run the program to see what happens. The contents of *secretFile.txt* should be printed to the screen. Now you can read the file without having to open it in a text editor like you normally would!

READING A LINE OF A FILE

Let's say you have a long text document and you want to look at only part of it. This is where the readline() function comes in handy. Unlike the read() function, which gets the entire contents of the file, the readline() function gets a single line of the file at a time.

To try the readline() function, first add a bunch of text to *secretFile.txt*. You can do this either by using a text editor or by using your fancy new Python abilities to write a bunch of information to it! If you use Python to write to your file, add \n to your strings whenever you want a new line. For example, if you write "Cool\nDance\nParty" to a file, Python places "Cool" on one line, "Dance" on the next, and "Party" on the last line, like so:

```
Cool
Dance
Party
```

After you've added text to *secretFile.txt*, write this code into a Python file and save the file as *showSecretLines.py* in a new folder called *files*:

showSecret Lines.py

```
secretFile = open("secretFile.txt", "r")

print(secretFile.readline())
print(secretFile.readline())
print(secretFile.readline())

secretFile.close()
```

Once again, you must open *secretFile.txt* before you can read from it using the readline() function. Because you want your *showSecretLines.py* program to read data from the file, you must pass in r (or r+) again. Next, include three print statements to print the first three lines of *secretFile.txt*. Finally, close the file again using close().

The readline() function starts with the first line of your file. Each time the readline() function is used, it reads the next line automatically. This function is very handy for printing a couple of lines from the beginnings of text files.

NOTE *The readline() function converts the file to a list of strings, where each item in the list represents a single line. If you want to print a line from the middle of a text document, you could write a loop to find and print a particular string in the list!*

MISSION #64: TO-DO LIST

Sometimes you might not have much spare time to play Minecraft. You might build complex structures across several days in short sessions. As you add programs to open doors or teleport the player somewhere, your builds will become more complex and might take longer to finish. Working on projects across several days could cause you to forget what you were doing and what you need to do next. This happens to me often. Fortunately, you can make a program to help you remember!

The programs in this mission create a to-do list and display it in the Minecraft chat. You can use this program to keep track of your Minecraft goals so when you have to stop playing, you can easily pick up where you left off.

To make the to-do list, you'll write two separate programs: one to write the list and the other to display the list. Let's start by creating the program that writes the list.

PART 1: WRITING THE TO-DO LIST

First, you need a program to create the items in the to-do list. Listing 11-1 starts you off, using a while loop and the input() function to add items to the to-do list. Copy it into a file in IDLE and save it as *inputToDoList.py* in the *files* folder.

```
  input  ❶ toDoFile =
ToDoList.py
         ❷ toDoList = ""

         ❸ toDoItem = input("Enter a to-do list item: ")

         ❹ while toDoItem != "exit":
         ❺     toDoList = toDoList + toDoItem + "\n"
               toDoItem = input("Enter a to-do list item: ")

         ❻ # Write the to-do list to the file
         ❼ # Close the file
```

Listing 11-1: The start of the program to write items in your to-do list

The program creates an empty string called toDoList ❷, which will store all the items for your to-do list when you enter them. Using the input() function, the program then asks you to enter an item into the to-do list ❸. The while loop then checks whether the input is not equal to "exit" ❹; if it's not, the program adds your item to the to-do list with a new line at the end using "\n" ❺. However, if you enter "exit", the loop no longer runs, and you won't be able to add any more items to the to-do list.

Your mission is to finish the program. To do that, you need to write the code that opens the file, writes toDoList to the file, and then closes the file. Use the open() function to open the file at the start of the program ❶. You should open it with write permissions. Name the file that the function opens *toDoList.txt*. Your program will create the file if it doesn't already exist in the directory.

At the end of the program, write the contents of the to-do list to the file so you can access it later. Use the write() function to write the toDoList variable to the toDoFile ❻. After the file has been written to, make sure you close it with the close() function on the last line ❼.

Figure 11-1 shows me writing a to-do list with the program. When I'm finished, I type exit.

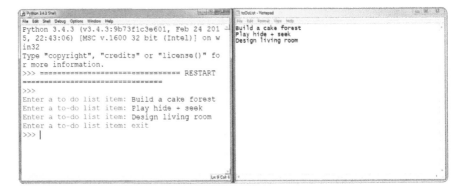

Figure 11-1: Entering things to do, like build a cake forest and play hide-and-seek

PART 2: DISPLAYING THE TO-DO LIST

Now that you have a program to write a to-do list to a file, you need to display the to-do list in the Minecraft chat, one line at a time. Listing 11-2 starts the program for you. Copy the listing into a new file and save it as *outputToDoList.py* in the *files* folder.

output
ToDoList.py

```
from mcpi.minecraft import Minecraft
mc = Minecraft.create()

❶ toDoList =

for line in toDoList:
❷    # Output "line" to the chat
```

Listing 11-2: Program to output the to-do list file to the Minecraft chat

Listing 11-2 uses a for loop to output each line in the *toDoList.txt* file to the Minecraft chat, one at a time. At the moment, the program is incomplete. To finish the program, add the open() function to open the *toDoList.txt* file that you created with *inputToDoList.py* ❶. Make sure the file has read permissions. After you open the file, add code inside the for loop to output the string stored in the line variable to Minecraft's chat ❷. You'll have to use the readline() and postToChat() functions to do this.

Figure 11-2 shows my to-do list in the Minecraft chat.

Figure 11-2: Now when I come back to building, I can see what I need to do.

USING MODULES

Modules are collections of functions that you can import into Python so you don't have to write those functions in your programs. A module usually has a specific purpose, such as performing scientific calculations or making games, and a wide variety of modules are available for Python. You might be surprised to know that you've been using modules throughout this book! The Minecraft Python API is a module: every time you've written `from mcpi.minecraft import Minecraft`, you've been using a module. The Minecraft Python API module lets you connect your Python programs to Minecraft. Because it's prewritten by someone else, you can use the module's functions without having to write the code yourself.

Python comes with a bunch of modules that you can use in your programs. These modules, together with all the Python you've learned in this book so far, are called the *Python standard library*. You can also install modules that are not part of the standard library; we'll do that in "Installing New Modules with pip" on page 252.

In this section, you'll learn all the ways that you can set up your programs to use modules. As an example, we'll use the `pickle` module, which provides more advanced ways to save and load data with files than just writing and reading data from them. Let's look at the `pickle` module now.

THE PICKLE MODULE

The `pickle` module is very useful when you're writing complicated data to a file. For example, dictionaries and multidimensional lists are challenging to store and retrieve using the standard functions that we used earlier in the chapter. This is where the `pickle` module comes in handy.

The `pickle` module can save you hours of writing and debugging your own solutions for storing complex data. You can also use the `pickle` module on simple data: for example, you can use it to store numbers without converting them to and from strings, which is necessary for standard file input and output.

In other words, you can use the `pickle` module to save a variable's value in a file and then read the variable's value directly into another program without any extra processing. The data type remains the same as when you stored the value, even if the data type is a string, integer, float, or Boolean.

Next, you'll learn how to import modules using `pickle` as an example. Then you'll use `pickle` to save some complex data—an entire Minecraft building!

IMPORTING PICKLE

To use any module's functions, you need to import them by using the `import` keyword. Actually, you've already used the `import` keyword to import modules, such as the `time` module, as well as functions from the Python Minecraft API.

After you've imported the module into your program, you can use the module's functions by using dot notation. Include the module name, a dot, and the function you want to use. Let's import the `pickle` module and use a couple of its functions:

```
❶ import pickle

   locations = {'John': 'Forest', 'Phillipa': 'Mountains', 'Pete': 'City'}

❷ secretFile= open("secretFile.txt", "wb")
❸ pickle.dump(locations, secretFile)
```

We import the `pickle` module at ❶. Next we open *secretFile.txt* with a special file permission, `"wb"` ❷. When you open a file with `pickle`, you must add `b` to the file permission. In this case, `"wb"` writes data to the file using a special format that the `pickle` module requires.

The `dump()` function writes to the file at ❸. The `pickle` module's `dump()` function stores a variable in a file. It takes two arguments: the data to be written to the file and the open file that it will write to. This example stores the locations of secret agents in a dictionary called `locations` and then dumps that dictionary in a file called `secretFile`. Because `dump()` belongs to the `pickle` module, you must use dot notation to specify both the module and the function with `pickle.dump()`. Unlike the standard file functions in Python, the `dump()` function saves the data to the file automatically—you don't need to close the file with the `close()` function.

The `pickle` module also lets you read stored data. You can use `pickle`'s `load()` function to read the contents of a file. It takes one argument, the file that you want to load, and returns the contents of the file. The following example loads the `locations` dictionary we stored earlier. Add this code to the program:

```
   import pickle

❶ secretFile= open("secretFile.txt", "rb")
   locations = pickle.load(secretFile)
```

First we open the file with the permission `"rb"` ❶, which allows your program to read a special data format that `pickle` uses. Then we load the dictionary.

Now that the dictionary has been loaded, you can treat it like any other dictionary. For example, you can access the value of one of the keys. Just add this code after the `pickle.load()` function:

```
print(locations['Phillipa'])
```

This will print `'Mountains'`, the value of the `'Phillipa'` key. That's because the dictionary in the file is unchanged when it's loaded into the program with `pickle`—it's still a dictionary, so we can access its keys and values and use it just like any other Python dictionary. You could do the same with a list or a variable as well.

IMPORTING ONE FUNCTION WITH THE FROM CLAUSE

Importing a module means you have access to all the functions in that module, but sometimes you need only one function in a module. If you want to import just one function, you use the `from` clause when you import the module. This clause lets you access the function without including the module name and dot notation every time you call a function. You would just write `function()` instead of `module.function()`.

Sometimes when you use the `pickle` module you might want to use only the `dump()` function, not its other functions. To do this, change the code that you wrote earlier so it looks like this:

```
❶ from pickle import dump

locations = {'John': 'Forest', 'Phillipa': 'Mountains', 'Pete': 'City'}

secretFile= open("secretFile", "wb")
❷ dump(locations, secretFile)
```

The first line uses the `from` clause to import only the `dump()` function from the `pickle` module ❶. The last line calls the `dump()` function ❷. Notice that it doesn't have dot notation. You just call the function name without referencing the module name.

You can also import more than one function from a module using `from`. All you need to do is separate the function names with a comma. For example, if you want to use the `dump()` and `load()` functions from `pickle` in the same file, you could import them both:

```
❶ from pickle import dump, load
locations = {'John': 'Forest', 'Phillipa': 'Mountains', 'Pete': 'City'}

secretFile= open("secretFile", "wb")
❷ dump(locations, secretFile)

❸ locations = load(secretFile)
print(locations['Phillipa'])
```

The first line uses the `from` clause with commas to import both the `dump()` and `load()` functions ❶. This means that later in the program, you can use these functions without having to include the function name and dot notation, which you can see at ❷ and ❸.

IMPORTING ALL FUNCTIONS WITH *

You can also import all the functions in a module so you don't need to include the name of the module with dot notation every time you use it. You do this by entering an asterisk (*) at the end of the import statement, like this:

```
❶ from pickle import *
   locations = {'John': 'Forest', 'Phillipa': 'Mountains', 'Pete': 'City'}

   secretFile= open("secretFile", "wb")
❷ dump(locations, secretFile)

❸ locations = load(secretFile)
   print(locations['Phillipa'])
```

Because this code imported all the functions in the module using an asterisk ❶, we don't need to use dot notation when we call the dump() ❷ and load() ❸ functions.

The * option is very handy, but it comes with a risk! If you're working with multiple modules, two modules might share the same function names. When this happens, Python will get confused and you might get an error. So when you're working with many modules, it's best to avoid using the * option and instead import only the functions you need to use.

GIVING A MODULE A NICKNAME

Sometimes you'll want to rename a module because its name is too long and you want to use a shorter name in your program. Or, you want to change the module's name to make it easier to remember. Or, perhaps you want to change its name because the module shares the same name as another module and you want to avoid conflicts.

You can use the as clause with the import statement to give a module an *alias*—a nickname. For example, this code imports the pickle module and renames it to p:

```
import pickle as p
```

Now, every time you want to use the pickle module, you can write p in your program instead of pickle. Here's an example of this in action:

```
p.dump(locations, secretFile)
```

Notice that p.dump() is used instead of pickle.dump(). This saves you time because you don't have to keep typing pickle!

MISSION #65: SAVE A BUILDING

Building things is my favorite part of Minecraft. I've spent hours building houses, castles, villages, and so many other things. But when I move to another part of the map or to a different world, I have to leave my creations behind. I'm sure you've also had to abandon some awesome creations.

Wouldn't it be cool if you could save your buildings and take them with you when you move into different worlds? Well, with `pickle` and the Python API, you can!

In this mission, you'll develop two programs that will save and load buildings into your Minecraft game. One program will store the building, and the other will load the building. Both programs build on *duplicateArea.py* from Chapter 10 (page 225).

PART 1: SAVING THE BUILDING

The first program will save a building into a file. Listing 11-3 includes the code to copy the building. Copy the listing into a file in IDLE and save it as *saveStructure.py* in the *files* folder.

saveStructure
.py

```python
from mcpi.minecraft import Minecraft
mc = Minecraft.create()

import pickle


def sortPair(val1, val2):
    if val1 > val2:
        return val2, val1
    else:
        return val1, val2


❶ def copyStructure(x1, y1, z1, x2, y2, z2):
    x1, x2 = sortPair(x1, x2)
    y1, y2 = sortPair(y1, y2)
    z1, z2 = sortPair(z1, z2)

    width = x2 - x1
    height = y2 - y1
    length = z2 - z1

    structure = []

    print("Please wait..." )

    # Copy the structure
    for row in range(height):
        structure.append([])
        for column in range(width):
            structure[row].append([])
```

```
            for depth in range(length):
❷                block = mc.getBlock(x1 + column, y1 + row, z1 + depth)
                structure[row][column].append(block)

    return structure

❸ # Get the position of the first corner
  input("Move to the first position and press ENTER in this window")
  pos1 = mc.player.getTilePos()

  x1 = pos1.x
  y1 = pos1.y
  z1 = pos1.z

❹ # Get the position of the second corner
  input("Move to the opposite corner and press ENTER in this window")
  pos2 = mc.player.getTilePos()

  x2 = pos2.x
  y2 = pos2.y
  z2 = pos2.z

❺ structure = copyStructure( x1, y1, z1, x2, y2, z2)

❻ # Store the structure in a file
```

Listing 11-3: Incomplete code to store a building in a file

The copyStructure() function copies an area in the game into a set of three-dimensional lists ❶. It takes two sets of coordinates as arguments. I've made a slight change in the copyStructure() function compared to *duplicateArea.py*. I've used the getBlockWithData() function instead of the getBlock() function ❷. Rather than getting just the block ID for a block at certain coordinates, the getBlockWithData() function also gets the block's state. This is useful for blocks like stairs, where the direction of the stairs is stored in the block state. When the structure is copied, stairs and other blocks that face a certain way will be built in the correct direction.

I've included some neat code so you can use the player's position to set the coordinates of a building you want to copy. When you run the program, it asks you to move to the first corner of the structure and then press ENTER in the Python shell ❸. The program uses the player's position to get the first set of coordinates for the building. Next, it asks you to move to the opposite corner of the structure and do the same ❹. As a result, you can just stand where you want to start copying your building instead of writing coordinates or hard-coding them into your program.

The values of these coordinate variables are passed to the function copyStructure() at ❺. The returned value is stored in a variable called structure.

To complete the code, you need to open a new file with pickle. Call the new file "pickleFile". Then write the code to store the building in the file. Do this by using the pickle module to write the value of the structure variable to a file ❻.

Figure 11-3 shows a tower that I built in my Minecraft world.

Figure 11-3: My tower that I want to copy

To copy the tower using *saveStructure.py*, I move to one corner and press ENTER in IDLE (Figure 11-4).

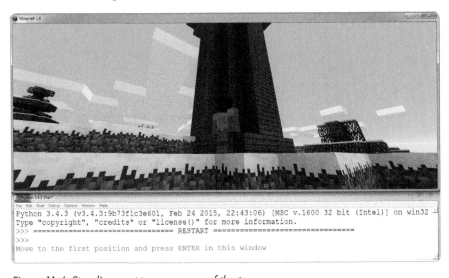

Figure 11-4: Standing next to one corner of the tower

Then I fly to the opposite corner of the tower and press ENTER in IDLE a second time (Figure 11-5).

Figure 11-5: Flying to the opposite corner of the tower

Follow the same steps to use *saveStructure.py* to save one of your own buildings. Next we'll complete the other half of the process and load our saved buildings into the game.

PART 2: LOADING THE BUILDING

The second program needs to load the building into the game from the file (named *pickleFile*) created by *saveStructure.py*. Listing 11-4 includes code from the *duplicateArea.py* program (page 225) that places a building stored in lists. Copy the listing into a file in IDLE and save it as *loadStructure.py* in the *files* folder.

*loadStructure
.py*

```
from mcpi.minecraft import Minecraft
mc = Minecraft.create()

import pickle


❶ def buildStructure(x, y, z, structure):
    xStart = x
    zStart = z
    for row in structure:
        for column in row:
            for block in column:
                mc.setBlock(x, y, z, block.id, block.data)
                z += 1
            x += 1
            z = zStart
        y += 1
        x = xStart
```

```
   # Open and load the structure file
❷ structure =

❸ pos = mc.player.getTilePos()
   x = pos.x
   y = pos.y
   z = pos.z
❹ buildStructure(x, y, z, structure)
```

Listing 11-4: When complete, this program will build a building from a file.

The buildStructure() function ❶ does most of the work in this program. It builds the structure in the game using four arguments: x-, y-, and z-coordinates and a structure stored in a three-dimensional list.

Import the pickle module so you can load the structure into the program, and then store it in the structure variable at ❷. Using the open() function, open the *pickleFile* file that you saved the structure into. Then load it into the structure variable using pickle's load() function. After the structure has been loaded, close *pickleFile* using pickle's close() function.

Also included in Listing 11-4 is some code that gets the player's position to use as the starting location for the structure ❸.

After the structure is loaded and the coordinates are set, pass the structure to the buildStructure() function along with a position ❹, which will build the saved structure.

Figure 11-6 shows the program in action. The building I saved earlier has been loaded into the game and rebuilt at a new position. Try it yourself—now you have the ability to take your creations with you wherever you go!

Figure 11-6: Look, it's a copy of my tower!

But what if you create a whole village and want to take it with you? You could save each building in its own file using pickle, but that's not very convenient. The pickle module works great for saving a single building, but it's not so good for saving a bunch of buildings. That's where the shelve module comes in. Let's look at that next.

STORING LOTS OF DATA WITH THE SHELVE MODULE

The pickle module can store only one piece of data at a time. In some programs, you might want to store several variables; if you use the pickle module, you'll need to create several files, which can be difficult to manage.

Python's shelve module solves this problem. It can store several items of data in a single file. It works like a dictionary in which each data value has a key that you can use to store and retrieve the data. Think of shelve like a shelf: each compartment in the shelf stores different data values.

OPENING A FILE WITH SHELVE

After importing the shelve module, you'll use its open() function to open a file. If the file doesn't already exist, a new one will be created.

The following code opens the *locationsFile.db* file and stores it in the shelveFile variable:

```
import shelve
shelveFile = shelve.open("locationsFile.db")
```

The open() function takes only one argument, the name of the file. You don't need to specify file permissions when you use the shelve module because it automatically grants read-and-write privileges.

When naming a file with the shelve module, you must include the *.db* extension at the end of the filename. You can see the *.db* at the end of my *locationsFile.db* file.

ADDING, MODIFYING, AND ACCESSING ITEMS WITH SHELVE

The shelve module works like a dictionary. To add data to the file, you use square brackets with a key name to store a value. For example, let's say a secret agent named Beatrice is on a submarine, and we want to store Beatrice's location in the shelveFile dictionary:

```
import shelve
shelveFile = shelve.open("locationsFile.db")
shelveFile['Beatrice'] = 'Submarine'
shelveFile.close()
```

First we open the file. Next, we give the shelveFile dictionary a key of 'Beatrice' and the value 'Submarine'. This line creates a new item in the shelveFile dictionary with the key 'Beatrice' and the value 'Submarine'.

Then we use shelve's close() function to add the new data to the file and safely close the file.

If a key already exists in a shelve file, this code would update the old value to the new value. Let's say that Beatrice finishes her mission and returns to headquarters. You could update Beatrice's location like this:

```
import shelve
shelveFile = shelve.open('locationsFile.db')
shelveFile['Beatrice'] = 'Headquarters'
shelveFile.close()
```

Now the corresponding value of the Beatrice key is 'Headquarters'.

Accessing a value from shelve works just like a dictionary, too. You use keys to access specific values. For example, to print Beatrice's location, we'd use the following code:

```
import shelve
shelveFile = shelve.open('locationsFile.db')
print(shelveFile['Beatrice'])
```

This will output Beatrice's location, Headquarters.

Just like a standard dictionary, the shelve module can store any data type, including floats, strings, Booleans, multidimensional lists, other dictionaries, and so on. In fact, in the next mission you'll store and access multi-dimensional lists to save and load multiple structures!

MISSION #66: SAVE A COLLECTION OF STRUCTURES

The programs in this mission will store and load all of your saved structures using a single file. This mission is once again divided into two programs: one for saving and the other for loading.

You'll need to convert the programs from Mission #65 to use the shelve module instead of the pickle module. You'll also add code to take user input so users can name their buildings. Open the *saveStructure.py* and *loadStructure.py* files and save them as *saveCollection.py* and *loadCollection.py*.

As we did in the previous mission, let's make the changes to these programs in two parts.

PART 1: SAVING A STRUCTURE TO A COLLECTION

Part of the original *saveStructure.py* file is included and annotated here to help identify where you'll make the changes. Here's the first line and the last few lines of *saveCollection.py*:

saveCollection.py

```
❶ import pickle

--snip--

# Name the structure
❷ structureName = input("What do you want to call the structure?")
```

```
# Store the structure in a file
❸ pickleFile = open("pickleFile", "wb")
❹ pickleFile.dump(structure)
```

An extra line is added to the file to ask what you want to call the structure when you save it with pickle ❷. For example, my version of the program asks "What do you want to call the structure?" and I can reply with something like "House" or "Cake forest." Make sure you call each new structure by a different name; if a new structure has the same name as another one, the old structure will be overwritten by the new one.

To change this program to use the shelve module instead of pickle, you need to make two changes. First, swap the module import from pickle to shelve ❶. Second, change the last few lines of the code to use shelve instead of pickle. Open a file called *structuresFile.db* and store it in a variable called shelveFile using the shelve.open() function ❸. Then store the structure variable in a shelve dictionary using the structureName variable for the name of the dictionary's key ❹. It should look something like this: shelveFile[structureName] = structure. Finally, close shelveFile on the last line by using close().

PART 2: LOADING A STRUCTURE FROM A COLLECTION

Now you need to change the *loadCollection.py* file. I've removed the middle of the file to save space here and to make the bits you need to change easier to see:

load
Collection.py
```
❶ import pickle

--snip--

❷ structure = pickle.load("pickleFile")
❸ structureName = input("Enter the structure's name")

pos = mc.player.getTilePos()
x = pos.x
y = pos.y
z = pos.z

❹ buildStructure(x, y, z, structureDictionary[structureName])
```

I've added an extra line to the code that asks for the name of the structure you want to build ❸. Also, I added a bit of code to the last line that gets the structure from the shelve dictionary and passes it to the buildStructure() function.

You need to make a couple of changes to this program. First, as in *saveCollection.py*, change import to shelve instead of pickle ❶. Second, load the shelveFile that you created in *saveCollection.py* by using shelve.open() ❷. Store the data returned by the shelve.open() function in the variable

structureDictionary ❹. The code should look something like the following:
structureDictionary = shelve.load("shelveFile").

All of the data for the structures, including their names and blocks, are stored in the *structuresFile.db* file, which means you don't need to make any changes to *loadCollection.py* before you run it. All you need to do is enter the name of the structure that you want to use when you run the program.

Let's see the program in action, using a structure from my Minecraft world. First, I copy the structure using *saveCollection.py* by flying to one corner of the structure and pressing ENTER (Figure 11-7).

Figure 11-7: I move to one corner of the structure I want to save.

Next, I fly to the opposite corner of the structure and press ENTER again (Figure 11-8).

Figure 11-8: I move to the opposite corner.

Then the program prompts me to enter a name for my structure. Figure 11-9 shows that I've called my structure "Cake tree".

Figure 11-9: I enter the name that I want to save the structure as.

Finally, I run *loadCollection.py*, fly to the location where I want to build a copy of the structure, and enter the name of the structure I want to build (Figure 11-10). The program starts building in front of me, just like magic!

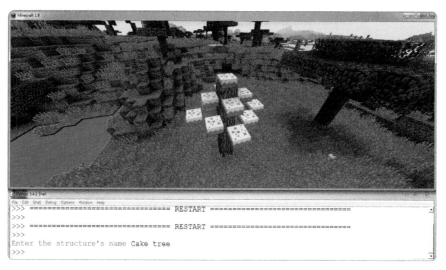

Figure 11-10: Now when I want to create a copy, I just enter the name of the structure and it builds.

You can repeat this process with as many buildings or structures as you want; for example, I've made a copy of a hut in Figure 11-11. After you've copied a structure once, you can load it anytime you want just by running *loadCollection.py* and entering the structure's name!

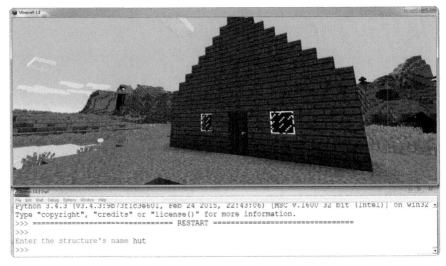

Figure 11-11: You can use the program to save multiple structures. Here I've copied a hut.

INSTALLING NEW MODULES WITH PIP

In addition to pickle and shelve, you can import thousands of other modules to use in your Python programs. With so many modules available, correctly installing them is very important. To simplify installing modules, Python provides a package manager called pip. A *package manager* is software that has a database of other software that you can install on your computer. It also includes features that make it straightforward to install, upgrade, and uninstall the other software.

The pip package manager can install, upgrade, and remove packages in Python. It also has a large collection of modules that you can use in Python. This section shows you how to install a package using pip and showcases the Flask module, which you can use to build a website!

If you're using the most recent version of Python 3, pip is preinstalled. If you're using an earlier version of Python, pip may not be installed. The easiest way to get pip is to install the latest version of Python. (See "Installing Python" on page 3 for Windows and on page 13 for Mac.)

Let's look at how to use pip. Depending on the operating system you use, you can use pip in a couple of ways. Be sure to follow the instructions that match your computer!

USING PIP ON WINDOWS

When using pip on Windows, you need to open the Windows command prompt. The command prompt is similar to the Python shell. It lets you input a single command on a line, which runs when you press ENTER.

To open the command prompt, press the Windows key or open the Start menu and search for cmd. When you open the program, you'll see a black window (Figure 11-12).

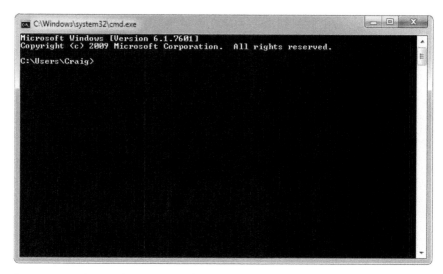

Figure 11-12: The Windows command prompt

To use pip in the command prompt, type pip followed by the action you want it to take. For example, let's install the Python module Flask, which you can use to make websites with Python. Enter the following command in the command prompt:

```
> pip install Flask
```

On the Python Package index website at *http://pypi.python.org/*, you can find many other Python modules that you can install.

USING PIP ON A MAC OR RASPBERRY PI

If you're using pip on a Mac or a Raspberry Pi, you'll need to include sudo at the start of the command to get it to work. For example, enter this line:

```
$ sudo pip install Flask
```

If you get an error, flip to Chapter 1 to double-check the Mac or Raspberry Pi installation instructions.

On the Python Package index website at *http://pypi.python.org/*, you can find many other Python modules that you can install.

USING A MODULE FROM PIP: FLASK

Flask is a Python module that you can use to develop websites. In this section, you'll learn how to set up a basic Flask website and then integrate the website with Minecraft so you can display your player's position on a website!

With Flask, you need only a few lines of code to make and manage a website. You just write the Python code as you normally would and add some extra information related to Flask. Next, you run your code, and it makes a website that your computer can access. You can then view the website in your web browser.

Listing 11-5 creates a basic Flask website that includes the most important piece of information about me: my name.

namePage.py

```
from flask import Flask
❶ app = Flask(__name__)


❷ @app.route("/")
  def showName():
❸     return "Craig Richardson"


❹ app.run()
```

Listing 11-5: A Python program that uses Flask to create a website

To use Flask, you first need to create Flask using the Flask() function ❶. The __name__ argument tells Flask that your Flask project is contained in this file, and it doesn't need to look anywhere else to find other parts of the program. Note the two underscores, not one, at the start and at the end of the __name__ argument.

The @app.route() tag uses a decorator. *Decorators* provide additional information to Python about your functions. For example, in this program the @app.route() decorator tells Flask which part of the website the function will be used on. In this case, "/" tells Flask the showName() function will be used on the home page ❷. The return statement in the function tells Flask what will be displayed on the page. In this example, it returns my name, so my name will be displayed on the page ❸. The last line of the program tells Python to start Flask when this file is run ❹.

Save this file as *namePage.py* in the *files* folder. Add your own text to make your own website.

To run the website, click **Run ▸ Run Module** in IDLE. The program runs and generates a website file that you can open in a web browser. To find the location of the website, you need to read the line of code that your program outputs when you start running it. When I run the program, the output looks like this:

```
* Running on http://127.0.0.1:5000/ (Press CTRL+C to quit)
```

From this line, I can tell that entering *http://127.0.0.1:5000/* into a web browser will take me to the Flask website that I just started running. Now when I open the web browser and go to this site, I can see my name displayed on the page (Figure 11-13).

NOTE *The website you create in this program is available only on your computer at the moment. Only you can access this website—nobody else on the Internet can look at it.*

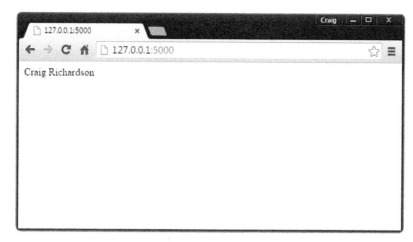

Figure 11-13: Look at my website! You can change what's displayed here to whatever you want. What will you write on your website?

To stop the program, go into IDLE and press CTRL-C or click **Shell ▸ Restart Shell**.

NOTE

This chapter covers only a very basic introduction to Flask. *Flask is very useful to learn because it allows you to build interactive websites quickly with Python. If you want to know more about* Flask, *check out this tutorial on the* Flask *website at* http://flask.pocoo.org/docs/0.10/tutorial/.

MISSION #67: POSITION WEBSITE

One of Python's best qualities is that it's easy to integrate the features of different modules into a single program. You've been using the Minecraft Python API module throughout the book and have just learned about the Flask module. With just a few steps you can integrate the two.

In this mission, you'll combine the Minecraft Python API with Flask to display a player's position on a web page.

Create a new file in IDLE and save it as *positionPage.py* in the *files* folder. You need to get the player's position from Minecraft and display it on the web page using a function with the Flask @app.route("/") tag. You can base the code on the example in Listing 11-5. Make the code display the position in the format "x 10, y 110, z 12".

Run the program and check out your web page. Pretty cool, huh? Using Flask you can create web pages with all kinds of information on them. You can even upload these pages to the Internet to share with your friends!

WHAT YOU LEARNED

In this chapter, you were introduced to using files with Python. You learned how to read and write to files using Python's standard library, giving you control over files when you create your own programs. You also learned how to use modules, which extend Python's capabilities and what you can do in Python.

You explored the pickle module, the shelve module, and the pip package manager. The pickle and shelve modules are used for different purposes. The pickle module saves the value of a single variable, especially when it contains a multidimensional list or dictionary, which would be difficult to store and open using the standard library. The shelve module has the same strengths as the pickle module, but it gives you more flexibility to store several values at once in a dictionary-like structure. With pip, you learned how to install new modules. You were also introduced to the Flask module, which is a quick and flexible way to build websites with Python.

With this knowledge, you completed four missions. The first allowed you to create to-do lists, which you can display in the Minecraft game to remind you what you're working on. The second made it possible to save buildings and load them into your current world and other worlds. The third mission modified the second mission so you could store all your buildings in a single file instead of a file for each building. The final mission showed you how to use the Flask module to create a web page that displays the player's current position.

You've done a great job so far! The next chapter is the final chapter. You'll learn about classes and object-oriented programming, a popular programming style that allows you to reuse code.

12

GETTING CLASSY WITH OBJECT-ORIENTED PROGRAMMING

Reusability is a very important aspect of programming. It saves time and effort. You've seen this with loops and functions, and now you'll learn about *object-oriented programming*.

Object-oriented programming is an approach to programming that groups functions and variables together to create *classes*. Each class can be used to create *objects* that share the same variables and functions as the class. You can create many objects from the same class, making the class's variables and functions reusable.

When a function is part of a class, it's called a *method*, and a variable that's part of a class is called an *attribute*.

In this chapter, you'll learn object-oriented programming and use classes to reuse code. Mastering object-oriented programming and classes makes building programs a breeze, and you can even use object-oriented programming to make games. In the missions in this chapter, you'll use classes to make some basic programs. You'll start by creating a simple building, but soon you'll build an entire town.

OBJECT-ORIENTED BASICS

Object-oriented programming is very popular, and you can use it to create all kinds of cool software, but it can be a tricky concept to understand. Let's relate it to something that's more familiar: you.

You're a person. You have a number of methods: you can eat, breathe, sleep, count to 10, and do lots of other things. You also have attributes: name, age, height, shoe size, and so on.

Your friend Mary has the same methods as you; she too can eat, breathe, sleep, count to 10, and do lots of other things. She also has the same attributes (name, age, and so on), although they contain different values.

In fact, everyone has these methods and attributes. You can describe people as a class. You and Mary are both people, so you could say you are both objects in the Person class.

In object-oriented programming, objects are called *instances* of a class. All objects share the methods and attributes of the class, but the values of the attributes can be different for each object.

Let's jump into Python and make a class.

CREATING A CLASS

You'll start by creating a class and then create all your objects from that class. To create a class, you use the class keyword, the name you want to call the class, and the object class in parentheses (I'll explain the object class in "Inheriting a Class" on page 274):

```
class ClassName(object):
    def __init__(self):
        # Body of init
```

It's good practice to capitalize the names of your classes. This makes it easier to tell the difference between classes and functions, which should start with a lowercase letter.

When you create a new class, you need to include the __init__() method and pass in self as an argument. The self argument is required by every method in a class. It references the class the method belongs to. The __init__() method tells Python what you want the class to do when you use it for the first time in a program. This is called *initializing* the class, which is what __init__() is short for.

For example, let's create a class called Cat and then make some cat objects. The Cat class will store two attributes for each cat, their name and their weight in kilograms. Each cat object will have its own name and weight values. Open a new file in IDLE's text editor and save it as *catClass.py* in a new folder called *classes*. Enter the following code to create a class called Cat:

catClass.py
```
class Cat(object):
❶    def __init__(self, name, weight):
❷        self.name = name
❸        self.weight = weight
```

In this example, the __init__() method takes three arguments ❶. The first is self, which is a required argument in every class method. The second argument, name, and the last argument, weight, are additional arguments to create attributes for all the cats.

The last two lines create the attributes name ❷ and weight ❸ and set them to the values of the name and weight arguments. When you create attributes inside a class, you use dot notation with self. Attributes are always identified by a self, which tells Python that an attribute belongs to the class.

Next, you'll learn how to use this class to create instances of objects.

CREATING AN OBJECT

Using the newly created class, let's create some cat objects, or instances of the Cat class.

Initializing an object is similar to creating a variable. To initialize an object, you enter the name of the object, an equal sign (=), and the class name. You pass arguments to the class in parentheses, just as you do with a function call.

For example, let's adopt a cat and name it Fluff. Using the Cat class, we can create a cat object called fluff by adding the following code on the last line of *catClass.py* (notice that it's not indented):

catClass.py

```
class Cat(object):
    def __init__(self, name, weight):
        self.name = name
        self.weight = weight

fluff = Cat("Fluff", 4.5)
```

When you create an object, the number of arguments you provide depends on the arguments in its __init__() function. Here we include two arguments, one for name ("Fluff") and one for weight (4.5). You don't need to include the self argument when creating an object because the self argument is added automatically by Python.

Creating an object is also known as *calling a constructor*. The __init__() method is often referred to as a constructor because it constructs a class when called. The __init__() method is a special type of method because you don't reference it by name. Instead, it runs when you create an object using the name of the class. For example, here the code fluff = Cat("Fluff", 4.5) calls the __init__() method, which constructs a Cat object called fluff.

Next, you'll learn how to access the fluff object's attributes.

ACCESSING ATTRIBUTES

You can access the attributes of an object to get more information about that object. For example, add the following code to *catClass.py* after the fluff object to print the weight attribute of the fluff object:

catClass.py

```
print(fluff.weight)
```

The value that prints when you run the program should be 4.5, because that's what you set the weight attribute to when you created the object.

Notice that we're using dot notation between the object's name, fluff, and the weight attribute. The dot means you want to use the attribute that belongs to a specific object. In this case, the value of the weight attribute belongs to the fluff object. Whenever you get or set the value of an object's attribute, you use dot notation.

You can change the value of an attribute as you would any other variable—by using an equal sign (=). For example, let's change Fluff's weight to 5 because he gained weight during the winter holidays. We do this by changing the weight attribute in the fluff object to 5:

catClass.py

```
fluff.weight = 5
```

Now whenever you access the weight attribute on the fluff object, it will be 5.

Using the knowledge you now have about making a class and creating an instance of it, let's make some cool stuff in Minecraft.

MISSION #68: LOCATION OBJECTS

Throughout the book, you've stored locations, such as your house, a castle, or a palace, in your Minecraft world. You've used variables, lists, tuples, and dictionaries to do this in a variety of ways.

You can also create and store related information, like locations, using object-oriented programming. For example, you can use objects to store the coordinates of a bunch of different locations.

Each location has an x-, y-, and z-coordinate, but the values for each location are different. By creating a location class, you can store and access the coordinates of different locations. That will help you keep track of all the awesome things you build in Minecraft. You'll be able to easily access the coordinates of all your Minecraft creations so you can teleport the player to them in an instant!

Listing 12-1 contains the start of the Location class. When the code is finished, it can be used to store the coordinates of a location in a single object. Copy the code into a new file called *locationClass.py* in the *classes* folder.

locationClass .py

```
from mcpi.minecraft import Minecraft
mc = Minecraft.create()

❶ class Location(object):
      def __init__(self, x, y, z):
❷         self.x = x
❸         # Add the y and z attributes here

❹ bedroom = Location(64, 52, -8)
❺ mc.player.setTilePos(bedroom.x, bedroom.y, bedroom.z)
```

Listing 12-1: The start of the Location class

To start the class, I included the class keyword and named the class Location ❶. At ❹ is the code to initialize an object called bedroom, which will store the location of the bedroom in my Minecraft home. The setTilePos() method sets the player's position to the bedroom's location—the bedroom object's x, y, and z attributes ❺. However, the program is incomplete. You need to finish the __init__() method of the class and set the y and z attributes to the values of the arguments passed to the __init__() method. I set the value of the x attribute ❷, but it's your task to do the same for the y and z attributes ❸. Don't forget to use the location of your own bedroom at ❹!

Figure 12-1 shows the completed program in action as it teleports the player into my bedroom.

Figure 12-1: The program has teleported the player into my bedroom.

BONUS OBJECTIVE: HOME SWEET HOME

Which other rooms in your house do you want to teleport to? Create more objects using the Location class to zip around your house in style!

UNDERSTANDING METHODS

Classes can contain methods, which are functions associated with the class. Writing class methods lets you create functions that all instances of that class can use. This is a great way to save time and reuse code, because you'll only have to write one method.

To create a method, you write a function in the body of a class using the def keyword. You've used the def keyword in previous chapters to create functions. Methods are also created with the def keyword, but they're indented under the class they belong to. For example, let's update the Cat class in *catClass.py*. We want the cat to be able to eat, so let's add a method called eat() to the Cat class. Enter the code and make the changes to *catClass.py* as you follow along:

```
class Cat(object):
    def __init__(self, name, weight):
        self.name = name
        self.weight = weight

    def eat(self, food):
        self.weight = self.weight + 0.05
        print(self.name + " is eating " + food)
```

Notice that the method definition and body of the method are indented by an extra four spaces so Python knows they belong to the class.

Like functions, methods can take arguments. Here the eat() method takes an argument called food that states what the cat is eating. The eat() method increases the weight attribute of the cat by 0.05 and then prints a message that the cat is eating the food.

After creating an object, you can call any of its class's methods. For example, you can call the eat() method using the fluff object. Add this code to the end of *catClass.py*:

```
fluff = Cat("Fluff", 4.5)
fluff.eat("tuna")
```

Here we see our earlier code, where we created an object called fluff that is part of the Cat class. Then we call the eat() method and give it the argument "tuna". When you run the program, the output will look like this:

```
Fluff is eating tuna
```

Now Fluff is happily eating tuna. Remember that the eat() method also increases the weight attribute. After calling the eat() method, add the code to print fluff's weight.

You can also call methods from inside the class by calling a method inside another method. Let's create another method called eatAndSleep() inside the Cat class. The eatAndSleep() method calls the eat() method and then prints that the cat is sleeping. Add this code to *catClass.py*, just after the eat() method (make sure you indent the new method as shown so Python knows it's part of the class):

```
    def eatAndSleep(self, food):
        self.eat(food)
        print(self.name + " is now sleeping...")
```

To call a method from inside the class it belongs to, you add self. to the beginning of the method name. Here the eat() method is called using self.eat(). Note that this is different from calling a method outside of a class. When you do that, you only have to enter the object name and the method you're calling. For example, the following code calls the new eatAndSleep() method on the fluff object. Add it to your *catClass.py* file. This should be the last line of code in your program:

catClass.py

```
fluff.eatAndSleep("tuna")
```

Here is the output that you should get when you run the program:

```
Fluff is eating tuna
Fluff is now sleeping...
```

Here's the full program so you can see where all the pieces belong:

```python
class Cat(object):
    def __init__(self, name, weight):
        self.name = name
        self.weight = weight

    def eat(self, food):
        self.weight = self.weight + 0.05
        print(self.name + " is eating " + food)

    def eatAndSleep(self, food):
        self.eat(food)
        print(self.name + " is now sleeping...")

fluff = Cat("Fluff", 4.5)
print(fluff.weight)
fluff.eat("tuna")
fluff.eatAndSleep("tuna")
```

Let's take the new skills you've learned into the world of Minecraft!

MISSION #69: GHOST HOUSE

The best thing about programming with Python and Minecraft is that you can start with a silly idea and run with it. Your idea might start small, but with just a few lines of code, you can build a fun program very quickly.

Wouldn't it be fun to build a ghost house that appeared in a game, only to disappear 30 seconds later? The house could then reappear somewhere else and then disappear again if you wanted it to.

Here's the first version of the ghost house program. Save Listing 12-2 in a file called *ghostHouse.py* in the *classes* folder.

ghostHouse.py

```python
from mcpi.minecraft import Minecraft
mc = Minecraft.create()

import time
```

```
❶  class Building(object):
❷      def __init__(self, x, y, z, width, height, depth):
            self.x = x
            self.y = y
            self.z = z

            self.width = width
            self.height = height
            self.depth = depth

❸      def build(self):
            mc.setBlocks(self.x, self.y, self.z,
                          self.x + self.width, self.y + self.height,
                          self.z + self.depth, 4)

            mc.setBlocks(self.x + 1, self.y + 1, self.z + 1,
                          self.x + self.width - 1, self.y + self.height - 1,
                          self.z + self.depth - 1, 0)
❹          # Call the buildDoor() and buildWindows() methods here

❺      def clear(self):
            mc.setBlocks(self.x, self.y, self.z,
                          self.x + self.width, self.y + self.height,
                          self.z + self.depth, 0)
❻          # Remove the doors and windows here

    pos = mc.player.getTilePos()
    x = pos.x
    y = pos.y
    z = pos.z

❼  ghostHouse = Building(x, y, z, 10, 6, 8)
    ghostHouse.build()

    time.sleep(30)

    ghostHouse.clear()
❽  ghostHouse.x = 8
```

Listing 12-2: The Building class creates a building.

Listing 12-2 uses a class called Building ❶ with an __init__() method to set the house's position and size ❷. It creates a Building object with the name ghostHouse ❼. The building appears and then mysteriously disappears after 30 seconds using the build() ❸ and clear() ❺ methods. The only problem is that it doesn't look like a house. Right now it looks like a large, empty shell made of cobblestone.

You need to make the ghost house look more like a house and less like a shell, because ghost shells aren't as scary as ghost houses. To make the building look more house-like, your mission is to add a method that builds a door at the front of the house and a second method that adds windows. Call these two methods from inside the build() method so they're built at the same time ❹.

After adding the methods to build a door and windows, you'll need to update the clear() method to delete them ❻; otherwise, they'll be left behind when the house disappears.

When you've added the extra methods, move the building to a new location by changing the x, y, and z attributes of the ghostHouse object and adding more calls to the build() and clear() methods. I've started this for you by changing the house's x position ❽.

When you run the program, the ghost house should suddenly appear and then disappear 30 seconds later, only to reappear somewhere else. Spooky!

Figure 12-2 shows my ghost house.

Figure 12-2: The ghost house appears and then disappears.

RETURNING VALUES WITH METHODS

Like functions, methods can also return values, or an object's attributes, using the return keyword. For example, let's say we want to convert Fluff the cat's weight from kilograms to grams. A kilogram is equal to 1000 grams, so to make the conversion, you multiply the weight attribute by 1000 and return it. Add the following getWeightInGrams() method to the Cat class in *catClass.py*:

catClass.py
```
class Cat(object):
    def __init__(self, name, weight):
        self.name = name
        self.weight = weight


    def getWeightInGrams(self):
        return self.weight * 1000
```

To output the value returned by the method, you create an object and call the method. In the following code, the fluff object is used, and the method is called inside a print() function to get the cat's weight in grams:

catClass.py
```
fluff = Cat("Fluff", 4.5)
print(fluff.getWeightInGrams())
```

Now when you run the file, it will output the following:

```
4500
```

In the next mission, we'll extend the ghost house program to include a method that returns information about the building.

MISSION #70: GHOST CASTLE

I have all kinds of names in mind for the different places I've built in my Minecraft world: the beach house, the plant farm, the animal farm, the storage room, the palace, the underwater palace, the underground palace, and loads more. The problem is that the names only exist in my head!

With classes, you can create attributes like location and size for things you build, as you saw in Mission #69 (page 263). You can also include names!

Let's name the ghost house and have Python remember it for us. We'll update the Building class from Mission #69 to add an extra method that returns the name of the building. Copy Listing 12-3 into a new file called *ghostCastle.py* in the *classes* folder.

ghostCastle.py

```
from mcpi.minecraft import Minecraft
mc = Minecraft.create()

import time

❶ class NamedBuilding(object):
❷     def __init__(self, x, y, z, width, height, depth, name):
           self.x = x
           self.y = y
           self.z = z

           self.width = width
           self.height = height
           self.depth = depth

❸          self.name = name

       def build(self):
           mc.setBlocks(self.x, self.y, self.z,
                        self.x + self.width, self.y + self.height,
                        self.z + self.depth, 4)

           mc.setBlocks(self.x + 1, self.y + 1, self.z + 1,
                        self.x + self.width - 1, self.y + self.height - 1,
                        self.z + self.depth - 1, 0)

       def clear(self):
           mc.setBlocks(self.x, self.y, self.z,
                        self.x + self.width, self.y + self.height,
                        self.z + self.depth, 0)

❹      def getInfo():
           # Add the body of the getInfo() method here

   pos = mc.player.getTilePos()
   x = pos.x
   y = pos.y
   z = pos.z
   ghostCastle = NamedBuilding(x, y, z, 10, 16, 16, "Ghost Castle")
   ghostCastle.build()
❺  mc.postToChat(ghostCastle.getInfo())

   time.sleep(30)

   ghostCastle.clear()
```

Listing 12-3: NamedBuilding is very similar to the Building class, except it has an extra attribute called name and an extra method that returns a description of the building.

First, I changed the name of the class to NamedBuilding so we won't confuse it with the Building class from the previous mission ❶. I've added an extra argument and attribute to the constructor called name ❷. The argument allows you to give a name to the building, and the constructor assigns the name to the name attribute ❸.

Your mission is to add a method called getInfo() to the new class NamedBuilding that returns the name and position of the building. I've added the start of the getInfo() method for you at ❹. You just need to add the body. The getInfo() method is called on the ghostCastle object at ❺ so it outputs the string returned by the method to the Minecraft chat. For example, if the ghost castle is located at x = -310, y = 64, z = 1081, the getInfo() method should return the string "Ghost Castle's location is at -310, 64, 1081".

Figure 12-3 shows my working program. Although the ghost castle is taller, it looks like the house from Mission #69. This is because the build() methods are the same for both, but feel free to change your version of the code so your building looks more like a castle.

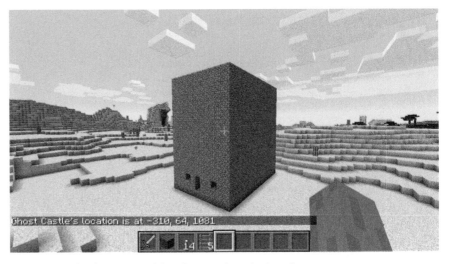

Figure 12-3: The description of the ghost castle is displayed.

BONUS OBJECTIVE: A WARM WELCOME

Wouldn't it be cool if the name of any building you walked into appeared in the chat automatically? Well, it's possible, but it's a bit challenging. If you want to try this, you can use the *shower.py* program from Mission #32 (page 120) as a starting point. The file should be in your *ifStatements* folder. You can use the program to detect the coordinates of the player and, if they're inside the building, call the building object's getInfo() method.

CREATING MULTIPLE OBJECTS

You can make several objects from the same class by creating objects with different names using the same class constructor (remember that *constructor* is another name for the __init__() method). For example, let's say we found a second cat named Stella who is now friends with Fluff. Open *catClass.py* and enter the following code to add Stella:

catClass.py

```
class Cat(object):
    def __init__(self, name, weight):
        self.name = name
        self.weight = weight

fluff = Cat("Fluff", 4.5)
stella = Cat("Stella", 3.9)
```

Now we have two cat objects, fluff and stella. Each has the same attributes, name and weight, but with different values.

Add the following code to *catClass.py* to print the cats' names:

catClass.py

```
print(fluff.name)
print(stella.name)
```

When you run the file, you'll get this output:

```
Fluff
Stella
```

The two cat objects also have access to the same methods. Both can call the eat() function. Add this code to *catClass.py*:

catClass.py

```
fluff.eat("tuna")
stella.eat("cake")
```

And the output will look like this:

```
Fluff is eating tuna
Stella is eating cake
```

Writing a class makes creating lots of objects very easy. Let's try creating multiple objects with Minecraft!

MISSION #71: GHOST TOWN

What's scarier than one ghost house? That's right, two ghost houses. But three ghost houses would be even scarier. And more than three ghost houses? I need to stop thinking about this, or I won't get any sleep tonight!

In Mission #69 (page 263), you made a class that builds a house that disappears. Now you can create several objects using the same class, and Python will remember each of the object's attributes and methods. You can make as many houses as you want, and you can make them appear and disappear with ease.

Your mission is to create four or more ghost house objects and arrange them in a village. After a certain amount of time, make them all disappear and reappear elsewhere on the map, just like a real ghost town.

Open *ghostHouse.py* in IDLE—we'll use this as a base. When you created a house in the *ghostHouse.py* program, your code should have looked like this:

```
ghostHouse = Building(17, 22, -54, 10, 6, 8)
ghostHouse.build()

time.sleep(30)

ghostHouse.clear()
```

Save *ghostHouse.py* as a new file called *ghostVillage.py*, and then create three or more objects in the file using the Building class to build the village. To help you get started, I've created a second object called shop in Listing 12-4. I've also set the variables x, y, and z to hold the player's current position, which we find using player.getTilePos(). This makes it easier to build the village all around you.

```
pos = mc.player.getTilePos()
x = pos.x
y = pos.y
z = pos.z
ghostHouse = Building(x, y, z, 10, 6, 8)
shop = Building(x + 12, y, z, 8, 12, 10)
# Create more ghost building objects here

ghostHouse.build()
shop.build()
# Build more ghost building objects here

time.sleep(30)

ghostHouse.clear()
shop.clear()
```

Listing 12-4: Creating multiple ghost building objects

Figure 12-4 shows my ghost village. After 30 seconds, the ghost buildings suddenly disappear.

Figure 12-4: Look at all the ghost buildings in the ghost village!

CLASS ATTRIBUTES

Sometimes you might want to set attributes that have the same value for every object instance in a class. It would be redundant to pass the same argument to the class every time an object is created. Instead, you can create a preset attribute in the class, and all the instances of objects in that class will share those attributes.

When multiple objects share the same attribute, it's called a *class attribute*. For example, all the cat objects we've created are owned by Craig (me). I can revisit the Cat class in the *catClass.py* file, create a class attribute called owner, and set it to "Craig":

catClass.py
```
class Cat(object):
    owner = "Craig"

    def __init__(self, name, weight):
        self.name = name
        self.weight = weight
```

As you can see, class attributes don't use self before their name. In this example, owner is a class attribute and self.name is an attribute. Notice that you define class attributes outside the __init__() function.

Class attributes work the same as any other attribute in an object. For example, you can access the value of a class attribute as you would a normal attribute. In this case, to find Fluff's owner, we can print the owner class attribute of the fluff object:

catClass.py
```
fluff = Cat("Fluff", 4.5)
print(fluff.owner)
```

The printed value should be "Craig". If we printed Stella's owner, the value would be the same because class attributes are the same for every object in that class:

```
stella = Cat("Stella", 3.9)
print(stella.owner)
```

The printed value here is also "Craig".

You can change the value of class attributes for individual objects. This will change the value of the attribute for that object, but no other objects in the class. For example, Stella has been adopted by my friend Matthew, so we need to change Stella's owner to "Matthew":

```
stella.owner = "Matthew"
print(stella.owner)
print(fluff.owner)
```

When the owner attribute of stella is printed, it shows "Matthew", but fluff's owner is still "Craig".

After all the changes we've made to *catClass.py*, the final program looks like the following. It's also available in the book's resources at *https://www.nostarch.com/pythonwithminecraft/*.

```
class Cat(object):
    owner = "Craig"

    def __init__(self, name, weight):
        self.name = name
        self.weight = weight

    def eat(self, food):
        self.weight = self.weight + 0.05
        print(self.name + " is eating " + food)

    def eatAndSleep(self, food):
        self.eat(food)
        print(self.name + " is now sleeping...")

    def getWeightInGrams(self):
        return self.weight * 1000


fluff = Cat("Fluff", 4.5)
print(fluff.owner)
stella = Cat("Stella", 3.9)
print(stella.owner)

print(fluff.weight)
fluff.eat("tuna")
fluff.eatAndSleep("tuna")

print(fluff.getWeightInGrams())
```

```
print(fluff.name)
print(stella.name)

fluff.eat("tuna")
stella.eat("cake")

stella.owner = "Matthew"
print(stella.owner)
print(fluff.owner)
```

Now that you've seen how to use objects, let's see how to make them even more powerful with inheritance.

UNDERSTANDING INHERITANCE

Inheritance occurs when classes share the same methods and attributes as other classes. For example, ducks are a type of bird. They share the same methods as other birds (flying, eating, and so on), and they have the same attributes as other birds (weight, wingspan, and so on). So you could say that *ducks* inherit their attributes and methods from the class *birds*. Figure 12-5 shows this relationship in a diagram.

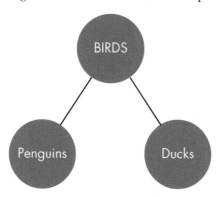

Figure 12-5: Penguins and ducks are both types of birds.

The class that other classes inherit from is called a *superclass*; the class that inherits from the superclass is called a *subclass*.

Inheritance is useful because it allows you to create subtle differences between similar objects. For example, penguins are also a type of bird, but they can swim underwater, unlike most birds. To represent penguins, you need to create a subclass that inherits from the bird class but has adaptations so the penguins can swim underwater. These adaptations are the reason you create subclasses: you can keep the main superclass features to avoid having to write the code again, and just add the methods and attributes you need in the subclass.

INHERITING A CLASS

When a subclass inherits from a superclass, the subclass can use all the superclass's methods and attributes. The subclass can also add extra classes and attributes without altering the original superclass.

Let's use the birds example to illustrate this. First, we'll write the code for the Bird superclass. Open a new file in IDLE, name it *birdClass.py*, and then add the following code to make the class:

birdClass.py
```
❶ class Bird(object):
❷     def __init__(self, name, wingspan):
           self.name = name
           self.wingspan = wingspan

❸     def birdcall(self):
           print("chirp")

❹     def fly(self):
           print("flap")
```

We create a class called Bird ❶, but notice that the Bird class inherits from object. The object class is a base class that all other classes will be built on top of. All classes inherit from the object class, and you use it when there are no other superclasses to inherit from. Even if there are several levels of inheritance where lots of classes inherit from each other, the object class will always be the superclass used on the highest level of inheritance.

The Bird class's __init__() method takes two arguments that set two attributes: the name of the bird and its wingspan ❷. It has two methods: birdcall() ❸ and fly() ❹. At the moment, the birdcall() method just prints "chirp" and the fly() method just prints "flap".

In the same file, create an object called gardenBird using the Bird class:

birdClass.py
```
gardenBird = Bird("Geoffrey", 12)
gardenBird.birdcall()
gardenBird.fly()
```

This code will output:

```
chirp
flap
```

Now that you've created a superclass, you can create a subclass that inherits from the superclass but gets its own method. You'll do that in the next section.

ADDING NEW METHODS TO SUBCLASSES

Let's add a class for penguins to *birdClass.py* and call it Penguin. Because penguins can swim underwater, you can add an extra method to the Penguin class called swim():

birdClass.py
```
class Penguin(Bird):
    def swim(self):
        print("swimming")
```

When you define a subclass and want it to inherit from another super-class instead of object, you put the name of the superclass to inherent from in parentheses. Notice that I didn't create an __init__() method for the Penguin class. The reason is that it inherits from the Bird class, so it uses the Bird class __init__() method. Let's use that __init__() method and test the swim() function by creating a penguin:

birdClass.py
```
sarahThePenguin = Penguin("Sarah", 10)
sarahThePenguin.swim()
```

This code will output the following:

```
swimming
```

The Penguin class can also use the fly() and birdcall() methods because it inherits them from Bird.

birdClass.py
```
sarahThePenguin.fly()
sarahThePenguin.birdcall()
```

In this case, the output will look like this:

```
flap
chirp
```

But flap and chirp don't make sense for a penguin because penguins can't fly and their birdcall is more of a quack! We'll learn how to override inherited methods and fix this in "Overriding Methods and Attributes" on page 278.

But first, let's return to Minecraft and create some new ghost buildings using inheritance.

MISSION #72: GHOST HOTEL

Houses and hotels are both types of buildings: they have doors, windows, rooms, stairs, and walls. Hotels are just fancy houses with extras like balconies, lots of rooms, and a pretty entrance.

How can you program some ghost hotels using the code you've already created for ghost houses? The basic structure of the buildings is the same. So let's say the only difference is that ghost hotels have extra methods to create carpets inside the rooms and add flowers around the edge of the building. That means the ghost hotel class can inherit all the methods from the ghost house class. Then all the ghost hotel class needs is two extra methods for the carpets and flowers.

In IDLE, create a new file and save it as *ghostHotel.py* in the *classes* folder. Copy and paste the code for the `Building` class from the *ghostHouse.py* program into the file.

Create a new class called `FancyBuilding` that inherits from the `Building` class. The `FancyBuilding` class should have a new method called `upgrade()` that adds carpet inside the building and flowers around the walls. Listing 12-5 shows my code for the `upgrade()` method, but feel free to customize your hotels.

ghostHotel.py

```
# Create a FancyBuilding class here

    def upgrade(self):
        # Carpet
        mc.setBlocks(self.x + 1, self.y, self.z + 1,
                     self.x + self.width - 1, self.y, self.z + self.depth - 1,
                     35, 6)

        # Flowers
        mc.setBlocks(self.x - 1, self.y, self.z -1,
                     self.x - 1, self.y, self.z + self.depth + 1,
                     37)
        mc.setBlocks(self.x - 1, self.y, self.z - 1,
                     self.x + self.width + 1, self.y, self.z - 1,
                     37)
        mc.setBlocks(self.x + self.width + 1, self.y, self.z - 1,
                     self.x + self.width + 1, self.y, self.z + self.depth + 1,
                     37)
        mc.setBlocks(self.x - 1, self.y, self.z + self.depth + 1,
                     self.x + self.width + 1, self.y, self.z + self.depth = 1,
                     37)

# Create an instance of the FancyBuilding class
# Call the build() and upgrade() methods
```

Listing 12-5: A method for the `FancyBuilding` class that adds carpet and flowers to the building

After you've created the class and added the new method, create an instance of the `FancyBuilding` class and call it ghostHotel. Build the ghost hotel using the build() method, and then add the extra bits using the upgrade() method.

Figure 12-6 shows my fancy ghost hotel.

Figure 12-6: Look at those flowers and that carpet!

BONUS OBJECTIVE: FANCY VILLAGE

In Mission #71, you created a ghost village in which all the buildings looked about the same. It's rare to see identical buildings in real towns. Change the ghost village program by creating several classes that inherit from the Building class. You could make a Shop class, a Hospital class, and a Restaurant class, for example. Then when you create the objects, you can choose which type of building to create by using the different classes.

OVERRIDING METHODS AND ATTRIBUTES

It's possible for a subclass to redefine methods and attributes from its super-class. This is useful when you want to use the same name for a method but you want it to behave differently in the subclass.

In "Understanding Inheritance" on page 273, we created a Bird class and a Penguin class. The Penguin class inherited from Bird so it shared all its methods. But penguins can't fly, and their birdcall is more of a quack sound than a chirp. So, we should change the fly() and birdcall() methods to reflect this. Open *birdClass.py* and add this code:

birdClass.py
```
class Penguin(Bird):
    def swim(self):
        print("swimming")

❶    def birdcall(self):
        print("sort of a quack")

❷    def fly(self):
        print("Penguins cannot fly :(")
```

I've made two changes to the Penguin class. I've added a birdcall() ❶ method and a fly() ❷ method. Because both methods are spelled the same as they are in the Bird superclass, they will override the superclass's methods.

Call the methods by adding this code to *birdClass.py*:

birdClass.py
```
sarahThePenguin.fly()
sarahThePenguin.birdcall()
```

Now when you run the program, you'll get this output:

```
Penguins cannot fly :(
sort of a quack
```

Overriding a method from a superclass will change what the method does for the subclass but not the superclass. So penguins won't be able to fly, but other birds that inherit from Bird will still be able to fly.

You can also overwrite the __init__() method in a subclass. This means that when the subclass object is created, it can have different attributes or behaviors than the superclass.

For example, let's create a Parrot subclass of Bird in the same file. Parrots can be different colors, so let's include an extra argument in the __init__() method for a color attribute:

birdClass.py
```
class Parrot(Bird):
❶    def __init__(self, name, wingspan, color):
        self.name = name
        self.wingspan = wingspan
        self.color = color
```

I've included a new __init__() method for the Parrot class that has an extra argument, color ❶, when compared to the original Bird class.

Now when we create a new Parrot object, we can access the color attribute. We can also access the birdcall() and fly() methods because they were inherited from the Bird superclass:

birdClass.py

```python
freddieTheParrot = Parrot("Freddie", 12, "blue")
print(freddieTheParrot.color)
freddieTheParrot.fly()
freddieTheParrot.birdcall()
```

This code will output the following:

```
blue
flap
chirp
```

Remember that you can overwrite any method that a subclass inherits from a superclass; you can even overwrite the __init__() method. This gives you a lot of control over objects and their many attributes and methods.

After all the changes we've made to *birdClass.py*, the final program looks like the following. It's also available in the book's resources at *https://www.nostarch.com/pythonwithminecraft/*.

birdClass.py

```python
class Bird(object):
    def __init__(self, name, wingspan):
        self.name = name
        self.wingspan = wingspan

    def birdcall(self):
        print("chirp")

    def fly(self):
        print("flap")


class Penguin(Bird):
    def swim(self):
        print("swimming")

    def birdcall(self):
        print("sort of a quack")

    def fly(self):
        print("Penguins cannot fly :(")


class Parrot(Bird):
    def __init__(self, name, wingspan, color):
        self.name = name
        self.wingspan = wingspan
        self.color = color
```

```
gardenBird = Bird("Geoffrey", 12)
gardenBird.birdcall()
gardenBird.fly()

sarahThePenguin = Penguin("Sarah", 10)
sarahThePenguin.swim()
sarahThePenguin.fly()
sarahThePenguin.birdcall()

freddieTheParrot = Parrot("Freddie", 12, "blue")
print(freddieTheParrot.color)
freddieTheParrot.fly()
freddieTheParrot.birdcall()
```

You'll try overriding methods and attributes in the next mission.

MISSION #73: GHOST TREE

You've created several forms of ghost buildings. Let's take it to the next level and create a ghost tree. That's an amazing idea, but how can we do it? The Building class is for buildings, which have walls and ceilings—trees don't have walls or ceilings. Worry not! You can work around this by modifying your ghost Building class.

Like the ghost buildings, the ghost tree will appear and disappear using the build() and clear() methods. But the methods need to work differently because trees look different from houses. So, you need to create a class that inherits from the Building class and then override the build() and clear() methods.

To get you started, I've grabbed the function that creates a tree from the *forest.py* file (page 149) and put it in Listing 12-6. Copy it into a new file called *ghostTree.py* in the *classes* folder.

ghostTree.py
```
from mcpi.minecraft import Minecraft
mc = Minecraft.create()

# Paste the ghostHouse.py program here
# Create a Tree class here

❶ def growTree(x, y, z):
    """ Creates a tree at the coordinates given """
    wood = 17
    leaves = 18

    # Trunk
    mc.setBlocks(x, y, z, x, y + 5, z, wood)

    # Leaves
    mc.setBlocks(x - 2, y + 6, z - 2, x + 2, y + 6, z + 2, leaves)
    mc.setBlocks(x - 1, y + 7, z - 1, x + 1, y + 7, z + 1, leaves)

# Create build() and clear() methods for the Tree class here
```

Listing 12-6: A function to create a tree

To finish the program, copy and paste the code for the Building class from *ghostHouse.py* into the new file. Then create a new class called Tree that inherits from the Building class. Inside the Tree class, add a build() method and a clear() method to override the methods from the Building class and build a tree instead of a house. Make sure you include the self argument in front of the attributes in the final growTree() method ❶.

After you've created the program, make a Tree object called ghostTree. Call the build() method to make the tree appear, wait a bit, and then make it vanish using clear().

Figure 12-7 shows the result of my program.

Figure 12-7: That's a spooky tree!

WHAT YOU LEARNED

You just learned the basics of one of the most important concepts in programming today: object-oriented programming! You learned how to write a class and create objects, and you learned how to use inheritance to customize classes and object behavior. You'll be able to apply this very useful skill not only in Minecraft but also in any kind of programming adventure that you choose to go on to next!

AFTERWORD

This is a momentous occasion. You've just finished the book. It's been a long journey, for me and for you! Since I started writing this book, I've grown several beards, lived in three different cities, and found out that bananas don't produce seeds. Honestly, I've had so much fun writing this thing. At moments it was hard and tiring, but I stuck with it because I wanted you to read it.

Since you started this book, you've covered a lot of ground. You've learned about the fundamentals of programming in Python and made some really cool programs that use these concepts to do amazing things in Minecraft. You've learned about variables, math operations, strings, input, Booleans, if statements, while and for loops, functions, lists and dictionaries, modules, files, and classes. You may have been a complete beginner when you started this book, but with this knowledge, you'll be capable of doing some really advanced things in Python.

Whatever you choose to do with programming in the future, I sincerely wish you the best of luck. For me, programming has been an amazing hobby that luckily turned into a full-time job.

If we ever meet in person, make sure we give each other a high five!

BLOCK ID CHEAT SHEET

Where two numbers are listed, the second number is the block state. Blocks marked with an asterisk (*) are available in Minecraft: Pi Edition.

196	Acacia Door Block
161	Acacia Leaves
6, 4	Acacia Sapling
162	Acacia Wood
5, 4	Acacia Wood Plank
126, 4	Acacia Wood Slab
125, 4	Acacia Wood Slab (Dbl)
157	Activator Rail
38, 2	Allium
1, 5*	Andesite
38, 3	Azure Bluet
138	Beacon
26*	Bed
7*	Bedrock
194	Birch Door Block
18, 2*	Birch Leaves
6, 2*	Birch Sapling
17, 2*	Birch Wood
5, 2*	Birch Wood Plank
126, 2	Birch Wood Slab
125, 2	Birch Wood Slab (Dbl)
38, 1	Blue Orchid
47*	Bookshelf
117	Brewing Stand
44, 4*	Brick Slab
43, 4*	Brick Slab (Dbl)
108*	Brick Stairs
45*	Bricks

39*	Brown Mushroom
99	Brown Mushroom Block
62*	Burning Furnace
81*	Cactus
92	Cake Block
171, 15	Carpet, Black
171, 11	Carpet, Blue
171, 12	Carpet, Brown
171, 9	Carpet, Cyan
171, 7	Carpet, Gray
171, 13	Carpet, Green
171, 3	Carpet, Light Blue
171, 8	Carpet, Light Gray
171, 5	Carpet, Lime
171, 2	Carpet, Magenta
171, 1	Carpet, Orange
171, 6	Carpet, Pink
171, 10	Carpet, Purple
171, 14	Carpet, Red
171	Carpet, White
171, 4	Carpet, Yellow
141	Carrots
118	Cauldron
54*	Chest
155, 1*	Chiseled Quartz Block
179, 1	Chiseled Red Sandstone
24, 1	Chiseled Sandstone
98, 3	Chiseled Stone Bricks

	82*	Clay			3*	Dirt
	173	Coal Block			23	Dispenser
	16*	Coal Ore			122	Dragon Egg
	3, 1*	Coarse Dirt			158	Dropper
	4*	Cobblestone			133	Emerald Block
	44, 3*	Cobblestone Slab			129	Emerald Ore
	43, 3*	Cobblestone Slab (Dbl)			116	Enchantment Table
	67*	Cobblestone Stairs			119	End Portal
	30*	Cobweb			120	End Portal Frame
	127	Cocoa			121	End Stone
	98, 2*	Cracked Stone Bricks			60*	Farmland
	58*	Crafting Table			31, 2*	Fern
	37*	Dandelion			51	Fire
	197	Dark Oak Door Block			140	Flower Pot
	161, 1	Dark Oak Leaves			10*	Flowing Lava
	6, 5	Dark Oak Sapling			8*	Flowing Water
	162, 1	Dark Oak Wood			61*	Furnace
	5, 5	Dark Oak Wood Plank			20*	Glass
	126, 5	Dark Oak Wood Slab			102*	Glass Pane
	125, 5	Dark Oak Wood Slab (Dbl)			95, 15*	Glass, Black Stained
	168, 2	Dark Prismarine			95, 11*	Glass, Blue Stained
	151	Daylight Sensor			95, 12*	Glass, Brown Stained
	32	Dead Bush			95, 9*	Glass, Cyan Stained
	31*	Dead Shrub			95, 7*	Glass, Gray Stained
	28	Detector Rail			95, 13*	Glass, Green Stained
	57*	Diamond Block			95, 3*	Glass, Light Blue Stained
	56*	Diamond Ore			95, 8*	Glass, Light Gray Stained
	1, 3*	Diorite			95, 5*	Glass, Lime Stained

95, 2*	Glass, Magenta Stained		18, 3	Jungle Leaves
95, 1*	Glass, Orange Stained		6, 3	Jungle Sapling
95, 6*	Glass, Pink Stained		17, 3	Jungle Wood
95, 10*	Glass, Purple Stained		5, 3	Jungle Wood Plank
95, 14*	Glass, Red Stained		126, 3	Jungle Wood Slab
95*	Glass, White Stained		125, 3	Jungle Wood Slab (Dbl)
95, 4*	Glass, Yellow Stained		65*	Ladder
74*	Glowing Redstone Ore		22*	Lapis Lazuli Block
89*	Glowstone		21*	Lapis Lazuli Ore
41*	Gold Block		175, 3	Large Fern
14*	Gold Ore		69	Lever
1, 1*	Granite		175, 1	Lilac
2*	Grass		111	Lily Pad
31, 1*	Grass		103*	Melon Block
13*	Gravel		105*	Melon Stem
172	Hardened Clay		52	Monster Spawner
170	Hay Bale		48*	Moss Stone
154	Hopper		98, 1*	Mossy Stone Bricks
79*	Ice		110	Mycelium
178	Inverted Daylight Sensor		112*	Nether Brick
101	Iron Bars		44, 6*	Nether Brick Slab
42*	Iron Block		43, 6*	Nether Brick Slab (Dbl)
71*	Iron Door Block		114*	Nether Brick Stairs
15*	Iron Ore		90	Nether Portal
167	Iron Trapdoor		153	Nether Quartz Ore
91	Jack o'Lantern		115	Nether Wart
84	Jukebox		87	Netherrack
195	Jungle Door Block		25	Note Block

	ID	Name		ID	Name
	64*	Oak Door Block		160	Pane, White Stained
	85*	Oak Fence		160, 4	Pane, Yellow Stained
	107*	Oak Fence Gate		175, 5	Peony
	18*	Oak Leaves		155, 2*	Pillar Quartz Block
	6*	Oak Sapling		38, 7	Pink Tulip
	17*	Oak Wood		33	Piston
	5*	Oak Wood Plank		34	Piston Head
	126	Oak Wood Slab		3, 2*	Podzol
	125	Oak Wood Slab (Dbl)		1, 6*	Polished Andesite
	53*	Oak Wood Stairs		1, 4*	Polished Diorite
	49*	Obsidian		1, 2*	Polished Granite
	38, 5	Orange Tulip		38	Poppy
	38, 8	Oxeye Daisy		142	Potatoes
	174	Packed Ice		27	Powered Rail
	160, 15	Pane, Black Stained		148	Pressure Plate (heavy)
	160, 11	Pane, Blue Stained		147	Pressure Plate (light)
	160, 12	Pane, Brown Stained		168	Prismarine
	160, 9	Pane, Cyan Stained		168, 1	Prismarine Bricks
	160, 7	Pane, Gray Stained		86	Pumpkin
	160, 13	Pane, Green Stained		104	Pumpkin Stem
	160, 3	Pane, Light Blue Stained		155*	Quartz Block
	160, 8	Pane, Light Gray Stained		44, 7*	Quartz Slab
	160, 5	Pane, Lime Stained		43, 7*	Quartz Slab (Dbl)
	160, 2	Pane, Magenta Stained		156*	Quartz Stairs
	160, 1	Pane, Orange Stained		66	Rail
	160, 6	Pane, Pink Stained		40*	Red Mushroom
	160, 10	Pane, Purple Stained		100	Red Mushroom Block
	160, 14	Pane, Red Stained		12, 1	Red Sand

	179	Red Sandstone		6, 1*	Spruce Sapling
	182	Red Sandstone Slab		17, 1*	Spruce Wood
	181	Red Sandstone Slab (Dbl)		5, 1*	Spruce Wood Plank
	38, 4	Red Tulip		126, 1	Spruce Wood Slab
	152	Redstone Block		125, 1	Spruce Wood Slab (Dbl)
	124	Redstone Lamp (active)		63*	Standing Sign Block
	123	Redstone Lamp (inactive)		29	Sticky Piston
	73*	Redstone Ore		11*	Still Lava
	93	Redstone Repeater (off)		9*	Still Water
	94	Redstone Repeater (on)		1*	Stone
	75	Redstone Torch (off)		44, 5*	Stone Brick Slab
	76	Redstone Torch (on)		43, 5*	Stone Brick Slab (Dbl)
	175, 4	Rose Bush		109*	Stone Brick Stairs
	12*	Sand		98*	Stone Bricks
	24*	Sandstone		70	Stone Pressure Plate
	44, 1*	Sandstone Slab		44*	Stone Slab
	43, 1*	Sandstone Slab (Dbl)		43*	Stone Slab (Dbl)
	128*	Sandstone Stairs		83*	Sugar Canes
	169	Sea Lantern		175	Sunflower
	165	Slime Block		46*	TNT
	179, 2	Smooth Red Sandstone		46, 1*	TNT, Hand Detonated
	24, 2	Smooth Sandstone		175, 2	Tallgrass (Dbl)
	78*	Snow		50*	Torch
	80*	Snow Block		132	Tripwire
	88	Soul Sand		131	Tripwire Hook
	19	Sponge		106	Vines
	193	Spruce Door Block		68*	Wall-Mounted Sign Block
	18, 1*	Spruce Leaves		19, 1	Wet Sponge

	59*	Wheat Crops		35, 13*	Wool, Green
	38, 6	White Tulip		35, 3*	Wool, Light Blue
	72	Wooden Pressure Plate		35, 8*	Wool, Light Gray
	44, 2*	Wooden Slab		35, 5*	Wool, Lime
	43, 2*	Wooden Slab (Dbl)		35, 2*	Wool, Magenta
	96	Wooden Trapdoor		35, 1*	Wool, Orange
	35, 15*	Wool, Black		35, 6*	Wool, Pink
	35, 11*	Wool, Blue		35, 10*	Wool, Purple
	35, 12*	Wool, Brown		35, 14*	Wool, Red
	35, 9*	Wool, Cyan		35*	Wool, White
	35, 7*	Wool, Gray		35, 4*	Wool, Yellow

INDEX

SYMBOLS & NUMBERS

+ (addition operator), 48–49
+= (addition shorthand), 62
* (asterisk), importing all functions
    with, 241
/ (division operator), 58
/= (division shorthand), 62
"" (double quotation marks), for
    strings, 66
= (equal sign), assigning values to
    variables with, 28
== (equal to), 84
** (exponential operator), 60–61,
    91–92
> (greater than), 88
>= (greater than or equal to), 89–90
(hash mark), for comments, 35
< (less than), 88–89
<= (less than or equal to), 89–90
* (multiplication operator), 58
*= (multiplication shorthand), 62
!= (not equal to), 86–87
'' (single quotation marks), for
    strings, 66
[] (square brackets), for defining
    lists, 168
- (subtraction operator), 48
-= (subtraction shorthand), 62
""" (triple quotation marks), for
    docstrings, 152–153
2D lists, 208–213, 216
3D lists, 218–225

A

a (append permission), 233
addition operator (+), 48–49
    shorthand (+=), 62
aliases, for modules, 241
and operator, 93

API (application programming
        interface), Minecraft
        Python
    installing on Mac, 15
    installing on Windows, 6
append permission (a), 233
append() function, 171–172
application programming
        interface. See API
arguments, 34, 147–148
    line breaks in, 153
    math operators in, 54–55
arrays. See lists
asterisk (*), importing all functions
        with, 241
attributes, 257. See also variables
    accessing, 259–260
    class, 271–273

B

block hits program, 180–182,
        196–198
    scoreboard, 192–194, 205–206
blocks
    changing, 52–53, 138–139,
        196–198
    finding highest, 90
    identifying, 85
    IDs
        cheat sheet, 285
        finding by, 97–98, 186–187,
            207–208
        reminder program, 155–156
    moving, 163–165
    placing, 49, 55–56
        by user input, 74–75
    random, 160–161, 183
    replacing, 173–174
    stacking, 49–50

blocks, *continued*
    state, 158–159
    wool, setting color by name,
        158–159
Boolean operators. *See* logical
    operators
Boolean values, 82–83
break statements, 139, 207
building quickly, 55–57

C

chat
    persistent, 139–140
    posting to, 67–68, 69–70
    usernames, 72–73
cheat sheet, block IDs, 285
choice() function, 182
class attributes, 271–273. *See
    also* attributes, global
    variables
classes, 257–260, 273–274
close() function, 233–234, 247–248
color of wool blocks, setting by
    name, 158–159
command prompt, 21, 23–24
comments, 35, 152–153
comparators, 83–91, 104–105,
    131–132
concatenation, 71–72, 83
conditions, 81, 104–105, 131–132
connecting to Minecraft, 34
constructor, 259
coordinates, 31–32
copying structures, 225–229,
    242–246, 248–252
count variables, 124, 127–128
crater program, 105–106
curse program, 128–129

D

dance floor, generating, 135–137
data. *See also* files
    storing with variables, 28
    types, 31
debugging, 42–44
decimal values, 37–38
decrementing values, 128

def keyword, 146
del keyword, 172–173
delays, setting in programs, 39–40
dictionaries. *See also* shelve module
    defining, 188–189
    items
        accessing, 189
        adding, 191–192
        changing, 191–192
        deleting, 192
        looping over, 205
        readability, 205
diving contest program, 132–134
division operator (/), 58
    shorthand (/=), 62
docstrings, 152–153
double quotation marks (""),
        for strings, 66
dump() function, 239–240

E

elif statements, 109–110, 112–113
else statements, 107, 141, 206–207
else-if statements. *See* elif
        statements
equal to (==), 84
equal sign (=), assigning values to
        variables with, 28
errors
    debugging, 42–44
    handling, 76–78
    index, 168–169
    scope, 162
    syntax, 30
    type, 147–148, 154–155
exception handling, 76–78
exponential operator (**), 60–61,
        91–92
expressions, 47–48

F

False (Boolean value), 82
files, 231–235
    opening, 232–233, 247
    reading, 234–235
    saving, 233–234, 247–248

shelve module, using with, 247–248
writing to, 233–234
Flask module, 253–255. *See also* modules, pip
floats, 37–38
converting to strings, 71–72
flower trail, creating, 130–131
forest, building, 148–150
for loops, 195–196
with dictionaries, 205
generating 2D lists with, 216
with multidimensional lists, 208–213, 218–225
for-else loops, 206–207
functions, 145. *See also* methods
arguments, 147–148
calling, 146–147
defining, 146
returning values with, 153–155, 179, 266

G

getBlock() function, 85
getHeight() function, 90
getPos() function, 56
getTilePos() function, 51
ghost structures
castle, 266–268
hotel, 275–277
house, 263–265
tree, 280–281
village, 269–271
gifts program, 110–111
global variables, 162–163
greater than (>), 88
greater than or equal to (>=), 89–90

H

hardcoded values, 68
hash marks (#), for comments, 35
"Hello, Minecraft World", posting to chat, 67–68
hot and cold game, 141–143

I

IDLE, 20–24
if statements, 103–105
with Boolean operators, 119–120
in functions, 157–158
with lists, 185–186
nested, 115, 137
with range checks, 117
importing modules, 39–40, 238–241
immutable
strings, 175
world, 82–83, 108–109
in operator, 185–186
increment, 127–128
indentation, 76, 104, 146
index, of a list, 168–169, 213–214, 223–225
infinite loops, 127–128
inheritance, 273–275, 278–280
__init__() method, 258–260, 278–280
input
numbers only, 77–78
placing blocks by, 74–75
input() function, 68–69
installation. *See* Mac, Raspberry Pi, Windows
int() function, 74
integers, 31
converting to a string, 71–72
range checks, 117, 135
iteration, 123–124

J

Java
installing on Mac, 14
installing on Windows, 4–5
joining strings, 71–72

K

keys, in dictionaries, 188–189

L

lava trap, setting, 52–53
len() function, 179

less than (<), 88–89
less than or equal to (<=), 89–90
lists, 167–169, 208–213
    copying, 183–185
    creating, 168
    generating with range(),
        198–199, 200–201
    index positions of, 168–169,
        213–214, 223–225
    items in
        accessing, 168–169
        adding, 171–172
        changing, 169
        deleting, 172–173
        finding, 185–186
        inserting, 172
    length, 179
    slicing, 184–185
    three-dimensional, 218–225
    two-dimensional, 208–213, 216
list slice, 184–185
list() function, 200–201
load() function, 241
local variables, 162–163
logical operators, 92–100
    and, 93
    and if statements, 119–120
    not, 96–97
    or, 95
    order of operations, 98–99
    and while loops, 134–135
loops. See for loops, while loops

M

Mac, setup instructions, 11–18
magic wand program, 196–198
math module, 142
math operators, 48–58
    addition (+), 48–49
    exponential (**), 60–61, 91–92
    division (/), 58
    multiplication (*), 58
    order of operations, 61
    shorthand, 62
    subtraction (-), 48
methods, 257, 261–263. See also
        classes, functions
    adding to subclasses, 275

inheritance, 274
    overriding, 278–280
    returning values with, 266
Midas touch program, 138–139
Minecraft
    API (application programming
        interface)
        installing on Mac, 15–16
        installing on Windows, 6–7
    connecting programs to, 34
    game
        installing on Mac, 12–13
        installing on Windows, 2–3
    playing offline
        on Mac, 18
        on Windows, 9–10
    server
        installing on Mac, 15–16
        installing on Windows, 6–7
    worlds, creating new
        on Mac, 17
        on Windows, 8–9
modules, 238–241
    installing with pip, 252–253
    nicknames for, 241
    pickle, 238–241
    shelve, 247–248
    time, 39–40
moving block program, 163–165
multiplication operator (*), 58
    shorthand (*=), 62

N

nicknames, for modules, 241
night vision sword program,
        186–187
not equal to (!=), 86–87
not operator, 96–97

O

object-oriented programming,
        257–258
objects, 257–260, 269–270
offline, playing Minecraft
    on Mac, 18
    on Windows, 9–10
open() function, 232–233, 247

operators. *See* logical operators, math operators
or operator, 95
order of operations
    logical operators, 98–99
    math operators, 61
OS X, setup instructions, 11–18

P

package manager, 252
parameters, of functions, 148
permissions, for files, 232–233, 239
pickle module, 238–241
pillars, building, 202–203
pip, installing modules with, 252–253
pixel art, 214–215
pollBlockHits() function, 180–182, 196–198
position, of player, 31–33. *See also* teleporting
    changing, 34
    finding, 51, 56
        in specific environments, 85–86, 87–88, 90–91, 93–96
        in specific locations, 91–92, 100–101
    highest and lowest, 169–171
postToChat() function, 67–68
print() function, 66–67
progress bar, 173–174
pyramid, building, 203–204
Python
    installing on Mac, 13
    installing on Windows, 3–4
Python shell, 20–21, 23–24

Q

quotation marks
    for docstrings, 152–153
    for strings, 66

R

r (read permission), 233
r+ (read-and-write permission), 233

randint() function, 62–63
random module, 62–63, 182–183
range checks, 117, 135
range() function, 198–199, 200–201
Raspberry Pi, setup instructions, 18–19
read-and-write permission (r+), 233
read permission (r), 233
read() function, 234
readline() function, 234–235
refactoring, 150–152
return keyword, 153–155, 179, 266
reversed() function, 201–202
running a program, 36

S

scope, of variables, 162–163
scoreboard, for block hits game, 192–194, 205–206
secret passage, building, 115–116
server
    installing on Mac, 15
    installing on Windows, 6
setBlock() function, 49, 158–159
setBlocks() function, 55–56
setPos() function, 38
setTilePos() function, 34–35
setting() function, 82–83
setup instructions
    for Mac, 11–18
    for Raspberry Pi, 18–19
    for Windows, 2–11
shell, 20–21, 23–24
shelve module, 247–248
shorthand operators, 62
shower program, 120–122
sightseeing guide, creating, 190–191
single quotation marks (''), for strings, 66
sleep() function, 39–40
slices, of lists, 184–185
sliding program, 177–178
smashing, preventing, 82–83, 108–109
Spigot
    on Mac, 15–18
    on Windows, 6–11

spires, creating, 58–60
sprint record, 78–80
sqrt() function, 142
square brackets ([]), for defining
lists, 168
square root, calculating, 142
stairs, building, 199–200
state, of blocks, 158–159
statements, 29–30, 47–48
str() function, 71–72, 83
strings, 66
accessing characters in, 175
concatenating, 71–72
converting to integers, 74
subclasses, 273–275, 278–280
subtraction operator (-), 52
shorthand (-=), 62
super jump program, 63–64
superclasses, 273–275, 278–280
survival mode
on Mac, 18
on Windows, 10–11
sword
hits, 180–182, 196–198
magic wand, 196–198
night vision, 186–187
syntax, 29–30

T

teleporting, 31–35, 40–42
by location name, 190–191,
260–261
by point score, 113–114
precisely, 38–39
to random locations, 125–126
restrictions, 118–119
text. *See* files, strings
text editor, 21–23
three-dimensional lists, 218–225
throwing an exception, 76
time module, 39–40
to-do list, 235–237
triple quotation marks (""""), for
docstrings, 152–153
True (Boolean value), 82
try-except statements, 76–78
tuples, 175–176, 179

two-dimensional lists, 208–213, 216
TypeError, 147–148, 154–155

U

UnboundLocalError, 162
usernames, adding to chat, 72–73

V

values
in dictionaries, 188–189,
191–192
of variables, 28
variables, 28–31, 168
assigning values to, 28
changing values of, 31
global, 162–163
local, 162–163
naming, 28–29
syntax, 29–30

W

w (write permission), 232–233
waiting, in programs, 39–40
wand, magic, 196–198
watery curse program, 128–129
weather-worn wall, building,
217–218
website, creating with Flask,
253–255
while loops, 123–124
conditions, 131–132
ending, 127–128, 139
with if statements, 137
infinite, 127–128, 130
with return statements, 160
while-else statements, 141
Windows, setup instructions, 2–11
wool blocks, setting color by name,
158–159
worlds (Minecraft), creating new
on Mac, 17
on Windows, 8–9
write permission (w), 232–233
write() function, 233–234

X

x, y, and z coordinates, 31–32

RESOURCES

Visit *https://www.nostarch.com/pythonwithminecraft/* for updates, program files for the Minecraft missions, and installation files.

REQUIREMENTS

Here's what you'll need in order to follow along with this book!

IF YOU'RE USING WINDOWS 7, 8, OR 10

- The official, paid version of Minecraft, available from *https://minecraft.net/*
- Python 3, available for free from *http://www.python.org/downloads/*
- Java, available for free from *http://www.java.com/en/download/*
- The book's accompanying setup folder, available for free from *https://www.nostarch .com/pythonwithminecraft/* (includes the Python Minecraft API and Spigot server)

  See "Setting Up Your Windows PC" on page 2 for detailed instructions.

IF YOU'RE USING OS X 10.10 OR LATER

- The official, paid version of Minecraft, available from *https://minecraft.net/*
- Python 3, available for free from *https://www.python.org/downloads/mac-osx/*
- The Java Development Kit, available for free from *http://www.oracle.com/ technetwork/java/javase/downloads/index.html*
- The book's accompanying setup folder, available for free from *https://www.nostarch .com/pythonwithminecraft/* (includes the Python Minecraft API and Spigot server)

  See "Setting Up Your Mac" on page 11 for detailed instructions.

IF YOU'RE USING A RASPBERRY PI

You shouldn't have to install anything at all—a free version of Minecraft comes installed on the Raspberry Pi! Read more about it at *http://www.raspberrypi.org/*. See "Setting Up Your Raspberry Pi" on page 18 for details.

-

CPSIA information can be obtained
at www.ICGtesting.com
Printed in the USA
LVOW05s0257211115

463307LV00001B/1/P